GW01463886

A CATERER'S GUIDE TO DRINKS

To Sandra —

I hope you enjoy
climbing my words.

Conal Gregory
February, 1985.

A Caterer's Guide to **Drinks**

Conal R. Gregory
MASTER OF WINE

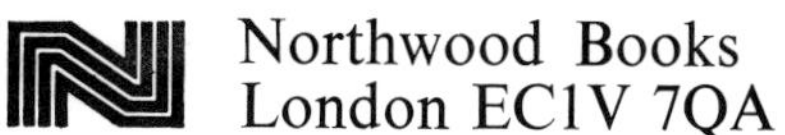

Northwood Books
London EC1V 7QA

Published 1979

ISBN 7198 2674 8

A 'Catering Times' book

Printed in Great Britain by The Anchor Press Ltd
and bound by Wm Brendon & Son Ltd,
both of Tiptree, Essex

Contents

To Rupert

Acknowledgements

I should like to thank the many shippers, producers and distributors who have answered my frequent questions. May I also thank those who gave permission to reproduce maps or diagrams in their possession: the Australian Wine Centre of London, the Brewers' Society, the Comité Interprofessionel du Vin de Champagne, Hallgarten Wines Ltd. and John Harvey and Sons Ltd.

May I add a special word of thanks for the quiet encouragement received from Miles Quest FHCIMA, Editor of *Catering Times*.

The inspiration and constructive criticism received from my students is evident within these pages and I hope will encourage future generations to study this fascinating subject.

Introduction

My aim is to fill a real gap in the books so far available on wines, spirits and other alcoholic drinks. This is to present an up-to-date guide in a form to which reference can be made without difficulty. It aims to identify the important fields for sales expansion in the last quarter of this century, and also to cover the important and often neglected areas of management control, sales and marketing promotion and legal constraints, without requiring constant reference to a diverse range of other publications.

I want to include within the scope of this book, the product knowledge and managerial material which will both guide a catering student through his or her studies and act as a ready aide-mémoire to the working caterer. The practical approach should appeal to all caterers, while the emphasis on modern material should invite the interest of general readers.

At the time of writing, this book covers the material required for the Certificate and Higher Certificate courses of the Wine & Spirit Education Trust Ltd, the Alcoholic Beverages Certificate of the City & Guilds of London Institute and for the Ordinary and Higher National Diplomas. Candidates as well as members of the H.C.I.M.A. should also find the book of value.

BEDALE — CONAL R. GREGORY

APRIL 1979

1. Background

'No! let me taste the whole of it,' Elizabeth Barrett Browning.

'What is Wine? Wine is the alcoholic beverage obtained from the fermentation of the juice of freshly gathered grapes; the fermentation taking place in the district of origin according to local tradition and practice.'

This Wine and Spirit Association definition therefore rules out products made from fruits other than the grape, such as ginger 'wine' and the various fruit 'wines' which are excluded as not fulfilling the above definition. It also rules out 'British' wine, which is a reconstituted concentrated grape juice that is generally fortified; this should not be confused with a naturally made English (or Welsh) vineyard wine.

U.K. Wine Consumption

Britain is a modest consumer of wines. In total clearances (the volume H.M. Customs and Excise pass into free circulation after the payment of duties), Britain consumed imported wines as shown below on p. 12.

Prior to 1 January 1976, wine was classified for revenue purposes as either 'light' or 'heavy' according to its proof spirit content; the dividing line being 27° proof spirit for Commonwealth and 25° for other wines. Corresponding to this division, there were two basic rates of duty – a lower rate for 'light' wine and a higher rate for 'heavy' wine. Before 1 July 1973, the duties applied to all imported wines other than imports from the Commonwealth and Eire. These imports were charged at lower rates of duty. Additional duties were charged on wines imported in bottle on sparkling wines, and on 'heavy' wine exceeding 42° of proof spirit.

On 1 January 1976, the structure of the wine duty was changed. The

Year	Million Hectolitres	Million Gallons
1966	1·286	28·3
1967	1·455	32·0
1968	1·605	35·3
1969	1·532	33·7
1970	1·614	35·4
1971	1·918	42·2
1972	2·264	49·8
1973	2·896	63·7
1974	2·977	65·5
1975	2·914	64·1
1976*	3·155	69·4
1977*	3·021	66·5

*Adjusted to new basis of wines moving into free circulation. (1 hectolitre, equals 100 litres, equals 22 imperial gallons.)

former customs revenue duty was replaced by separate duties of customs and excise; the customs duty being levied as an import duty.* The wine excise duty is applied to all wine of fresh grapes, including that produced in the U.K. All other fermented beverages, except for beer, cider and perry, are now liable to 'made-wine' duty, whether imported or U.K. produced. The previous 'two-strength' duty structure has also been changed to a 'three-strength' structure, determined by the percentage of alcohol by volume at 68°F (20°C). Wine excise duty is charged at different rates of duty for strengths of not exceeding 15 per cent, over 15 and up to 18 per cent, and over 18 and up to 22 per cent.

Wine of a strength exceeding 22 per cent is subject to an additional

Litres per capita

Country	1955	1960	1965	1970	1975	1976	1977
Italy	103·5	108·3	110·1	113·7	103·9	99·7	93·5
France	138·7	126·9	117·6	109·1	103·7	101·3	100·9
Luxembourg	36·8	31·3	30·1	37·0	41·3	45·3	49·3
West Germany	8·9	10·8	16·8	17·2	23·3	23·6	23·4
Belgium	7·1	7·8	11·2	13·9	17·2	16·7	17·5
Denmark	2·7	3·1	4·1	5·9	11·5	12·6	11·7
Netherlands	1·2	1·9	3·3	5·1	10·2	11·4	11·7
U.K.	1·1	1·6	2·2	2·9	5·2	5·6	6·4
Eire	2·3	2·0	2·4	3·3	4·1	4·5	4·3

(1 litre equals 1·75 pints.)

*Replaced by Common External Tariff (C.E.T.).

charge per 1 per cent or part of 1 per cent by which the strength exceeds 22 per cent. Such wines may not, under E.E.C. regulations, be imported or delivered for direct human consumption; they may be used for distillation, and for the production of vermouth and of vinegar. Sparkling wines remain subject to a flat-rate surcharge.

Only Eire consumes less wine per capita within the E.E.C. than the U.K.

The broad categories of wine consumption in Britain may be seen from three comparative years:

Clearances in 1000 Hectolitres

Category	1975	1976	1977	1976–7 Total Rise or Fall	1976–7 Percentage Rise or Fall
Light Wines					
E.E.C.	985·1	1173·6	1111·0	−62·6	−5·3
Non E.E.C.	697·3	641·9	592·6	−49·3	−7·7
Total	1682·4	1815·5	1703·6	−111·9	−6·2
Heavy Wines					
E.E.C.	6·5	15·2	9·1	−6·1	−40·4
Non E.E.C.	577·9	771·4	602·3	−169·1	−21·9
Total	584·4	786·6	611·4	−175·2	−22·3
Sparkling Wines					
Champagne	33·7	45·1	41·3	−3·8	−8·5
Other E.E.C.	82·5	91·3	80·6	−10·7	−11·7
Non E.E.C.	5·0	5·9	6·4	+0·5	+8·5
Total	121·2	142·3	128·3	−14·0	−9·8
Vermouth	524·9	546·3	516·5	−29·8	−5·5
Others*	N/A	N/A	61·2	N/A	N/A
Total imported wines	2912·9	3290·7	3021·0	−269·7	−8·2

*This is for unclassified wines.

(Source: Adapted from H.M. Customs & Excise *Wine Bulletin.*)

Outside the E.E.C., wine consumption was 11·8 pints (6·7 litres) per head in the U.S.A. and 23·4 pints (13·3 litres) in the U.S.S.R. (for the year 1977).

Future Wine Consumption Trends

Several estimates have been made which suggest consumer expenditure on wines will increase by 6 per cent per annum as real incomes rise after the economic recession of the 1974–7 period; although this growth is likely to be arrested by any duty increases or higher rates of Value Added Tax beyond 15 per cent. With the full impact of E.E.C. entry now passed, French wines of Appellation d'Origine Contrôlée status (A.O.C. or A.C. – explained in Chapter 5) from the better known districts are markedly more expensive and are unlikely to see the growth that non-A.O.C. and the lower generic A.O.C. will enjoy over the 1978–83 period. Although West Germany suffered during 1975–6 from an inadequate quantity of QbA and price increases in 1977 on Italian wines caused a set-back, caterers can expect an overall forward-demand trend in these two countries' wines here in the next five years. Champagne sales are again buoyant but Asti has become relatively expensive. The growth in non-Champagne sparkling wines is also likely to continue in the next few years; aided probably shortly by legislative terms in the cases of both France and West Germany.

A much greater interest in table wines for the British market is likely from Spain, Portugal and Greece, particularly if they are successful in their applications to join the E.E.C. In good quality fields, like the Rioja of northern Spain, substantial price increases are foreseen.

In the mid 1970s caterers saw a substantial rise in demand and sales for vermouth, due in part to the much higher price of Sherry and similar fortified wines (see Chapter 6). The 'extra dry' style vermouths are catching up the 'bianco' sweet ones in popularity. Brand awareness is high in this drinks sector. The larger 52 fluid ounce (1·5 litre) bottle is a help to the busy catering barman because it means fewer optic changes.

Shipments of port have not been as encouraging as many shippers would like of late; but caterers were among those who took up the 1975 vintage port declaration (made during 1977) within weeks of the opening offers. There are no signs that the French habit of consuming port prior to a meal as an appetiser is developing in Britain.

U.K. Spirit Consumption

The British drink less spirits per person than any other E.E.C. country; although there has been a gradual upward trend:

Consumption in Litres at 100 per cent

Country	1955	1960	1965	1970	1975	1976	1977
Luxembourg	0·84	0·97	1·23	1·90	3·50	4·09	4·70
Netherlands	1·16	1·14	1·89	2·04	3·04	2·50	2·90
West Germany	1·30	1·92	2·73	2·97	3·00	2·84	2·90
France	2·31	2·02	2·49	2·30	2·50	2·50	2·50
Belgium	0·67	0·77	1·12	1·32	2·00	1·93	2·10
Italy	1·20	1·00	1·40	1·80	2·00	2·00	2·00
Eire	0·75	0·77	1·06	1·46	2·00	1·99	2·20
Denmark	0·40	0·62	0·96	1·27	1·70	1·87	1·80
U.K.	0·62	0·76	0·84	·094	1·50	1·65	1·40

Outside the E.E.C., the comparative consumption for the U.S.A. has been static for several years at 5·5 pints (3·1 litres) per person. In the U.S.S.R., it is 5·8 pints (3·3 litres) per person.

Caterers will better appreciate the pattern of spirit consumption in Britain by considering the trends in recent years.

Clearances in '000 Hectolitres at 100 per cent

Category	1975	1976	1977	1976–7 Total Rise or Fall	1976–7 Percentage Rise or Fall
Home-produced spirits					
Gin	136·78	152·13	124·31	−27·82	−18·3
Vodka	73·79	88·73	82·18	−6·55	−7·4
Whisky (inc. other mature spirits)	424·49	485·53	402·88	−82·65	−17·0
Other	1·33	3·71	6·83	+3·12	+83·9
Sub Total	636·36	730·10	616·20	−113·90	−15·6
Imported spirits					
Rum	86·42	86·52	76·08	−10·44	−12·1
Cognac	40·31	42·36	37·09	−5·27	−12·4
Other brandy	19·71	24·05	20·44	−3·61	−15·0
Liqueurs	28·83	29·84	27·61	−2·23	−7·5
Other	9·61	13·01	14·52	+1·51	+11·6
Sub Total	184·88	195·78	175·74	−20·04	−10·2
Unclassified	N/A	N/A	2·52	N/A	N/A
Total spirits	821·24	925·88	794·46	−131·42	−14·2

Source: Adapted from H.M. Customs & Excise *Spirits Bulletin*

Trading in Wines and Spirits

Although there is a growing market in English vineyard wines, its overall production is sadly tiny. This means the vast amount of wine sold through the catering trade has to be imported. However, such imports have to be equated with the much more substantial exports of spirits and both the export and re-export of wines:

1976	Imports (exc. duty)	Exports (exc. duty)
Wines	£148,820,000	£ 17,680,000
Spirits	£ 64,110,000	£482,270,000
Total	£212,930,000	£499,950,000

Source: Department of Trade.

Seventy per cent of our table wine imports originate in other E.E.C. countries which are the U.K.'s second largest export market for Scotch whisky, after the U.S.A. In view of the European trading, the following table shows a breakdown.

1975	Wine Imports £	Scotch Whisky Exports £
France	37,760,000	18,300,000
West Germany	11,790,000	12,300,000
Italy	9,620,000	13,900,000
Netherlands	210,000	7,000,000
Eire	70,000	3,000,000
Belgium/Luxembourg	60,000	11,600,000
Denmark	—	2,700,000
E.E.C. States	59,520,000	68,800,000
Non E.E.C.	39,670,000	297,800,000
Total	99,190,000	366,600,000

Spirit sales are noticeably income-sensitive, but white spirits have enjoyed increasing popularity among younger consumers in the last five years. An overall 7 per cent increase in the spirit market has been predicted for the 1978–82 period with a definite price barrier emerging as a disincentive to wider purchasing. This is seen, for instance, in the growth in grape brandy sales, although the rise in these do not equal the fall in Cognac imports. Caterers are likely to continue to see the benefit of lower-strength spirits; but the 'benefit' [*sic*] of the smaller-size bottle in this area is largely for the consumption-at-home sector, rather than for the trade. Liqueurs in the heavily marketed branded sector look likely to progress at the expense of the lower-strength and little known liqueur lines.

Wine and Spirit Duties

Overall consumption in the wine and spirit field can vary considerably, depending upon the financial constraints imposed by the Government. It may be helpful initially to compare the nine E.E.C. states for excise duty and Value Added Tax purposes, together with the effect their rates have on a wine which retails at £18 per case of 12 bottles (£1·50 per bottle) in the U.K.:

E.E.C. Member State	Excise Duty per litre p.	VAT Rate %	Effect on U.K. retail price
U.K.	71·49	8*	£1·50
Denmark	67·93	18	£1·59
Eire	50·57	10	£1·35
Belgium	18·85	25	£1·26
Netherlands	18·90	18	£1·19
Luxembourg	9·44	10	£1·04
France	1·03	17·6	£1·04
Italy	—	14	£1·00
West Germany	—	12	£0·98

(Exchange Rates in House of Commons reply, 7 November 1977.)

*Increased to 15 per cent on 18 June 1979.

The term 'proof gallon' is frequently used by the trade and is defined as 'a gallon (4·54 litres) of a 100° proof spirit which at 51°F (11°C) contains 49·28 per cent of ethyl alcohol by weight and 57·06 per cent by volume'. See also footnote, page 56.

Caterers should appreciate the costs involved, other than the intrinsic value of the alcoholic beverage. This may be seen in the diagrams overleaf. The actual items will vary from shipper to shipper and fluctuate with trading costs, but it does give a rough indication. The diagrams will also be of benefit when read in conjunction with the section on importing and the structure of the licensed trade (see Chapter 2). This is particularly so where a number of caterers are considering the establishment of a bond

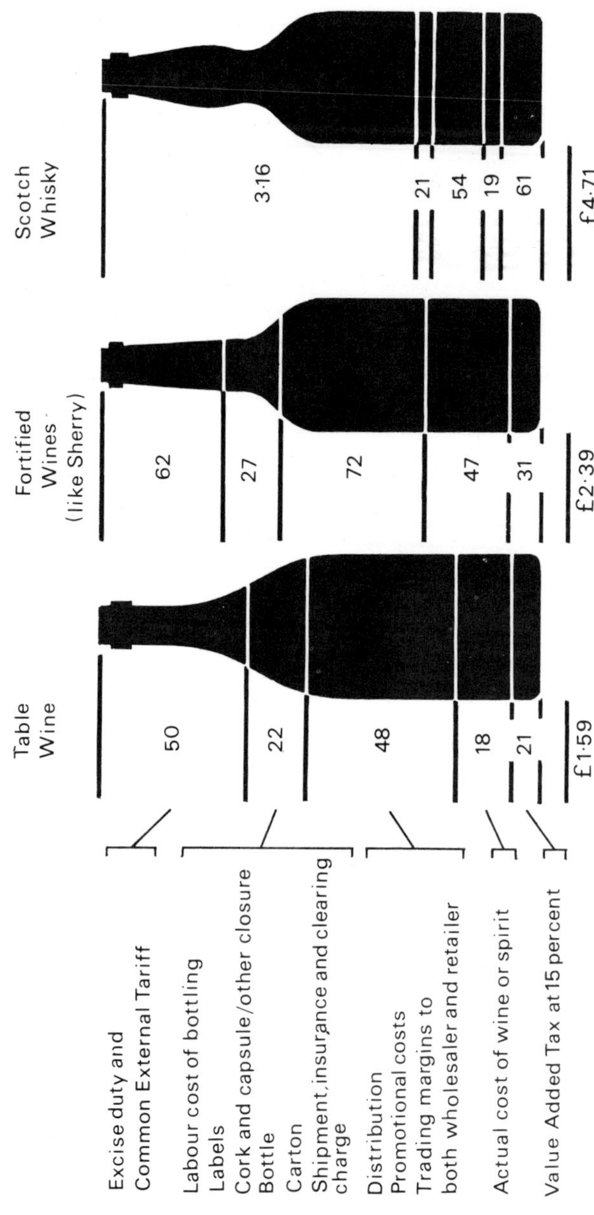

Schematic breakdown of production costs for wines, fortified wines and Scotch.

or other means of direct importation. It will also be of use when considering the costs for a catering division of a larger company which includes a wine and spirit shipping or distribution side.

Excise duty is liable on alcoholic beverages cleared by H.M. Customs and Excise for U.K. consumption. The common external tariff is applied additionally to non-E.E.C. alcoholic beverages which are imported. The excise duty operates on the basis of the stronger the beverage, the greater the levy – regardless of intrinsic value. Hence a bottle of Bordeaux Rouge pays the same excise duty as a First Growth claret, assuming the same volume content! However a higher rate of Value Added Tax will be levied on the beverage of greater sales value. Better wine is clearly better value, since every extra 20p spent per bottle of wine represents an additional 100 per cent wine value.

The Market for Beer

Caterers should consider the size and importance of the beer sector in alcoholic beverages. Britain was placed tenth in a table based on per person consumption internationally:

	Pints (568 ml) per capita				
Country	1977	1976	1975	1972	1968
West Germany	261·6	265·4	259·4	255·7	227·7
Australia	239·2	246·2	250·1	225·6	211·2
Czechoslovakia	239·2	245·3	250·3	246·2	233·6
Belgium	228·8	242·9	237·1	235·8	218·2
New Zealand	225·6	230·5	234·4	213·7	194·5
Denmark	224·0	229·3	227·0	213·0	165·4
East Germany	222·4	219·1	207·0	187·4	151·9
Eire	222·4	216·5	230·6	202·4	158·9
Luxembourg	214·4	225·3	225·3	211·2	204·3
U.K.	208·0	209·3	207·0	189·2	166·7
Austria	181·6	179·5	182·7	182·5	172·8
U.S.A.	150·4	145·2	151·0	126·4	114·4
Canada	149·6	149·4	151·2	134·6	118·4

Beer production in the U.K. saw a decline in 1977 after many years of consistent growth:

Year	Bulk Barrels
1947	29,802,800
1950	25,163,500
1955	24,354,000
1960	26,514,500
1965	26,514,500
1970	33,698,100
1975	39,452,900
1976	40,104,400
1977	39,862,800

(Each barrel equals 36 gallons/506·8 litres.)

While beer production in Britain is a useful indicator of the mark, caterers should be aware of the variety of imported beers and lagers available, as this is a sector that is showing increased sales interest. After Eire (Guinness), West Germany was the largest importer to the U.K. in 1977 with 93,500,000 pints (53,131,000 litres), a 36 per cent increase on 1976. This may be placed into perspective by examining the following table which shows U.K. beer consumption (both home and export produced) deducting beer exports:

Year	Bulk Barrels
1967	31,836,000
1968	32,601,000
1969	34,032,000
1970	35,013,000
1971	36,296,000
1972	36,896,000
1973	38,915,000
1974	39,910,000
1975	40,722,000
1976	41,459,000
1977	40,899,000

The caterer, particularly in the hotel field and outside catering trade, should be aware of the composition of this market by style. Figures are for the calendar year 1977.

Draught Beers	Percentage
Mild	12·5
Premium Bitter and Stout	15·2
Ordinary Bitter	30·7
Lager	18·6

Packaged Beers	Percentage
Light, Pale and Export	10·6
Lager	5·2
Brown	2·4
Stout	4·2
Strong Ales and Barley Wine	0·6

Draught beer accounts for approximately 75 per cent of sales, although bottle beer has been commercially available since the late seventeenth century. It has risen in popularity from the 1880s when the import of Continental lager began.

HISTORICAL BACKGROUND

The first references to wine appear on the sealing inscriptions of some pre-dynastic Egyptian amphorae, while some Egyptian archaeological evidence suggests cylinder seals and recessed brick niching identical to that used by the Sumerians in Mesopotamia (modern Iraq between the Tigris and Euphrates) about 3100 B.C. Wine-making spread slowly, particularly along the banks of the Nile. Wine in Egypt was the monopoly of the Pharaoh and priestly hierarchy; paintings in the tombs of the Pharaohs depict the Egyptian harvest. Grapes were placed in rush baskets, pressed by foot and then in sacks, and subsequently stored in amphorae, mostly being sweet white in style. During the later dynastic period (1075–525 B.C.), imported wines from Greece displaced local wines. The Greeks enjoyed a terrain and climate better suited to viticulture (grape cultivation) than the Nile; the Greeks' finer wines dominated the European market far into the Roman era.

Both the Old Testament and the Talmud, which was composed in Babylon, make frequent allusions to the vine and Nebuchadnezzar, King of Assyria, was known to have held extensive vineyards. The vine spread across all the eastern Mediterranean and into Persia and Arabia during the first millennium before Christ.

Unlike the Egyptians, all sections of Greek society – except the women of Sparta – enjoyed wine, although it was normally diluted with water. The Mediterranean economic triad of grapes, olives and cereals shared the soil, particularly during the eighth to sixth centuries B.C., with the woods and pastures. Merchant seamen brought the vine to southern Europe

(Cadiz and Málaga) about 1000 B.C. About 600 B.C., the Greeks founded colonies in Provence, Languedoc, southern Italy and the Crimea.

Wine kept well in airtight earthenware jars (*amphorae*), each holding about 48 to 67 pints (27 to 38 litres). It was usual to pour a little olive oil on to the surface of the wine to prevent oxidation. While earthenware was usual for wine that had to be transported, sewn-up skins or leather vessels were used for local purposes. Wood was also to be found. Herodotus, the Greek historian of the fifth century B.C., gives an account of the Armenian–Babylonian wine trade which used palm-wood casks.

After the death of Alexander the Great in 323 B.C., Greek power declined and gradually a common agricultural policy, including the vine, was enforced by Rome. The vine was noticeably cultivated in Italy, Spain and Syria. Corks are found in some fifth century B.C. Roman amphorae. They then almost disappear until the sixteenth century. Dionysus, known to both Romans and Greeks as Bacchus, god of wine, is credited in mythology with having spread the cultivation of the vine through Asia. Pliny the Elder (A.D. 23–79) referred to 24 classified growths in his *Historia Naturalis*: an indication of the amount of interest taken in viticulture.

With the extension of the Roman empire, it was impractical to transport wine over long distances. New vineyard areas were started: the Rhône in the first century A.D.; in Bordeaux and Burgundy a century later; in Alsace, the Loire and Mosel by the third century; and the Rhine a century later. Cleared banks offered suitable terrain for vineyards. Not only were the legionaries given freedom to plant vines which encouraged them to settle in their distant outposts, but the privilege was also extended to the more reliable of the local tribes as a way of attaching them to the soil and making them Rome's allies in defending it. This practice represents the foundation of European wine-making.

The wine of the Gauls gradually grew to rival Italian wine; which led in part to Emperor Domitian's edict of A.D. 92 that the vines beyond Italy were to be uprooted. In addition, he wished to provide outlets for Rome's wine surplus, because exports were dwindling in the face of local production in the external provinces. He also wanted these territories to switch to grain cultivation. Replanting restrictions were lifted in A.D. 280 by the Emperor Probius.

Although no evidence has been found in Egyptian and Greek times for the use of cork to seal wine, it was used in late Roman days as Pliny the Elder records, describing in his *Historia Naturalis* how it was used for bungs, *cadorum opturamensis*. Later wax became the general sealing agent used and cork appears to have fallen into disuse until glass bottles became commercially available in the fifteenth century. The Phoenicians had blown some exquisite glass; their techniques were developed later in Moslem countries.*

Widespread religious foundations followed the conversion of Emperor Constantius to Christianity in A.D. 312 and with them viticultural skills. The Church required wine for sacramental use and established vineyards throughout the empire, including some in Wales. Although Britain (like France) appears to have had no native vine, a grape-fermented drink was not unknown in the country. The Belgae tribe had imported Italian wine a century before Caesar invaded.

The fall of the Roman Empire was followed by the Muslim invasion of Spain and Portugal. Although the Koran declared that there was a devil contained in every berry of the vine, viticulture continued. Expansion occurred under the Holy Roman Emperor, Charlemagne (742–814) who initiated replanting on the Rhine and gave support to it in Burgundy and Alsace. Frisian merchants traded at this time with Britain, bartering French and German wines for English iron and wheat.

In the laws of Alfred (871–901) there is mention of an English vineyard. In the tenth century trade was temporarily upset by Viking pirates, although a wider trading pattern involving wine had emerged by now. At the same time, the Arabs are thought to have discovered the method of distilling alcohol. The most significant developments were near the coasts; areas like Burgundy did not fully establish themselves until the late thirteenth century.

Monastic influence spread under Norman rule and with it the vine. Yet it was the marriage of Prince Henry, later to become Henry II of England, with Eleanor of Aquitaine in 1152 that brought the important French western vineyards into trading contact with England. Henry also purchased Rhine, Mosel and the tributary Ruwer wines for his household. At a penny per gallon (4·5 litres), wine became a popular drink in twelfth-century England.

With the relaxation of taxes, the wine merchants of Bordeaux gained a strong foothold on the English market. In 1190, the Third Crusade,

*Hyams, E. – *Dionysus: A Social History of the Wine Vine* (1965), p. 239, for an account of a 13th century Tartar embassy that indicates the use of glass wine bottles a century before their development in Europe.

which was led by Richard I the Lionheart and Philip II of France, led to interest in the heavier Mediterranean wines; Alsace was also enjoying a developing trade in wine, which rose to 22,000,000 gallons (10,000,000 litres) being exported in 1400 to England, Germany and the Low Countries. Despite a 2s (10p) per cask tax rate being imposed on Aquitaine wine by Edward I to finance a war against Scotland, which was followed by the Hundred Years' War and the Black Death, wine trading continued between Bordeaux and England until the war ended in 1453. During this time, Gascon wine grew in popularity, not exceeding 2d (1p) per gallon (4·5 litres) on average in the thirteenth century, and accounted for 80 per cent of the English wine imports by the next century, amounting to 3,000,000 gallons (13,638,300 litres), at an average price of 3½d (1½p) per gallon. This compared favourably with German wine (1s 2d/6p per gallon), Italian (2s/10p), and Cretan (4s/20p), although this variety certainly included Spanish. Geoffrey Chaucer (*c.* 1340–1400) speaks, no doubt with experience as the son of a wine merchant, about the latter in *The Pardoner's Tale*, which is one of the *Canterbury Tales*,

> Now kepe yow fro the whyte and fro the rede,
> And namely fro the whyte wyn of Lepe,*
> That is to selle in Fish-strete† or in Chepe.‡
> This wyn of Spayne crepeth subtilly§
> In othere wynes, growing faste by,
> Of which ther ryseth swich fumositee,
> That whan a man hath dronken draughtes three,
> And weneth that he be at hoom in Chepe,
> He is in Spayne, right at the toune of Lepe,
> Nat at the Rochel, ne at Burdeux toun.

Edward III had granted Letters Patent to the Vintners in 1364 (though their trade was limited to Gascon wines). In 1437 the mystery of the Vintners of London was incorporated by Charter.

However, the Bordeaux trade later switched to Spain and Portugal.

*Spanish town, not far from Huelva, but outside the delimited Sherry Consejo zone.
†Fish Street leads out of Thames Street near the end of London Bridge. Chaucer's father was a wine merchant in Thames Street.
‡Cheapside today, an important street in the City of London.
§ An allusion to the practice of blending wines, probably with higher strength ones.

There is a 1485 record of a shipment from the Sherry region to 'Plemma', which was probably Plymouth. After the final defeat of the Moors by Fernando and Isabel in 1492, non-Jewish traders took over as part of the Spanish monarchy's drive for Roman Catholicism. Many of these merchants were English in the southern Spanish areas of Jerez and Málaga; they helped to select wines and facilitated the trade with England where Sherry* was to become known as *sack*. Spanish wines also began to be exported to the Spanish conquests in the New World. While this Iberian trade was continuing, Chianti was mentioned for the first time in the early fifteenth century in trade.

With the added protection of Henry VIII's navy, trade with Málaga, Jerez (capital of the Sherry region) and the Canaries expanded further. Some 60,000 butts (6,476,240 gallons/294,408 hectolitres) were shipped from Jerez in 1548; of which 40,000 butts (4,317,450 gallons/196,272 hectolitres) were despatched to England and Flanders. Merchants and underwriters in Spain, with little or no protection from Philip's navy, dealt direct with the English privateers and made private arrangements to ensure the safety of their shipping. This explains the continued consumption of Spanish wines during the long, undeclared war. Drake's raid on Cadiz in 1587 and capture of 2,900 butts of Sherry helped the English popularity for this wine still further!

The dissolution of the monasteries under Henry VIII led to a decline in English and Welsh viticulture, which did not revive for economic reasons until effectively after the Second World War. It appears that climatical deterioration was not as important a factor in leading to the reduction in English (and Welsh) viticulture after the 1530s, even though an analysis† has indicated cool springs, May frosts and a slight‡ fall in summer heat. The cheapness of imported wines and home-made beer (and cider) tended to undermine the commercial grape growing in southern England where greater efforts were required to make a smaller yield than across the Channel. It became the hobby, among others, of the occasional estate gardener and sometimes his gentleman master.

During the sixteenth century, the Riesling, Muscat and Traminer vines were first planted in Alsace; but the expanding trade in Bordeaux and

*Wines from Málaga and the Canaries also probably went under the name *sack*.
†By Lamb, H. H. – *The Earlier Mediaeval Warm Epoch and Its Sequel* (1965).
‡From 60·6°F (15·9°C) in 1500 to 1550 for the months of July and August to 59·6°F (15·3°C) for 1550 to 1600.

Burgundy was interrupted by religious warfare. During the late sixteenth and early seventeenth centuries, a thriving wine trade was built up between Portugal and ports in the West Country, notably Bristol. This 'Portuguese connection' can be traced back intermittently, as far as 1353 when a treaty between Edward III and Alphonso IV ratified commercial benefits between the two countries. A number of merchants set up trade in Portugal and also on the Portuguese island of Madeira.

Commercial distillation generally began in Europe in the early seventeenth century which was to set the later reputation for Cognac, even though Armagnac claims to have made their *ayga ardenterius* since at least 1411 – the date of a legal document housed in the Departmental Archives of the Haut-Garonne and said to have authenticated the sale of brandy about 1460 in the Landes market of St Sever. Armagnac therefore predates both Calvedos, originating about 1553, and the better known Cognac by almost two centuries. It is said that the volume of some crops in France led to the idea of distilling to reduce the stock holding. They intended to reconstitute the distillate with water later; but the distillate as it was caught on.

In another development about 1670, the monk Pierre Perignon achieved the capture of the sparkle within Champagne, after being appointed cellarer to the Abbey of Hautvillers. Closer-fitting corks replaced the poor cork or oiled hemp tied down with thread on to the string-ring which was prevalent until then. The first corkscrew is mentioned in 1686. The proper corking of wine permitted wines to develop in bottle. This was referred to by Shakespeare, for example, in *As You Like It* (III. 2.).

The shape of the wine bottle altered dramatically in just over a century. In the early eighteenth century, wine was bottled in a squat bottle with a short, wide tapering neck. This shape increased in height, becoming slightly carafe-like, until by the mid eighteenth century the neck was two-thirds of the main body height. It assumed its more usual modern appearance in shape by about 1810. This shape allowed wine to be binned and hence the cork did not dry out; accordingly, from the late eighteenth century, the concept of maturing vintage wines developed.

The English trade came under greater legal control in the seventeenth century, with fines such as that of 1661 which imposed £100 on vintners and £40 on retailers who 'mingled, corrupted or vitiated' wines. Price controls were introduced four years later. The variety of wines on sale was noticeable, although Rhenish, shipped via Holland to the port of

Deal, was the most popular in Restoration England. It corresponded to the modern 'Hock'; although this term dates from the eighteenth century.

Liqueur production commenced at varying dates and has not always been well recorded owing to the secrecy involved with the various compositions. A monk, Don Bernardo Vincelli, is attributed with discovering Bénédictine about 1510 at Fécamp in northern France. The first caraway liqueur is credited to Lucas Bols in 1575 in Amsterdam. Many recipes were devised about this time, often from a religious community's base, using flowers and their scents as well as other flavouring agents. They came to be taken for other reasons than *digestif* use; any ailments were said to be eased by their consumption.

In 1638 a Charter was granted to the Compound Distillers or Rectifiers to make juniper-flavoured spirits of a cordial nature, largely for medicinal use; the spirit was imported from France prior to flavouring. The Government opened this spirit trade in gin to development when French supplies were cut off at the end of the seventeenth century when France was at war with England and Holland. The quality was soon lowered and abuse set in. It went largely unchecked owing to the agricultural interest which needed an outlet for the surplus cereal crops. By 1725 there were 6,187 spirit shops in the City of London alone; it was claimed, just over 25 years later, that 9,300 children under five years of age died annually from the ill effects of spirit consumption. Various Acts were ineffectual until 1751 and it was to take almost two centuries before the licensing of grocers' shops was to be permitted on any scale again.

Preference to Portugal was further extended by the Methuen Treaty of 1703 which gave her wines one-third less duty than that imposed on French wines. The establishment of the Oporto Wine Company in 1756 by the Portuguese Government led to wine-making (vinification) improvements and ultimately to the creation of vintage port. By the late eighteenth century, 60 per cent of our imports originated in Portugal. The links with Britain had been sown for well over a century in the formation of Port Houses. Both port and Madeira continued to be shipped in quantity even after Gladstone terminated the Methuen Treaty in 1860. The first Port House, Kopke, claims its foundation in 1638. It is followed by Warre in 1670, Croft in 1678, Quarles Harris in 1680, and so forth.

This emphasis switched back towards Spain after 1814 at the end of the Peninsular War, with the formation of many Sherry Houses that supply leading brands to today's market. Indeed, Spanish wines have entered many an export market, from the Málaga enjoyed by Tsarina Catherine II (the Great) of Russia to the district wine of La Mancha, Valdepenas, which Emperor Charles V appreciated.

Irish whiskey was hardly known in England and Scotch whisky was largely confined to the crofting community, until the late eighteenth century. It had been made for centuries although the first written record does not appear until 1494 with the entry in the Scottish Exchequer rolls 'Eight bolls of malt to Friar John Cor, wherewith to make aqua vitae'. The term *aqua vitae*, meaning water of life, could have applied to a spirit other than using a barley base. It was not until 1618 – in the reign of the first joint English and Scottish monarch, James I of England and VI of Scotland – that the Gaelic for 'water of life', *Uisge beatha*, is recorded. Thereafter it is made clear it is a reference to a malted barley distillate. Appropriately enough, the 1618 reference was to a drink in the Highlands at a chieftain's funeral. During the seventeenth century, considerable expertise in whisky production was built up in Scotland, particularly in the Highlands, but its so-called fiery qualities did not appeal much south of the Border. It was not until the blends with grain Scotch were introduced about 1890 that the English took to Scotch whisky.

Scotch whisky was forced to submit to excise duty. It was divided for this purpose into three zones by 1797. The first licence was issued by 1824 against intense opposition from the many illicit stillmen. The illegal distillate, poteen or potheen, appears to have continued for some years. Today no stories appear of Scotch poteen, but an occasional Irish bottle can be offered. It is curious that it is illegal to distil in the U.K. *except* on a commercial scale; but the law permits the home brewing of beer and the making of wine from freshly gathered grapes as well as the fermentation at home of other produce. In 1832 a Customs officer, named Coffey, invented a continuous still which enabled merchants of Scotch whisky to reduce the strong peaty aroma and flavour of the malt whiskies and which led to the blends so well known today.

Rum was made in the West Indies, largely as a slave drink, in the seventeenth century. A Boston distillery was established by 1667 using West Indian molasses – this is a thick viscid syrup which is drained from raw sugar during production. The rum became the drink of North America, yielding wealth to New England at the cost of trafficking slaves in the venture. The British sought through the first Molasses Act of 1733 to gain from this trade, while the French prohibited exports of rum from her colonies in 1713 to avoid competition with brandy. Rum consumption grew in Britain in the nineteenth century; mainly mixed with sugar, spices and fruit juices as a 'Shrub' cocktail.

The Champagne Houses had suffered not only from the delaying actions by Napoleon's troops across their vineyards, but through the 10 to 40 per cent loss of breakages during the secondary fermentation. In 1836 M. François devised the sucre-Oenomètre which reduced the losses to an average of 10 per cent by 1842. A subsequent improvement in the strength of bottles used and better yeast selection – the latter brought about by the studies of Pasteur, Robinet, Salleron and Buchner – reduced the loss further.

Ale replaced the gin days of Hogarth's *Gin Lane* in the nineteenth century, with red Bordeaux (claret) being shipped via the Channel Isles. Pitt the Elder succeeded in sponsoring a Treaty with France to allow her wines to be imported at the same price as those of Portugal. The light qualities of many clarets were improved by both Rhône wines, like Hermitage, and by Spanish shipments. Free trade policies brought in many wines in the early nineteenth century, including the first from the Imperial lands of Australia and South Africa, such as Constantia. Madeira enjoyed popularity after the island was occupied by the British from 1807 to 1814, during the Napoleonic Wars.

By the mid nineteenth century, the light French and German wines started to rise in popularity, following a half-century dominated by fortified wines. Some of this appeal can be traced to the monarchy. In 1850 Queen Victoria visited Hochheim in the Rheingau of Germany and not only allowed a 12·4 acre (5 hectare) estate to be renamed Koenigin Victoria-Berg (or Koenigin Viktoria-Berg), but gave the generic term *hock* to Rhine wines. No doubt it was, and is, easier to pronounce and remember for many non German-speaking buyers.

Reforms, aimed at encouraging the sale of light wines, were made in the 1860s. Wine duties were reduced to 3s (15p) per gallon (4·5 litres) and simultaneously the Government introduced excise licences for refreshment rooms. A year later, in 1861, a sliding scale for duty was devised, based on alcoholic strength, whose principle is still in operation today.

The French Revolution broke up many large French vineyard estates into small parcels, as happened in Burgundy; it was not until 1803 that

German vineyards were secularized. The custom of naming German wines by their village and site name originated about 1830. German sales prospered under the Gladstone Acts of the 1860s until the onset of the aphid *Phylloxera* in the Palatinate in 1874.

This aphid originated from the eastern states of the United States of America and was able to survive the Atlantic crossing only because of the development of fast steamships. It had been discovered in Europe initially in 1863 in a Hammersmith greenhouse and seems to have reached France the same year, although it was not observed until 1866–7 in the vineyards near Arles. It was prevalent in Bordeaux by 1873 and had reached the Loire by 1876. *Phylloxera* was officially recognised in Burgundy in 1878 and in Champagne some twelve years later. It cost the French economy alone more than twice the 5,000,000,000 franc indemnity paid to the Germans after the Franco-Prussian war. In the U.S.A., the aphid did not kill certain vines although it did form galls on vine leaves. In the 1870s and 1880s, it spread across Europe and reached South Africa.

Its effect on output was dramatic. France saw her (quantitively) important wine department of Gard drop from 229,812 acres (93,000 hectares) of vines to 19,770 acres (8,000 hectares). After 1877, when the insect really made itself felt, French production was halved. Vineyard workers left the wine districts, some 6,000 from the Côte d'Or of Burgundy alone, and the value of vineyards was halved. France became a wine importer on any scale for the first time. This was a worldwide problem with *Phylloxera* evident in 1871 in Turkey and Portugal, 1872 in Austria–Hungary, Switzerland by 1874, Italy the following year and Spain by 1878. It is possible that *Phylloxera* was discovered earlier than these dates, but these are recorded confirmations of its evidence.

Prolonged controversy ranged over the possibilities for control and for the *cure* sought by the terms of the major French prize money (300,000 francs were offered in July 1874 by her National Assembly). Scientists did not know if the damage was a result of such favourable conditions for *Phylloxera* as drought, unsuitable soil or poor viticulture or was caused only by the insect itself. *Phylloxera* cannot, for example, survive in sand. This explains why the vineyards of Colares in Portugal (where the vine travels through a layer of sand to the soil below) have resisted the aphid.

All manner of treatments were attempted, of which the most immediately effective were chemical ones, such as the injection into the soil of carbon bisulphide. Others looked more dramatic, like large-scale flooding.

The shortage of quality wines, prior to the discovery in 1889 that certain American root stocks were *Phylloxera*-resistant, led to blending between French and Spanish wines. In turn, this forced the French Government to bring in a regional control by naming vineyards. Cognac was delimited in 1909, Champagne and Bordeaux by 1911, and the Rhône in 1923. Controls were instituted in Italy in 1925 and in Germany by 1930.

Phylloxera was not wiped out by vineyard reconstitution with resistant stocks. The aphid continues its infestation, but without lethal effect. It seems that the old 'national' vines had longer lives and many have been less productive; but no firm comment can be made on whether the wine made pre- or post-*Phylloxera* was better. Many other factors come into play, such as the more severe pruning given to grafted vines and the very different vinification methods used today.

The late nineteenth century saw Champagne come into its own with sales rising from 1,250,000 cases in 1868, to 2,120,000 cases by 1890, over 2,600,000 by 1902 and a staggering 3,250,000 cases by 1909. In the period after monastic suppression, houses like Ruinart, Veuve Clicquot and Moët had not had the competition that was to result from the founding of firms in the first half of the nineteenth century. These include Ernest Irroy in 1820, Mumm seven years later, Bollinger in 1829, both Deutz and Geldermann and Pommery and Greno in 1836, Krug in 1843 and Pol Roger in 1849. In Britain, duty reductions and music hall songs – like Leybourne's *Champagne Charlie* of 1869* – created the climate for Champagne sales. Exports doubled between 1844 and 1865 and doubled again by the turn of the century. Champagne, with a lead from the Prince of Wales, became the drink of society and whilst those dominant days have passed, it remains the festive drink of quality.

With higher consumption went an interest in a drier style and Perrier-Jouët shipped a little of their 1846 vintage without *dosage*. From the 1860s, shipments with low dosage levels became increasingly popular and by 1874 almost the entire shipment to England consisted of this dry type. France remained attracted to the sweeter style and it is still popular there. Like whisky, port and Sherry, dry Champagne was a British invention.

*The title of his first song was actually *Moët and Shandon for me* (spelt very much as the Cockneys pronounced it).

Sherry gradually became more popular during the early twentieth century with a setback temporarily during the Spanish Civil War, and as a fortified wine, gradually took the place of port. Legal protection was accorded to port by British law (a 1914 Treaty which was ratified in 1916) and later, by case law, to Champagne and Sherry. France passed the first *Appellation d'Origine Contrôlée* regulations in 1919, though they were largely ineffective. She had developed these further by 1935.

Further afield, the formation of the Co-operative Wine Growers Association or K.W.V. in 1918 and the reintroduction of Imperial preference helped the marketing of South African wines. Australian shipments similarly prospered. The first commercial shipment of Australian wines to Britain was in 1854 with a steady expansion building up to 703,000 gallons (3,195,910 litres) by 1896. The first budgetary move to encourage goods of British Empire origin was made in 1919. Imperial preference for 'Empire' wines in 1925 gave Australia an opportunity to export fortified dessert wines to Britain which reached 4,000,000 gallons (18,184,400 litres) within two years. Australia has since expanded her export markets beyond Britain, selling 1,678,000 gallons (7,628,120 litres) overseas in a year like 1962.

The cocktail fashion arrived, from the United States, in Britain in the 1920s although the cocktail had probably been created in the early nineteenth century. The U.S.A. attempted prohibition from 1920 to 1933 with the 18th Amendment to its Constitution. Its repeal led to local decision-making: Mississippi was the last state to allow alcohol sales in 1961. On a much smaller scale, the Welsh county system to allow local communities to decide about Sunday licensing may be compared. Cocktail trade is still significant on the catering and domestic side.

The export of South American wines can be seen growing during this time. They have a long history for the Spanish had planted vines in Mexico in the early sixteenth century. The Jesuits planted a vineyard at Cuyo, Argentina, in 1556. However, little of note has emerged over four centuries later, despite the aspirations of revolutionary Miguel Hidalgo in 1810 and the work of the Irish-American grower James Concannon last century. Italian work last century contributed largely to the prolific output of Argentina, utilising the snow waters of the Andes. Irrigation is used largely to combat *Phylloxera* there. The Argentinian reds, made from the Cabernet Sauvignon vine and found particularly in the north of the Province of Mendoza, are among those exported today. Brazil has developed its viticulture this century, using largely the Trebbiano and Riesling for the whites and the Cabernet and Merlot for the reds in such climatically favourable regions as the southern Rio Grande do Sul which lies in the southern temperate zone. Both Chile and Peru had vines planted by Spanish missionaries with sacramental wines in mind, but it took Italian influence last century to expand and develop the potential. In Chile, this impetus came in 1851 from Silvestre Ochagavia who persuaded French experts to help. This explains much of the technical skill seen there today. The smaller state of Uruguay saw its viticulture established in the 1890s near Montevideo, but little is exported for there is a fair consumption within the country.

In the post-1945 era, boosts to wine consumption have come from the halving of table wine duty in 1949 and the reduction of the fortified wine duty nine years later. A substantial proportion of Government revenue is still derived from alcoholic beverages, including new taxes like VAT. Holidays overseas and probably the home wine-making kits have developed wine interest. This is likely to increase now that Britain has joined the E.E.C. which has the stated aim of Customs harmonisation.

In recent years, vermouths have increased in popularity at the partial expense of Sherry, port and Madeira, while newer white spirits – like white rum and vodka – have increased sales out of all recognition from pre-1955 levels. Vodka has had a long history in central and eastern Europe with some historians dating its origin to fourteenth-century Russia. Its western popularity stems from the 1917 Russian Revolution which caused the Smirnoff formula to be taken, via Paris, to the U.S.A. where production was established.

The wine-shipping and distributive trade has consolidated into a much smaller number of large purchasing and retailing units, reducing the number of independent small merchants and shippers, but opening new doors in the field of supermarkets and multiple off-licences. Wine and spirit sales in the catering sector have grown out of all recognition from the pre-1945 situation and further new outlets – like wine bars and quick food chains – are emerging to act as extra sales points for alcoholic beverages. The increased size of many such wine firms has led to improved transportation and handling of wines and spirits, substituting maritime containers and road tankers for wooden casks, metered pumps for syphons, and fully automated filtering, bottling and labelling lines for manual labour. While the handling reflects twentieth-century technology, many in the wine and spirit trades ensure that the traditions of interest and expertise are fostered for the continued growth and service to the catering trade.

2. Personnel, Training, Purchasing, Storage and Service

'Such and so various are the tastes of men', Mark Akenside.

WINE SOURCES

Most caterers purchase wines from a shipper at wholesale prices. The shipper is responsible for importing the wine, warehousing the stock, despatching it to meet your orders and for payment of both C.E.T. and Excise duties (as appropriate). Regional wine merchants usually purchase from shippers, make their mark-up and sell to local caterers as well as on the retail side through off-licences and mail order. The merits of the various U.K.-based sources for wine purchase are discussed in Chapter 3.

For larger-scale caterers, for those who wish to combine in a purchasing co-operative or consortium, and for an appreciation of the problems involved for your shipper or merchant, it is useful to understand the shipping and bottling aspects of the operation.

In France a vineyard proprietor will sell his grapes for pressing and later sale by a co-operative, or will vinify it – i.e. make it into wine – and sell it in bulk or in bottle. In the latter case, it will normally be sold to a broker, called a *négoçiant*; although a *courtier* may be employed to search out an appropriate wine or parcel of wines. The *négoçiant* will usually sell to his export agents or may act as a direct seller in an export market, with a subsidiary company and representatives working there. In West Germany and on other markets, it is usual to rely on the agent, who may actually own some vineyards, and to purchase within its export list. Large caterers, supermarket chains and similar organisations may be able to enjoy favourable discounts by buying directly. However, they should also have the staff expertise to buy accurately, ship, treat and bottle;

although there are contract bottlers and shipping agents prepared to undertake much of this.

Purchasing

Purchases may be effected in five ways:

1. Ex-cellars:
This method of sale is used for wine despatched to a customer direct from the supplier's cellar in the country of origin. This is a common method used for West German purchases on export markets. If an export shipper is used, only a small commission is payable (which is frequently included in the price quoted) and a minimum order requirement is frequently stipulated. This may well be 1,000 dozen bottles (or equivalent).

2. F.O.B.:
This method is similar to ex-cellars, although the prices quoted include transport from the cellars to the port of embarkation. The customer has only to pay for freight and transport to and within the country into which the wine is being imported. The initials stand for 'free on board'. As for ex-cellars, this type of purchase requires capital to be ready to pay the appropriate duties, unless the wines are going into bond.

3. Under Bond:
Caterers may purchase under bond, where the shipper or merchant moves goods to the bond of the caterer or to the public bond that the caterer nominates, without payment of duty. The shipper is then not responsible for the duty element or the financing of it.

4. Notional Under Bond:
If a purchaser has not a bond and does not want access to one, he can still take advantage of buying under bond on a notional basis. The under bond price (as in 3. above) is quoted where the purchaser submits a cheque or other payment for the full duty element at the time his order is placed. The shipper is thereby able to save on the financing involved in having to pay the duty. The customer in this sequence will normally receive two invoices: one for the duty element and the second for the wine.

5. Duty Paid and Delivered:
This is where the shipper or merchant pays the duties liable and the paid price by the customer includes the duty element. Several shippers offer discounts for 'cash with order' D.P.D., which means the shipper is not financing either the duty or the intrinsic value of the wine after clearance of the payment.

Shipping

Wine is shipped increasingly in bottle and this trend is likely to continue. Various quality wine-producing regions have made this one of their regulations. Small wood-cask shipments are not common owing to both high freight charges and the costs involved in the maintenance of casks. Most bulk wine is shipped in 530–580 gallon (2,410–2,640 litre) capacities in containers of glass-lined mild steel or stainless steel with an external polyester cladding. Metal contamination is more frequent in the former owing to the greater chance of the glass lining coming loose and exposing wine to the metal.

Upon arrival, the containers should be sterilised, usually with a quarternary ammonium compound.* Bulk storage equipment is necessary for receiving wine in this way, although it is usual to sample for taste and analysis prior to pumping. Increasingly road tankers with a variety of compartment sizes are being used, which speeds the transit of wine; but there should be adequate staff and equipment available to receive it. Wines may be stored in wooden casks (where controlled oxygen supply and tannin through the wood are beneficial), mild steel tanks, glass-lined concrete vats, stainless steel tanks, fibreglass tanks, and occasionally aluminium containers.

Wine usually requires treatment after shipment, which involves filtration (i.e. clarification of the wine) prior to bottling. This can be undertaken by laboratory staff for a contract bottler† if the volume does not justify the employment of such qualified staff normally.

*This may be in solid or liquid state. It is preferable to a hypochlorite compound which tends to be alkaline by nature and can leave an odour.

†One who undertakes bottling for another organisation, usually requiring a regular order. The labels are generally supplied by the firm for whom the wine is intended. Some wine merchants will undertake this trade, but usually it is a specialist business.

STORAGE

Wine Storage

Wines are best stored underground to remove the light and to keep the temperature variation reduced economically. The best temperature is 50–55°F (10–13°C). Above-ground cellars can have the temperature variations by insulating walls and ceilings and by installing air-conditioning. Air humidity should also be controlled because dry air can lead to a loss of wine through evaporation while excess humidity can lead to the development of unwanted micro-organisms and in rust forming on equipment. A 70 to 80 per cent hygrometer reading is best. The cellar should be free from draught and away from any central heating source. It is advisable to install a maximum/minimum temperature gauge in each store and to take regular readings. The cellar should be kept clean and free from vinegar, fuel oil or other odours.

With the exception of the fastest moving *vin ordinaires* which can be kept horizontal within their cartons, all other wines with corks should be binned in order to keep an appropriate check, and to ensure that the corks do not dry out by keeping the wines in a horizontal position. In this way the wine keeps the cork expanded and stops oxidation. Normal sizes of bins are discussed in Chapter 3; the sizes selected should reflect your trade in litres (35 fluid ounces), 1½ litres (52 fluid ounces), double litres (70 fluid ounces), magnums (80 fluid ounces/2·27 litres) and other similarly larger units. It is important to structure the wine cellar so that all the wines that are in regular demand are housed in the most accessible order and within geographical context. Finer quality wines, and those ordered less regularly, can be still stored by regional reference but in a further bin. Ensure that gangways are clear and that any necessary equipment, such as ladders for tall bins or trolleys, are in position prior to each meal occasion.

The careful control of wines received forms part of one's general control system; but, for practical purposes, it is usually best to designate a particular member of staff. Stress the importance of complying with the wine carrier's terms regarding non-delivery, which may be checked against a potential arrival sheet and for any claims that may arise. Most shippers have to comply with strict carriers' terms, which require firstly the reporting of damage to *both* the shipper and carrier within three days in writing; and secondly the signing-in as 'unexamined', if in a hurry, or actual checking at the time of receipt. Control must include easy checking of a goods-in book and the reconciliation of wine orders. A reorder level must be set for each line and bottle size, in order that a fresh requisition is called for automatically when that level is reached. Allow extra ordering time at peak periods like Christmas, Easter and Jewish religious holidays. Check that the banqueting staff know the ordering-time periods well and that forthcoming commitments are conveyed to the cellar staff.

Spirit Storage

Spirits, and all other alcoholic beverages without corks, should be stored vertically. It is usually advisable to place spirits in a separate store from wine for security. Careful monitoring, as for wine, is required for spirits; since most of the needs will be in the cocktail bar area and drinks trolley, it may be appropriate that the ordering for and control of the spirit store should be the responsibility of a separate member of staff.

Importance of Control

As outlined above, the correct foreknowledge of wine and spirit deliveries is important. This should go hand-in-hand with maintaining an up-to-date wine list. If one merchant is supplying the outlet's needs, ensure that adequate notice is received for stocks which are to be de-listed and that arrangements are made for sampling and approval, as well as subsequent listing, of the replacement. Wines and spirits are intrinsically some of the most valuable assets of the caterer's property and are also an area of temptation due to their ease of movement and ready resale value. Therefore full controls are essential. These should include a duplicate order book or, preferably, triplicate – one copy to the cellars, one for accounts and one for retention in the buying office – a goods-in receipt book and attached delivery note system, an invoice file which is matched with the original order and the delivery note, an appropriate credit note system with allowance for stock returned and which cross-checks, where necessary, with customers' bills and sommeliers' order pads. Stocktaking at least quarterly is advisable. Bin numbers and well-marked bin cards with a system for designating the bottle size are desirable for speedy cellar movement.

Although the bulk of wines and spirits should be kept within the respective stores or cellars, a small stock for the next meal occasion's use should be kept in the refrigerator for white wines, rosés and spirits like vodka, and at room temperature for reds. Occasionally bottles have a return value and such goods-out should be noted in the control system. Good standards of hygiene should be maintained throughout. Any breakages, although reported and noted for stock purposes, should be cleared promptly, especially as this nearly always involves glass with alcoholic beverages.

Staff Training

An important element in achieving the correct interplay of the control system and in ensuring the profitable, efficient service of one's alcoholic beverages is to provide adequate staff training. This is sadly too often neglected.

A number of bodies organise courses on alcoholic beverages, other than for the City and Guilds, H.N.D., O.N.D. and Hotel Catering and Institutional Management Association examinations, such as the Brewers' Society with their residential courses.

The Wine and Spirit Education Trust runs three other courses that might be appropriate: an eight-session Certificate; a more advanced Higher Certificate on full day release, or 15 evening sessions; and the Diploma, which is for advanced product knowledge candidates and is split into two sections which most candidates take over a two-year period. Successful Diploma students may be eligible for the course and examination that leads to the coveted Master of Wine qualification, held by slightly over than one hundred people to date. A Master Sommeliers' examination is also open to eligible candidates which leads to membership of the Court of Master Sommeliers. Usually all these courses allow candidates to taste wines and spirits; this is of real benefit in their work, as well as naturally giving them an insight into the problems and developments in the field of alcoholic beverages.

Identify the talents of those likely to perform well in the service of alcoholic beverages and the weaknesses of others. Self-motivation and enthusiasm are key factors in this specialist, but highly profitable, sector of catering. Newcomers should be given clear guidance as customers regularly seek advice.

SERVICE

How to Appreciate Wine

The length of time wines may be stored is a vexed one, but the various vintage charts make fair attempts – with the proviso that they can never take into account all wines made in any one year in a given region. There will always be better wines made and worse ones; therefore such charts are only a rough general guide. The best method is to taste regularly, making notes and comparing your comments with others.

Spirits do not benefit from keeping once bottled; their ageing is undertaken in wood prior to bottling.

Three main factors should be examined when evaluating a wine, apart from considerations such as price, shipper and potential for a given outlet:

1. Appearance:

Is the wine bright? Cloudy? Has it a deposit? Is it pétillant? Has it a mousse? On the colour, violet shows immaturity on a red wine which fades through mahogany to tawny. Whites, if dry, commence light green frequently to mid-straw; sweet whites start as mid-straw and develop into a rich gold. Rosés vary in colour, dependent upon the length of time the skins have been in contact with the grape juice during fermentation.

2. Nose:

This should be clean and of good character, demonstrating the wine's regional origin (such as Cabernet fruit on a Médoc from Bordeaux or the Riesling from the Mosel). As a wine develops, so will or should the nose.

3. Palate:

Is the wine dry, medium-dry, medium-sweet, or sweet? How much fruit is there in the mouth? What is the overall acidity and tannin? Judge the alcoholic strength to see if it is in character. What is the length of the wine? When is it ready for drinking?

By means of this three-fold appraisal, one will recognise the best time at which to serve such wines and place them in terms of their suitability for listing. It is surprising how many medium-priced wines from regions such as Rioja in northern Spain, Chianti, Rhône, and the Dão of Portugal are sold prematurely without realising their potential.

For tasting terminology, see the Glossary.

Glasses for Alcoholic Beverages

Wine and cocktail glasses should have stems which allow them to be held easily and prevent the heat of the hand from being transmitted to the beverage. The glassware should be thin and clear to allow a true appreciation of the wine's appearance. Tulip-shaped glassware is ideal, although the 5 fluid ounce (140 millilitres) round 'Paris' goblet is regularly found. German wines may be served in longer-stemmed glasses with wider bowls but tulip-shaped ones will certainly suffice. Avoid the saucer-shaped creations which are still produced for sparkling functions; they do not allow proper consideration of either the appearance or nose, and ensure the *mousse* disappears at an early stage, which is quite the opposite of the intention!

Fortified wines can similarly be served in a tulip-shaped glass with good length of stem, but Sherry is often presented in a 'copita', a small glass with a short stem and larger bowl than the tapering top. Spirits are often served in square-shaped clear glasses; the exceptions are brandy and liqueurs, which are best served in 'balloon' glasses, provided they are not cumbersome.

Wash glasses in hot water only with no detergent; the latter leaves an off-flavour. Dry with a clean linen towel as soon as possible after washing in order to avoid smears. Use calibrated carafe vessels, preferably with a wide neck to make them easier to clean. If several wines are to be served, assemble the glasses before each cover; although it is usual to leave the liqueur or port glass until later, when a decision has been made by each guest, unless this forms part of the set menu. Even where liqueurs are included or a spirit, it is difficult to pour the correct quantity over someone's shoulder: far better to undertake this in the bar area beforehand.

TAKING ORDERS AND SERVING

Make wine and spirit ordering as easy as possible. The wine list should be in a form that allows regular updating; this is often best achieved by having a loose-leaf system with an appropriate plastic cover. Tent cards and other aids can bring attention to special offers, including your bin ends. Use number references for ease of both customer reference and cellar ordering; short descriptive phrases also help. Have adequate numbers of lists and always keep several in the cocktail bar area to allow early ordering. If an order for alcoholic beverages has not been received by the time a cover is seated, ensure the wine list is presented simultaneously with the menu. Check if an apéritif is required while the food order is considered. It may help to have a short apéritif list printed; this can include dry white and sparkling wines by the glass and/or half bottle.

When taking an order for wine, follow this procedure:

1. Check that you have the order correctly by repeating it. Your lists should be up to date and therefore it should not be necessary to check on the available stock.
2. Ask when the wines will be required, giving – if appropriate to the occasion and type of customer – several options. Check if the wine or wines are to be decanted with the inference, wherever possible, that you are able to do this unless totally under-staffed. If the choice is a wine that may be served at different temperatures, such as young Beaujolais, ask how the customer would like it served.
3. Adjust glasses as necessary to be appropriate to the alcoholic beverage orders. Check if a mineral water is additionally required. Offer soft drinks to children and others not participating in the alcoholic orders.
4. Ensure the wine, wherever possible, is at the right temperature. Almost all reds should be served at room temperature (about 60°F/16°C), while dry and medium whites and rosés should be slightly cooler (about 54°F/12°C). Dessert whites and sparkling wines should be chilled (about 45°F/7°C). The drier fortified wines and many white spirits, like rum and tequila, should be served at a similar temperature to the rosés above. Other fortified wines and spirits can be enjoyed at room temperature. These are suggested guidance levels and are subjective.

   If an order is received for a wine that is too cold, do not try to raise its temperature too quickly. Explain the situation to the customer, place in the room where it is to be served, and suggest that the wine is poured early so that it may be warmed through the cupping effect of the hand around the glass.
5. Check the labels prior to presentation to the customer against the wine list. Look for vintage, bottler and similar information that may have been in the list or alternatively may be enquired about upon presentation. If it is a wine with some sediment, ensure it is brought from the bin in a horizontal position and carried in the same way to the customer. Wine baskets usually disturb a wine's sediment more

than necessary. Only use one if you are totally happy that this will not occur.

6. Present the wine to the customer, main label facing towards them. If there has unavoidably had to have been any change, such as the next vintage or a different shipper, explain this now and offer to switch the order for the customer if your suggested replacement is not acceptable. Mention any price difference, if appropriate, to the replacement, prior to asking if it is acceptable.
7. If the wine is acceptable in bottled form, remove the top of the capsule to below the first lip of the bottle or, ideally, bend the foil back in the first lip section. This will allow you later to place the cork in an inverted position within the top of the foil which has been turned back.
8. Clean the top of the bottle. Remove the cork, ideally with a double series corkscrew with a long enough screw that will not allow claret and port corks to fracture. Port tongs can be used where there is a source of natural heat and time permits. Remember to perform 7 and 8 *in front* of the customers so that they may watch the operation.
9. Smell the cork to see there are no 'off' aromas; this may be your first sign of trouble, other than weeping between the bottle and capsule. Invert the cork in order that the stain – if it is a red wine – which shows the length of time the wine has been in contact with the cork may be seen and/or the crystalline deposit. Hold the cork there by placing a rubber band around it and the neck of the bottle or by placing it within the folded-back foil lip section.
10. Thoroughly clean the inside and top of the bottle. If the offer to decant has been accepted, remember that the slower the decanting, the greater the final quantity of clear wine. With mature wines – perhaps clarets of 20 years or so, Burgundies and Rhônes of 12 years or so and vintage ports of 25 years – it is preferable to decant only a few minutes before the wine is required, in order that it is not oxidised prematurely. Although the wine should, as far as possible, be carried to the table or trolley near the customer in a horizontal position, if notice has been given that a really mature, old wine is required, stand the bottle upright for 24 hours beforehand to allow any soft deposit or, in vintage port, loose crust to fall and settle at the bottom. A candle is best to show clarity but not essential and some restaurants prefer a reading lamp.

Decanting serves two prime objectives: to remove the sediment and to refreshen the wine. In a very young wine, the effect of decanting will be artificially to aerate or oxidise the wine a little and so to bring it to a more mature state.

After uncorking, pour the wine into a funnel in which a washed clean muslin has been placed. A funnel with a hook at the end is preferable as this allows the strained wine to fall gently down the side of the vessel and not into the centre, with the resultant unfortunate effect of frothing. The candle flame or light should be placed below the shoulder of the bottle in order to see the movement of the wine and deposit as pouring continues. Stop when the deposit or crust starts falling into the muslin or when the wine begins to turn muddy, whichever is the sooner. The final part may be strained into a waiting glass. If you feel particularly competent at decanting, pour straight into the decanter without a muslin until the last stages. 'Beeswing' is part of the deposit and the gummy tissue that separates the cells (sugar and water sacs) that compose the grape. Deposit or 'crust' is simply the bottle equivalent to the more speedy process of depositing the lees in the barrel.

11. After uncorking and possibly decanting, it is quite in order to check the wine prior to presentation to the host. Examine the clarity and other aspects of appearance – such as *pétillant* on a still table red wine would indicate malo-lactic fermentation (see pages 50–4) – as well as clean factors on nose and taste. Taste is optional in this context as it should merely confirm the appearance and nose.

12. Pour a small but adequate amount (about one-third normal serving) to the host. This tradition started in the eighteenth century when oil was floated on top of a wine to preserve it: some might still be present when the first glass was poured and therefore the host took it. Upon receiving acceptance from the host of the wine, check – if this has not been asked or advised earlier – as to who is to receive the wine. Proceed to fill each glass to between half and two-thirds full. Do not pour more as that would not allow proper appreciation of the appearance and nose, which involves agitating the wine in the glass.

13. Return the decanter and original bottle to the table and check if any further orders are required. By now an extra bottle or wines for later courses may have been decided upon, although it is better to obtain such orders on the first occasion of ordering.

14. Return regularly during the course or courses at which the wine is being served to top up, but still do not exceed the half to two-thirds level in each glass.

15. Once the wine is finished, enquire if another bottle or a different wine is required. If a later course – such as the dessert – is commenced and the earlier bottle not completed, check if the wine is to be continued or if another wine would be liked. Remember not to lose sales by not having half bottles and wines by the glass available and visibly seen to be available. Several restaurateurs encourage greater overall consumption by offering to charge for only that proportion of each bottle poured.

16. Do not forget to offer liqueurs, brandies and digestives towards the end of a meal. This can be done subtly by ensuring that the staff clearing plates at the appropriate course leave two tent cards per five covers which describe your liqueur and brandy range and mention the coffee specialities (see Chapter 8). This will allow discussion to take place before the wine and spirit staff approach. Remember to check out the legal aspects of serving alcoholic beverages which is currently dependent upon the outlet's licence (see Chapter 4).

The service of beer is covered in Chapter 9.

When preparing for each function, check on:

1. Wine, spirit and other beverage stocks in order that the lists are up to date;
2. Location and clean state of ice buckets, decanting vessels, carafes, muslin and funnels for decanting;
3. Location of corkscrews, sparkling stoppers, rubber bands, alcoholic beverage order pads and pencils or pens;
4. Special requirements for the function, menu specialities, and closing hours.

These are the advance aspects of preparation in addition to the normal management ones of staff hours, reordering, payment procedures for particular customers, and layout.

Serving Sparkling Wines

Sparkling wines should be brought prechilled to the table and, after presentation, have the foil around the cork and lip of the bottle removed. Then, holding a tea towel, place a thumb or index finger firmly over the cork and unwind the wire muzzle. It is unwise to remove the wire entirely

Gradually untwist the wire

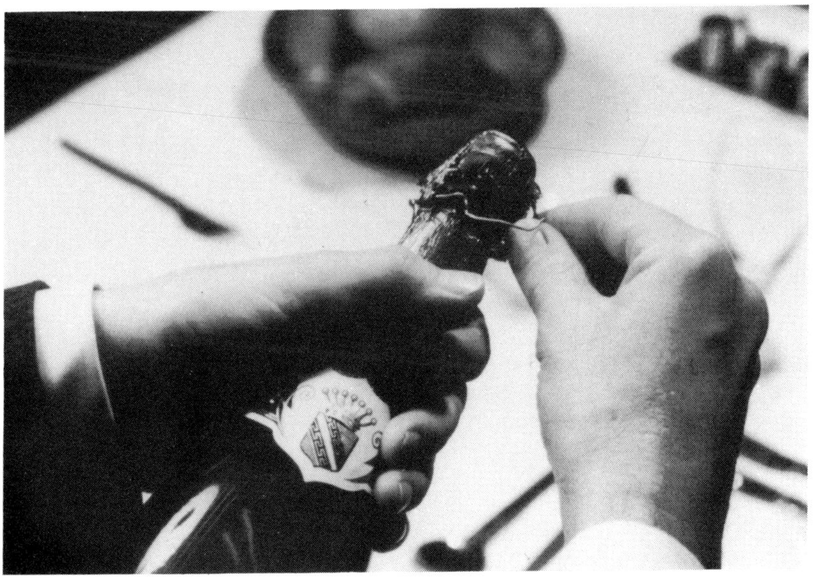

After removing the foil, slowly release the wire muzzle

With the muzzle removed, retain a firm hold on the cork

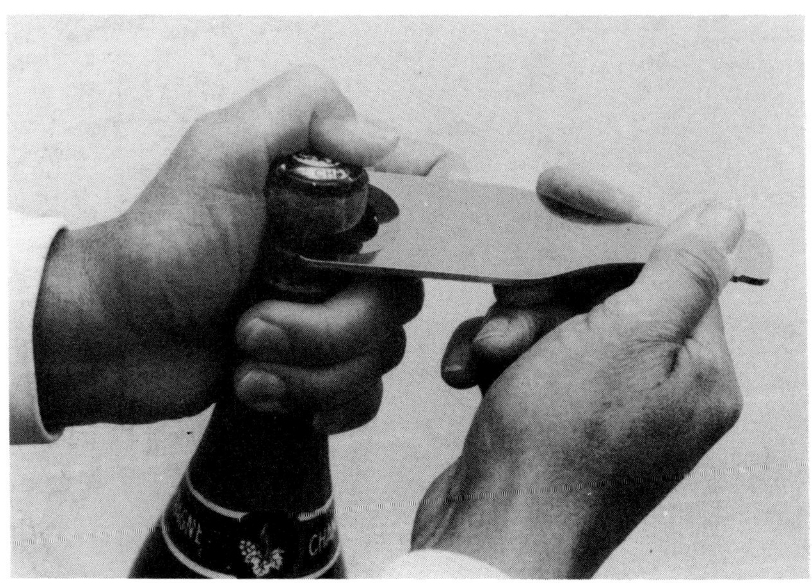

Grip the cork neck with the tweezers, still retaining hold on the cork

Pour slowly — and enjoy it!

as this action may allow the cork to eject prematurely. Simply undo the wire, so that it is loose, and then grip the cork firmly in one hand, while still ensuring it is not ejected. Then, holding the bottle in the other hand, twist the cork in the opposite direction to the bottle trying to produce a gradual movement, not a vertical jerk. Listen for the sound as the carbon-dioxide gas escapes which should mean the bottle can be served without any spillage. After serving, place a sparkling stopper over the top of the bottle to retain the sparkle.

COMPLAINTS

Be prepared for complaints in connection with alcoholic beverages by knowing the main faults that one may find. It is emphasised that faults are not common, but like any branch of catering, can occur. Sometimes, however, the condition of a wine is not a fault but a natural development that should be recognised and explained as appropriate to the customer.

If you are inexperienced at recognising common faults, ask your wine merchant – whether it is a tied trade one (where it owns outlets and has both managers and tenants who are obliged to purchase their beverages either through the company or the company's nominated or approved suppliers) or an independent – to show you examples in order that they may be recognised.

Here are those most likely to be found:

Excess Iron

Symptoms: A haze (or casse), often associated with a metallic taste. In a pronounced state, an unpleasant pungent nose is evident through the formation of sulphides.

Cause: Probably the use of iron implements during the making or transit of the wine.

Treatment: Return to wine supplier who will add citric acid. This will stop the haze but not the bad nose problem.

Excess Fruit Acid

Symptoms: A tart flavour to the wine.

Cause: Use of unripe grapes during the wine-making, or excessive use by the vintner of tartaric acid or citric acid.

Treatment: Blend with other wine of just below normal fruit acidity, particularly if this is a running carafe or house wine. Alternatively add calcium carbonate; however, this may lead to an excess of calcium, requiring refrigeration additionally.

Excess Sulphur

Symptoms: A strong sulphur nose and, often, a reduction in colour which can even lead to a bleaching of a wine.

Cause: Although the body naturally needs sulphur and is applied as the standard preservative for wine, it may have been overapplied. There are E.E.C. restrictions on its use; the U.K. used to have higher tolerances before E.E.C. entry.

Treatment: If the sulphur is not oppressive, uncork a good hour or two hours in advance and preferably decant. If the sulphur is still pungent, return to supplier who will probably disgorge and rebottle with a similar wine of lower sulphur level to bring it up to normal adjustment.

Excess Copper

Symptoms: Occasionally a haze or copper casse, which will need to be confirmed by analysis. The effect of this, if left to continue to a marked degree, will be oxidation.

Cause: It may be spraying too late in the vineyards, but is more probably the result of the wine coming into contact with brass, bronze or copper implements in the winery or in transit if bottling takes place at a different point.

Treatment: None for the caterer; return to the supplier.

Corked or Corky Wine

Symptoms: The cork will smell unpleasant and the wine will frequently have a taste of fungus.

Cause: A disease of the cork, usually the work of cork weevil.

Treatment: None. Replace as others in the same stock may not be affected.

Over-Chaptalised

Symptoms: An unbalanced wine with too much alcohol in relation to other properties. It can have too sweet an edge for the style.

Cause: Excessive use of beet or cane sugar or sugar syrup from starch. In proportion, such a procedure is reasonable but must be within balanced limits.

Treatment: Uncork and blend with a wine from the same place or, if this is not practical, return to merchant.

Protein Haze

Symptoms: A cloudy haze will appear in the wine, which may be table or fortified. (Sherry is quite susceptible.)

Cause: Inadequate fining or filtration.

Treatment: Return to supplier who will disgorge. He will treat it with bentonite and isinglass and subsequently refilter it.

Tartrates

Symptoms: Thin flakes or small crystals which fall to the bottom of the bottle.

Cause: Wine has been stored in too cold a cellar, thereby precipitating the tartrates.

Treatment: Since the tartrates are harmless, the sensible view is to make a note in the wine list that the bottle contains harmless precipitated tartrates as 'it has been stood/stored in too cold a cellar'. Brief your wine staff fully on the reasons and apply a back label, if possible, to the bottle with the reason. If you are not responsible, or consider that customers will not accept the wine in spite of the explanation, return it to your supplier who will disgorge and refrigerate for one week at 18°F (−8°C) and/or add cologel or metatartaric acid.

Flabbiness

Symptoms: Lacks distinction and 'finish' or length of taste on palate.

Cause: Absence of acidity usually.

Treatment: If a carafe wine, blend with next shipment, adding tartaric or citric acid.

Oxidation

Symptoms: These vary depending upon the degree of oxidation. Faults include a distinctly unpleasant aroma and a deepening of colour on rosé and white wines.

Cause: Oxygen has contaminated the wine, either before or more likely after bottling. Often a faulty cork or a bottle which has been stood upright, whereupon the cork will dry out, is the cause of the oxygen seeping in.

Treatment: If only mildly 'off', it can be uncorked and have both ascorbic acid, i.e. Vitamin C, and sulphur dioxide added. If strongly oxidised, return to supplier.

Excessive Tannin

Symptoms: The wine shows a real 'bite' with a film across your teeth immediately after tasting. It is often associated with a slight haze in the wine.

Cause: The wine has been stored for too long in new wood, or has been left to ferment on the grape skins for too long, or excess tannin may have been added artificially.

Treatment: It is usually best to continue storing until the tannin chemically breaks down and the wine becomes palatable. If it is not simply the case of a young wine and is clearly out of balance, particularly in relation to total acidity, return it to the supplier. He will probably uncork and give it a gelatine treatment if actual tannins are present. If it is the haze which is more noticeable, a supplier may try to treat potential tannins by adding polyvinyl pyrrolidine (a white, free-flowing powder).

Refermentation

Symptoms: Probably the cork will blow. The wine will show excessive carbon-dioxide bubbles for a still wine (not to be confused with *pétillant* wines), but will probably not have the overacid taste of a wine suffering from a malo-lactic fermentation (see below).

Cause: Yeast in the bottle which led to an unwanted secondary fermentation.

Treatment: Return to supplier, who will uncork, add sorbic acid, give a better filtration than the first time and rebottle.

Malo-lactic Fermentation

Symptoms: Presence of bubbles (carbon dioxide) associated with excessive acidity, plus an off nose and flavour at the same time.

Cause: The malo-lactic fermentation is a natural wine development, but producers aim to complete it in the vat before bottling. The main exception is a Nouveau wine. The best known example of this is Beaujolais Nouveau, where the wine is bottled in late October for sale in mid November and at a time when the malo-lactic fermentation has not taken place.

Treatment: Since the malo-lactic is completed within a fortnight, wait until this time has elapsed and retaste. If found to be excessively acidic subsequently, return it to supplier; but it may well have settled sufficiently to continue selling. This is a condition not to be confused with young Chianti, vinho verde and light Mosels where they are frequently *pétillant*.

Volatile Acidity

Symptoms: A vinegar nose and taste.

Cause: The wine has been exposed to the air and the vinegar bacteria has multiplied. Often found on old wines that have been badly cellared.

Treatment: If really mild, uncork and blend with the same wine which has not been contaminated. However the likelihood is that other bottles from the same source are in the same condition. In this case, it should be returned to the supplier.

If too many preservatives and treatments are given, an overall unpleasant taste – often of a chemical nature – can be found. Alternatively, the wine may be limpid and lack character. In either event, return to the supplier for large-scale blending.

Wine is complex. Much research in the last 150 years has given a man a better understanding of its composition and of how to treat disorders, such as those described above. The final appreciation is undertaken by the taster (i.e. the purchaser) and not by analysis. In this, it is important to understand how wines mature.

Wine Ageing

Table and sparkling wines prefer to mature, once bottled, with a minimum of oxygen. At bottling stage the air space created between the bottom of the cork and the start of the wine amounts to about $\frac{1}{4}$ ounce (9 millilitres). By storing horizontally, the cork stays expanded and does not usually allow very much air to penetrate. The traditional wire around a sparkling stopper enforces this on a wine where an atmospheric pressure of 3 atmospheres and above needs to be maintained.

As a generalisation, dry whites may be consumed earlier than medium-sweet and sweet table styles. The former are better while they are fresher and can show their evident fruit; oxidation does not normally improve them. Dessert styles can benefit from ageing further in bottle. During the ageing process, salts precipitate, the acidity decreases, and a gradual transformation turns the acids, alcohol and other properties into such compounds as aldehydes and esters which give wines of maturity their character. Reds with a fair tannin content, like most Rhône, Burgundy and Bordeaux wines, benefit from several years' bottle age in addition to their 2 to 4 years in vat.

Fortified wines enjoy being in the presence of oxygen. Ageing open to the air is traditional; Madeira, vermouth and Sherry are good examples.

Once a bottle of fortified wine has been opened, it will not deteriorate at the speed of a table wine in the same situation unless it is already of distinct age.

The red wines which need the longest cellar ageing are those that have been made with a fairly high degree of tannin and whose other characteristics will allow such ageing to take place. This traditionally means vintage claret, Rhône, northern Burgundies, the Rioja of north-eastern Spain, such Italian wines as Barolo, and the firmer Californian, South American and Australian wines. A steady cool temperature is best for ageing, rather than a considerable seasonal variation.

No ultimate age can be given for wine as it varies from district to district and vintage to vintage. Some fine years, like 1945 in Bordeaux, may never be sufficiently balanced to drink on account of their high tannin, while much southern and eastern European wine is clearly aged in cask for too long at present. The taster's decision is, like art, subjective and what may please one – such as the youthfulness seen as attractive to many a French taster – may be seen as 'immaturity' to another national, who prefers aged or even decadent [*sic*] wines. It is vital to appreciate the occasion and to relate the style and age of the wine to the time at which it is served. In this way, the greatest value may be derived from any wine, regardless of its age.

In terms of vintage ports, where the wine is traditionally bottled between its second and third year following the harvest, there is considerable variation. The following is intended as a guide:

Pre-1945: A few good bottles at high prices are to be found that need no further ageing.
1945: Can be served now and for many years, as late as 1990.
1947: Reaching its end; serve now. The brandy is beginning to become pronounced.
1948: Similar remarks as for the '47.
1950: Over the top.
1954: Ready to drink; it will continue to benefit by keeping to 1980.
1955: Can be served now; will continue to mature to the late 1980s.
1958: Ready to drink. It will keep for less time than the '55, probably to about 1985.
1960: Fine style, ready to drink but will continue to mature to late 1980s.

1963: Almost ready to drink; will benefit by 8 to 10 years more bottle ageing.
1967: Probably ready from 1983 onwards.
1970: Likely to be ready to first serve around 1986.
1975: Good quality; likely to be ready about 1991.

Alcoholic Strength

Historically wine was taxed on the quantity imported. A system of 'prisage' took place where, for instance, a merchant importing between 10 and 20 tuns, paid the equivalent of 1 tun (252 gallons/1,146 litres) in tax. Coinage duty or customs duty was introduced under Charles II for both wines and spirits. The revenue went towards defraying the expenses of the Mint. The double rate of both Customs and Excise duty was applied until 1825 when the gallon (4·5 litres) – as opposed to the tun – was introduced as a unit of charge.

The modern system is to tax alcohol by its strength, not merely by its volume. In 1862, a Customs and Inland Revenue Act placed the dividing line between high and low strengths for wines at 26° proof. A higher rate of duty was introduced for wines above this strength up to 42° proof and then an additional 3s (15p) for each degree above this level. Since then strength bands have been amended. Today wine is split into three strength categories: up to 15°, between 15° and 18°, and between 18° and 22°. Common external tariff still applies to non-E.E.C. imports in addition to the excise duty. This is consolidated in the 1979 Act.

Britain works largely on the Sikes scale, but is moving on 1 January 1980 over to the metric (Gay-Lussac) scale. In the Sikes scale, 175 divisions are made between no alcohol (water) at zero and absolute alcohol at the top of the scale. 'Proof' is roughly an equal proportion of water and absolute alcohol and is fixed at 100° (out of 175) on the Sikes scale* In practical terms, distillers refer to so many degrees over or under proof; thus '30 under' means 70° Sikes. Most European countries wanted to put the emphasis on wine or beer (or both) and developed a different system.

*The exact measurement is by a Sikes' hydrometer where a beverage containing 57·06 per cent alcohol by volume at 51°F (11°C) is proof. The relevant technical extract is the Customs & Excise Act, 1952, which states that proof is '. . . the volume of the ethyl alcohol contained therein made up to the volume of the spirits with distilled water (which) has a weight equal to that of twelve-thirteenths of a volume of distilled water equal to the volume of spirits, the volume of each liquid being computed as at 51°F (11°C).' (Replaced by the consolidated Customs and Excise Management Act 1979 and Alcoholic Liquor Duties Act 1979.)

The metric or Gay-Lussac scale fixes absolute alcohol as 100°.* Degrees proof may be converted into degrees G.L. (the abbreviation normally used for Gay-Lussac) by dividing by 7/4. For instance, 25 degrees under proof Sikes is 42·9° G.L. The following guide may help:

	Gay-Lussac Scale (% of absolute alcohol)	Sikes Scale (% of proof)
Water	0 degrees	0 degrees
Table wines	10 degrees	17·7 degrees
Vermouth	18 degrees	31·6 degrees
Fortified wines	24 degrees	42 degrees
Most spirits	40 degrees	70 degrees
British proof	57 degrees	100 degrees
Absolute alcohol	100 degrees	175 degrees

Like the French with the Gay-Lussac scale, the American scale has 100 degrees but with 200 gradations which makes their 'proof' at 50 per cent absolute alcohol. Several countries, such as Italy and the U.S.S.R., follow France in measuring by volume, but West Germany measures in degrees of absolute alcohol by weight.

It is important to understand the different duty categories, as these have a significant bearing on the consumer price and label presentation. It is likely that wines will shortly have to state their alcoholic content on their labels as spirits already do.

*On the Gay-Lussac scale, measurement of volume is at 59°F (15°C) by comparison with the 51°F (11°C) of the British Sikes scale.

3. Marketing of Alcoholic Beverages

'Come, give us a taste of your quality', William Shakespeare.

The successful marketing of alcoholic beverages commences with research. Much of the research need not cost anything for local caterers are often prepared to share information. Libraries can give data on local wine companies whose representatives may well be prepared to give frank information on regional purchasing patterns. Libraries should also be able to assist on published material on drinking habits. Consumption trends can be evaluated from the advertisement sections of newspapers while help is often available through commercial radio stations. The local catering college and other centres of training may have research material from studies undertaken, in addition to the experience of the local depots of national wine and spirit shippers.

The practical side of the consumption pattern can be obtained from sections of your forthcoming clientele. For instance, if the outlet is a hotel, contact the local Rotary and Round Table clubs and the Chamber of Commerce to find out their usual function requirements for drinks and, through their membership, individual drinks, dining-out regularity and requirements.

Marketing Outside

Outside the catering outlet, successful drinks promotion can be obtained through a combination of seven basic methods:

1. Direct Mail:

Both nationally-held and locally-produced direct mail lists exist for practically every socio-economic class and occupation. If you see your outlet appealing to a particular clientele, expert direct mail houses will undertake a special mailing. However, postage is expensive, even with the bulk and other rebates available. You may like to link this to a drinks offer, such as inviting customers to enjoy a complimentary glass of Beaujolais Nouveau (if during the late November to Christmas period) or sparkling wine (for the rest of the year) for those who book for a certain date of the mailing.

2. Leaflet Distribution:
Potential customers are often worried over the likely drinks prices and need reassurance. A simple reproduction of part of your wine list, or the drink themes of the month, should allay such consumer fears. One marketing idea here is to show how you see the marriage of food and wine, for instance, in Spanish or Italian food. You could perhaps offer an inclusive price for a dish and a certain glass of wine.

3. Local Newspapers and Quality Periodical Media:
This may be by direct advertising, or on a semi-complementary basis by suggesting an idea using your outlet for the local 'wining and dining' column, or by using the personal column of the local newspaper. Evening papers or glossy periodicals are generally more effective than morning dailies.

4. Inviting the Press:
Show the range and versatility of your wine list to the press and stress the helpful, practical approach taken by the staff. If appropriate, indicate the value for money of your drinks.

5. Combined Telephone and Sales Letter Approaches:
Local libraries keep a file on local societies and clubs, including those specifically interested in wine like the local branch of the International Wine & Food Society and the Epicure Society. Most such society secretaries are happy to mention your outlet to their members and this may lead to an actual function at your outlet.

6. Use of Local Radio and/or TV:
Personalities can be useful here. If you purchase your Sherry or port

ranges from a particular national or other well-known shipper, useful publicity can be obtained for your outlet's wines by inviting the overseas principal of that particular wine speciality to be interviewed on your premises. Local entertainers of theatres can similarly be used.

7. The Personal Approach:
Promote all aspects of alcoholic beverages in the outlet, not only the wine list, and link such promotion to interest groups where appropriate. For instance, you could suggest several English vineyard wines for a reception for the local branch of the National Farmers' Union, combined with traditional English fare.

Staff training is a vital key to successful drinks sales (see Chapter 2); it leads logically on to promotion within the outlet.

Marketing Within

Within your outlet, it is your wine list that should primarily work for you. Before consideration can be given to your supplier or several suppliers of alcoholic drinks, use the research gathered to consider four factors:

1. Clientele:
Appraise your potential clientele for their wine, spirit and other alcoholic drinks requirements. What degree of *quality* will be required? Is it necessary to list several French bottled (or even Domaine bottled) wines in addition to U.K. bottled wines? The *quantity* factor is significant for the storage space available; is the outlet placed in a district known for regular wine drinking or wine consumption with food? With this factor settled, greater consideration can be given to minimum stock holdings. It will also allow you to know for later negotiation whether you qualify for quantity discounts. Knowing your clientele also means catering for specific tastes, which might mean Irish whiskey or a similar trolley/cocktail bar choice that might otherwise be omitted from the planning. A vital factor to decide is whether high priority is to be given to drinks sales: is a good wine list going to be a feature of your outlet?

2. Cuisine:
The relationship between wine and the cuisine needs to be thoroughly investigated. An Italian restaurant needs a fair range of Italian wines – and probably spirits – to stay in character; while an outlet specialising in

game requires a wine list that reflects a fair range of appropriately matched wines.

3. Storage Space:
The practical question of what are your outlet's physical limitations? Wine bins are the most suitable method of housing wines and can be surprisingly economical within a particular space. As a guide, 10 dozen bottles can be fitted into a $4 \times 3\frac{1}{2}$ foot ($1{\cdot}22 \times 1{\cdot}07$ metre) or 14 square foot (1·3 square metre) space. Wine bins also make a good display feature and can be a positive marketing aid, providing the risk of pilferage is overcome by their position in the outlet. The most popular wines which require to be served at room temperature, rather than the whites, rosés and larger cellar stock, can be placed in such publicly accessible wine bins and thereby achieve the further benefit of reducing service time since the bottles are nearer the point of sale.

Apart from storing wines at room temperature, adequate storage space is required for wines which need chilling. Reserve stock can be located elsewhere, but then a decision must be reached on how quickly wines are needed and the speed of withdrawal and delivery by a merchant, especially if the wines are held in bond. It may be fair with obscure or rare vintage wines to ask for warning to be given.

4. Finance:
The financial situation should be carefully evaluated. How much finance is available to invest in wine? If there is a substantial amount, it becomes feasible to lay down stocks on a long-term basis, purchase more widely and try to ensure greater continuity on the lines selected. Purchase sources were considered earlier (Chapter 2) but, should finance prove a likely stumbling element to the proper provision of alcoholic beverages, you could approach one of the wine shippers that operate 'own cellar' schemes. These work on the basis that a reserve stock is loaned to the caterer, which is invoiced at the prices ruling at the time of delivery plus Value Added Tax. The account is not paid unless it is closed when the outlet simply pays for the amount used on the stock not returned. The drawback to such a system is that the supplier usually stipulates that only that company is represented on the wine list.

With these four factors – clientele, cuisine, storage and finance – properly evaluated, you can decide on the basic choice of supplier and, in turn, on your wine list or lists. Remember that you may require different lists for separate parts of the outlet.

Wine Merchants

Wine suppliers may be divided basically into two: general ones, who are regional wine merchants or a district division of a national one (or both); and specific, where the caterer decides on specialist suppliers of wines and spirits which he will need, and other sources such as wine auctioneers.

The choice of a general wine merchant for supplies will bring several distinct advantages. Such a merchant will, for example, usually print free, twice a year, the outlet's wine list and provide an attractive cover. He will often provide optics and sometimes other bar counter aids, like ice buckets, tent cards (for the wine of the week or month) and corkscrews. There will be the service of a company representative and the occasional offer of remnants or ends of bin. Accounts will be simpler with one wine merchant: one invoice, usually monthly, means one cheque. It also means valuable time saved for the busy caterer in administration: one telephone call can cover your complete wine order and one delivery saves the time of bar and cellar staff.

A general wine merchant may help to train your staff and should invite you and leading members of your wine staff to trade tastings. There may be an extra discount on overall orders, such as a six-monthly gallonage figure, which would not be obtainable by using several specialist shippers. Yet a general wine merchant does tend to stratify the choice of wines within brands and to certain styles; he may not be able to offer the range you would like or be as price competitive as individual shippers. This can be vital if the outlet is in a very price-conscious position. However, a general merchant will try to assist when supplies become limited in a particular area, particularly if you are purchasing all the outlet's alcoholic beverages from him.

There are three distinct advantages in using specialist wine merchants. Firstly, better prices should be obtained by using the direct importers, rather than the general merchants who are purchasing at wholesale rates from the importer. The specialist does not have to finance the expensive staff representation or the trade and consumer advertising and promotion considered necessary by the general wine merchant. Secondly, a much wider range is available from which to form a list that will be envied by both customers and competitors. For example, few general merchants offer many quality Rhône or Spanish wines. If, therefore, you wish to offer several of these good value but lesser known wines, your buyer must go to a specialist. Thirdly, you will be in a position to take advantage of special offers, often made when new lines are introduced. You may feel that a certain wine or new style would be suitable, but the terms of your present supplier do not make it viable to test out the idea. Finally, it is a good idea not to 'have all your eggs in one basket' or to have to depend totally on the expertise for wine and spirit purchasing of your catering buyer. An independent consultant is therefore used by some outlets or groups of caterers.

If a specific number of wine merchants is chosen, give marketing consideration to the presentation of your list, as a general merchant may have a prearranged type. Several firms offer leather, leather-cloth or another outer material for the list, which can display your outlet's motif. You may want to have the pages duplicated to allow greatest flexibility on line or price change or the better presentation of printing.

SELECTING FOR THE WINE LIST

It is essential that customers find it easy to handle the list and obtain what your local research has indicated will be required. Therefore, if there is a local demand for rosé, it is helpful to list rosé styles in a separate section in addition to their individual regional listing. A customer looking for this type of wine may not be aware that the medium-sweet, fruity Cabernet wine enjoyed recently actually comes from the middle Loire, or that the branded rosé *bocksbeutel* shape is from Portugal!

It may be practical to set aside those lines which are becoming ends of bin and where you cannot obtain further continuity, together with the older vintages, and list such entries on a specific page where alterations are more acceptable. At a simple level, it is right to explain how basically dry and sweet are the wines you offer, particularly for countries like West Germany, and for all wines offered by the glass and carafe. This removes the necessity for many customers of having to ask the wine staff. A taste indication can be given by using letter symbols; if in doubt, ask your supplier. Remember that the British enjoy overstating the dry nature of comparatively sweet or medium-sweet wines in description.

House Choice

Our House wines have been carefully selected so that they offer particularly good value for money in these days of rising wine prices:

1 House Red – rich red from Bulgaria
Carf.(Ltr)£ Hlf Carf.(Hlf Ltr)£

2 House Dry White – a crisp white from Spain's eastern coast. Served chilled: ideal for fish or light dishes.
Carf.(Ltr)£ Hlf Carf.(Hlf Ltr)£

3 House Sweet White – golden-coloured sweet wine from Central Portugal. Shipped for us.
Carf.(Ltr)£ Hlf Carf.(Hlf Ltr)£

RED BORDEAUX (Claret)

8 Médoc 1975 . . . from the outstanding region of Bordeaux, this vintage is now ready for drinking. Fairly fruity and on the dry side.
Shipper Btl £ Hlf Btl £

9 St Émilion 1975 . . . on the lighter side by comparison with the Médoc 1975, perhaps because a softer grape was used that matures more quickly.
Shipper Btl £ Hlf Btl £

WHITE BORDEAUX

14 Graves Dry Non Vintage . . . a crisp, dry white wine that reflects the trend in Bordeaux away from making only dessert wines. Excellent with fish dishes.
Shipper Btl £ Hlf Btl £

15 Sauternes Non Vintage . . . a rich, honey-coloured dessert wine. Why not try a half-bottle with the sweet course?
Shipper Btl £ Hlf Btl £

BURGUNDY

18 Côte de Beaune 1973 . . . a well matured, red Burgundy that has a quality fullness.
Try this with roast meat.
Shipper Btl £ Hlf Btl £

19 Beaujolais 1978 . . . a crisp, light Beaujolais chosen for its freshness. Goes well with poultry or meat dishes. French bottled.
Btl £ Hlf Btl £

20 Chablis 1977 . . . a light, dry white, fresh and cool. Why not try a half-bottle for your first course? Now at its peak for drinking. Excellent for fish and cold dishes.
Shipper Btl £ Hlf Btl £

RHÔNE

25 Côtes du Rhône 1973 . . . a rich, fruity red with a flavour that lasts. It is unusual to be able to offer such an old Rhône vintage. This wine is very suitable for game or highly spiced foods.
Shipper Btl £ Hlf Btl £

ITALY

30 Chianti Classico 1974 . . . a single vineyard Chianti, strongly flavoured but smooth tasting, from the finest region of Tuscany. It complements the heavier dishes. Estate bottled.
Btl £ Hlf Btl £

HUNGARY

35 Riesling Non Vintage . . . a medium dry, light wine, made from the best variety of Central European Riesling grapes. Recommended for fish or light meat dishes.
Shipper Btl £ Hlf Btl £

GERMAN

39 Liebfraumilch Qualitätswein, Non Vintage . . . a fruity wine, medium sweet, that has the quality wine designation as given in the new German wine law. Palatinate.
Shipper Btl £ Hlf Btl £

40 Bereich Bernkastel Qba 1977 . . . a lovely fresh Mosel of quality, medium dry, from the outstanding 1977 vintage. German bottled.
Btl £ Hlf Btl £

SPARKLING

45 Vertus et Cie Brut Non Vintage . . . a dry, crisp Champagne that is excellent value for money in relation to the more advertised Champagnes. French bottled.
Btl £ Hlf Btl £

46 Asti Spumante Non Vintage . . . a medium sweet, sparkling fruity wine. Italian bottled.
Btl £ Hlf Btl £

ROSÉ

50 Anjou Rosé de Cabernet Non Vintage . . . a Loire wine from grapes that impart a delicate orange-pink hue and fruity taste: medium dry.
Shipper Btl £ Hlf Btl £

WINE OF THE MONTH

. . . .

. . . .
Shipper Btl £ Hlf Btl £

Selecting Wines

When selecting for the list, consider the cuisine factors earlier mentioned. Stock a fair range of whites if you are purchasing for a fish bar, including some lesser known wines, like the still Champagne Appellation Coteaux Champenois. This will give originality and flair to your list, invite comment, and should encourage wine sales.

If most of your clientele is likely to purchase the cheaper range of wines or if it is a quick-food outlet, give greater weight in the list to single glass measures and to carafes. If single glasses are not available of at least two or three wines, sales may be lost. Give full marketing and purchasing considerations to this field as, in most instances, single glass sales will be from your carafe choices. Evaluate the outlet's carafe choice in five ways:

1. Range of Styles:

There is a need for several styles to be available; probably four will be adequate: dry white, sweet white, red and rosé. However, certain outlets would list only one white (a medium-dry) and others would not include a rosé, depending upon local demand.

2. Quality:

There is no point in sacrificing one's reputation or boosting the gross profits temporarily by selecting wines that are of unsound quality. This means not receiving white wines with tartrates – in themselves not harmful, but in no way aesthetically pleasing – or accepting cloudiness in your carafe selection. Customers expect a *vin ordinaire* (or its equivalent from other countries) to be star-bright in appearance, unlike quality higher priced bottles. Furthermore your busy staff do not have the time to decant every bottle.

3. Consistency and Continuity of Supply:

Customers will expect to find the same carafe or 'by the glass' choice without undue switching over a fair period of time and it should not be necessary to add an extra purchasing burden by having to seek alternative sources at short notice. Customers will not have faith in brands which they have had problems with themselves. Therefore obtain assurances on continuity from your supplier; check out the political and other trade restrictions; and discuss, wherever possible, with other caterers the reliability of different wine merchants.

4. Price:
One must be competitive while achieving the other purchasing objectives. Consider any savings made by purchasing in 1 gallon (4·5 litre) jars, poly-kegs of 5 gallons (22·7 litres), direct cask importation (see Chapter 2) or, even at a smaller scale, in 70 fluid ounce (2 litre) bottles.

5. Presentation:
This can be as important as you make it. If the carafe is to be served in its original bottle, then the appearance of a driven cork and long capsule is worth paying extra for. Few outlets find the service of a bottle with a metal R.O.P.P. capsule acceptable to consumers, although it may be if all such wine is to be decanted.

An attractive label plays its part; consideration in the carafe – as in other fields of alcoholic drinks – should be given to an outlet's own label. This may be a shipper's label on which your outlet name and motif have been printed, or a wine bottled specifically for your outlet or a group of caterers, which you may have shipped or asked a wine merchant to undertake for you. It gives greater weight to an outlet in terms of individuality and makes it much more difficult for customers to make price comparisons with competitors. When using your own labels, ensure you conform to the legal requirements (see Chapter 4).

For your carafe choice, there is a wide range to select from in country of origin. Most French ones are drawn from the Mediterranean coastal belt of Corbières-Roussillon and show good fruit on the reds, balance on most of the medium-sweet and sweet whites, and quite attractive quality for the rosés. However, they frequently lack adequate acidity for the drier whites. Italy provides a keenly priced range, many of which are D.O.C. and can thereby be listed in both the carafe and regional sections of the list. Increasing quantities of Spanish and Greek wines are being offered to caterers which reflects their membership application to the E.E.C. Grape varietal styles can be appealing in carafe choices from West Germany and from central Europe, such as Yugoslavia, Hungary and Bulgaria. The latter have the advantage of being handled by the major wine distributors if space is limited.

Your carafe choice may double as the house wine, which should have size versatility: half, bottle (usually 25 or 26 fluid ounces/700 or 720 millilitres), and carafe quantities. It can also reflect any regional atmosphere that is being created in the outlet by offering, wherever possible, that region's wine. Continuity of supply and some price safeguards on likely increases of cost are factors to consider particularly when choosing a house wine, in addition to the elements discussed earlier for carafe selections. Three house wines should be adequate: a red, probably Burgundian in style with underlying fruity softness (as opposed to the often harsh or astringent nature of youthful claret) which could come from central Europe or Spain if French prices are too high; a hock style from the Rhineland, northern Italy (like the Trentino-Alto Adige), or Yugoslavia; and a sweeter style, probably from Spain (the eastern seaboard of Catalonia) or Portugal.

Apart from these three house choices for a basic list, in the regional field consider a fruity Médoc and a St Emilion from Bordeaux; a Riesling from Yugoslavia, Hungary or northern Italy; a Champagne (a Buyer's Own Brand (B.O.B.) is adequate and offers good value for money); and a non-Champagne sparkling wine. Burgundy could be represented by a Mâconnais or Côte Chalonnaise if the Côte d'Or is too expensive; and a southern Burgundy such as Beaujolais; a white Burgundy need not be Chablis or Pouilly Fuissé but could come from one of the slightly lesser known districts. Alternative red wine regions – probably Chianti from Italy and a straightforward Côtes du Rhône – will see that there are wines to accompany most fare, such as game. Rosés are optional but, if there is demand, consider the value in several Loire ones in relation to the advertised brands. The whites could be reinforced by a crisp dry Bordeaux (like Entre-Deux-Mers) or medium-dry (like much Graves); and by a dessert Bordeaux, which might be St Croix du Mont or a similar district if Sauternes is too expensive. Curiously it remains one of the best value areas in any trade list. A general Liebfraumilch category will be looked for. This may or may not be a popular brand, depending upon both your sources of supply and the type of clientele for this basic list. A single *bereich* West German wine may also be appealing and prove popular, in contrast to the French selections, when it comes to staff recommendations with fish and poultry dishes.

Selecting Fortified Wines

Having secured a good basic wine list, you should now turn to your fortified choices. A range of both Sherry and sherry styles is normally needed. For the latter, select three types: dry, medium and sweet. It could be a draught Cyprus but careful calculations should be made with any draught wines as they have relatively short shelf lives, even with the new collapsible containers. There is now keen non-Sherry competition from Australia, Montilla – which lies only 120 miles (192 kilometres) north-east of the Jerez district – and South Africa. In the branded Sherry field, two examples for each style should be adequate but this can be expanded upon the needs created locally. Ensure good stock rotation and that your staff take as adequate a time on the service in this field as they do in the table wine sector; for example, by chilling a manzanilla Sherry.

In the port field, many outlets will not require a ruby (except in certain punches or in the kitchen) and therefore a tawny style should be adequate with the possible addition of a late bottled port. Crusted or vintage ports – as well as white port which is an attractive apéritif – are for more extensive lists. Ensure the tawny served is indeed tawny in colour and has evidence of good cask age; certain cheaper styles are now available that may not help your outlet's reputation.

In view of its comparative good value, consideration should be given to Madeira. This can be by promoting it by the glass – the drier Sercial or medium-dry Verdelho at apéritif stage – or having it accessible at the post-meal trolley point in the Bual or Malmsey styles. An outstanding list will include Solera and even the rare vintage Madeiras but a shorter list could reasonably include one or two of the basic styles, particularly because once a bottle has been opened, it does not deteriorate for many weeks, provided it is recorked after service.

A range of spirits, including one Cognac and possibly an Armagnac in view of its increasing importance, with the usual branded liqueur selection, plus aromatised wines like vermouths, mineral waters and possibly beers would complete a basic selection. The beers, which may include lagers, can be either bottled, draught or both (see Chapter 9); even here, there is scope for the individual marketing and purchasing approach by selecting one of the high quality or low carbohydrate lagers available.

Selecting Speciality Wines

The speciality wines should be built on to such as basic list. In Bordeaux, Burgundy, the Loire and Rhône Valley, start to include single parish or village wines, like St Julien or Margaux within Bordeaux, or Fixin or Pommard in Burgundy, or a village like Fleurie within Beaujolais. If it will aid the marketing and subsequent sale, individual estates can be selected, with careful consideration given to the vintages and likely stages of maturity. Areas like Alsace come into their own in the speciality field as they are usually good value, of high quality control and enjoy continuity without marked vintage differences. In Alsace, as in Burgundy, select and name your shipper on the list, for this is a cardinal point in the style.

Districts like Muscadet in the western Loire or the medium dry to medium sweet Vouvray or Montlouis of the middle Loire fall into the slightly more elaborate list; while the B.O.B.* Champagne of the basic wine list could now be augmented by a Grande Marque Champagne. A number of non-French wines will assist the list at this stage. These might be a vinho verde from northern Portugal (especially if the outlet serves sea food), a good Rioja from northern Spain, or a regional Italian like Barolo for game. The Australian table wine selections and the small number of American lines imported are also worthy of consideration. In West Germany, single Qualitätswein choices that reflect district personality should be featured, such as Schloss Böckelheim from the Nahe, or Forster from the Palatinate.

The final category for a wine list is the estate or more specialised wines. In claret, this means a single vineyard. Château bottling does give a cachet but does not necessarily mean a higher standard, although estates are increasingly insisting on bottling at source. Listing such wines raises one's wine investment substantially, but if a shared cellar scheme with caterers in the district or a shipper's cellar scheme is used, this cost is reduced. Much of your listing in this field will depend upon the speed with which replacement stocks can be provided; many merchants will hold small unpaid reserves for caterers while a wine list is in operation. For better value, consider the less well-known sites in Burgundy and the Rhône and the little seen West German ones of higher status (QmP). The opportunity to order an expensive *auslese* or *beerenauslese* may not come often, but a wine-orientated caterer will give the stimulus by quoting in half-bottles and possibly also by the glass. At the rarity end, do not forget dessert styles like Tokay Essencia and dry whites like Château Grillet, the only Appellation Contrôlée applied to a single vineyard. It may bring few sales for those particular lines but will cause enough comment to lure a wine-appreciative clientele.

*Buyer's Own Band.

A Guide to Wine Selection

Unless the caterer wishes to offend, allow customers to enjoy what drinks they want. Wines go in fashion. Edward VII liked dessert styles, such as Sauternes, with fish; society followed suit. Today this is almost unheard of. The following hints are not intended to be dogmatic, but to guide wine staff when they are asked to suggest an accompaniment to a specific dish:

Apéritif	Dry or medium-dry Sherry; or Madeira; a wine apéritif or dry vermouth; a sparkling wine; or a light dry white table choice.
Hors-d'œuvre	No wine if the food is too pungent; if not, dry Sherry or dry Madeira.
Crab, oysters, lobster, smoked salmon	Dry white wine (like Muscadet or Chablis); Alsatian (like the spicy Gewürztraminer); or Champagne.
Clear soup	Medium-dry Sherry; Madeira; or Marsala; dry white wine; Champagne or another sparkling wine.
Fish	Dry and medium-dry whites (such as Mosel and Alsace); the richer the sauce, the sweeter the wine.
White meats, poultry	Alsatian (particularly Riesling); dry Loire whites; northern Italian whites (like Soave); dry and medium-dry Mosel and Rhine choices.
Roasts	Claret, Burgundy, Australian reds and Italian reds (like Valpolicella and Bardolino).
Game	Robust reds like Rhône or such Italian wines as Barolo.
Cheese	Continuation of the wine that accompanied the roast or game dish; claret and red Burgundy apt, but try drier styles of Madeira and Amontillado Sherry.
Dessert	Sweet whites (like Sauternes, Tokay or West German *auslese, beerenauslese* and *trockenbeerenauslese*); sweeter styles of Champagne.
Fruits and nuts	Madeira (Bual or Malmsey); port (tawny ideally, crusted or late bottled also appropriate); Oloroso Sherry (particularly brown); dessert white wines.
Coffee	Port (vintage, crusted or an old fine tawny); fine Madeira (probably a named Solera); brandy (Cognac, Armagnac or other) or liqueurs.

Aids to Selling Drinks

With a strong base in the wine list that reflects your research, you could employ the following aids to ensure you maximise drinks sales. Coasters that feature your bar, outlet or chain; cocktail sticks with your 'logo' or up to five words; cocktail stirrers can also be used. Maps around the walls, posters or reproduction wine labels help to create the right drinks-conscious atmosphere. Many of these can be obtained from the relevant tourist office of the country concerned or, for specialist ones, from the promotional syndicate of the wine and spirit region itself. Two good examples are the Alsatian wine village map and the map of the Scotch Whisky distilleries. Diplomas and awards can be effectively displayed and give further encouragement to your staff as well as reassurance to customers. The results of such awards can be additionally effective by appropriate publicity through the local media.

Use of a blackboard to publicise your wine of the week or month, such as Beaujolais Nouveau in November–December. Make by-the-glass offers on Champagne and other sparkling wines, using special closures that retain the pressures of atmosphere. Many customers are not prepared to purchase a whole bottle (or even half) of a sparkling wine as an apéritif, but will purchase if available by the glass. Display fortified wines from the barrel and spirits from optic measures; do not use optic brackets for a different spirit or brand than the one stated on the optic as this is illegal. Wine-based apéritifs can be offered, like Sangria in summer or a mulled wine in winter.

Display drinks-related items, such as old glasses, corkscrews, decanters, tastevins (the saucer-shaped tasting vessels used largely in Burgundy) and bottle tickets. Several caterers have made small collections of period glass which attract custom; others have combined with local glass dealers to display cut-glass items which can be ordered in the catering outlet, thereby forming an additional item of sale.

Tent cards, composed of stiff card folded once to about $5\frac{1}{2}$ by $4\frac{1}{2}$ inches (14 by 10 centimetres) may be printed locally quite cheaply or given by a shipper to promote a particular wine. The advantages of using tent cards are that extra product information can be given beyond the space in a wine list, often accompanied by a map of where the wine comes from; and that a wine additional to the main list, such as one on special offer or being test-marketed prior to main line inclusion, can be marketed in this way. It is also an extra sales point to a customer.

Quarter or half bottles, placed ready on the table with the appropriate glasses, induce a feeling that wine is a natural part of the meal which follows. The sommelier (or wine waiter) may remove both the quarter and half bottle(s) upon his arrival with the list but the psychological marketing will have by then been achieved.

The element of choice can be overdone, particularly if your staff's product knowledge or your space are fairly limited. However, if your research has suggested that there is the need for a specialist side, fulfil it by a wine bar or by offering more unusual wines by the glass. For instance, it is most unlikely that anyone will order Madeira by the bottle, but good sales can be created by selling it regularly by the glass.

The drinks function can be well served in the capacity of the host who can present a complimentary glass on arrival or at the table. This need not be expensive and can be a light Montilla or Kir (the blackcurrant syrup-based Burgundian apéritif mixed with Bourgogne Aligoté). If such a glass is complimentary, ensure the staff are not slow in producing it. Otherwise it will lose its point and may even aggravate if delivered after the first drinks ordered have arrived!

A further sales aid is the outlet's 'own label', which is discussed elsewhere (page 89–95;) it gives originality and makes direct price comparison with competitors difficult.

The physical aspect of service is important in creating drinks sales. Many customers do not order vintage port or crusted port because they do not see it, except tucked away on the list. Therefore open port bottles at a central point in the restaurant and use port tongs, wherever possible, to remove the cork. This is done by placing the tongs or iron jaws in an open fire or over a gas-ring to warm to red heat. While they are heating up, place a feather to soak in a glass of cold water, near to the bottle to be opened which should be standing upright. Remove the tongs from the heat and allow to cool to 'just red'; then use them to grip the bottle neck for 30 seconds and immediately apply the wet feather. This will cause the neck to break cleanly, without the trouble of removing a broken cork.

Another practical aid, which is also eye-catching, is the Austrian wine dispenser. Some models have a candle to allow a mulled wine to be easily made.

Apart from wine, consider offering mineral waters; several natural ones are imported as well as a number of U.K.-produced waters.

Boosting Wine and Spirit Sales

In addition to these aids, drinks marketing can be taken an additional stage to boost sales:

1. By holding special wine-tasting dinners:
Several caterers have combined in recent years with shippers to hold dinners when a particular region or country's wines are offered beyond the normal list. The meal uses recipes traditional to that same region or country.

2. By organising special wine weeks or week-ends with visiting shippers:
On these occasions talks, films, slide-shows and other presentations can be given, in addition to tastings and special wine-orientated meals. Such occasions bring in additional custom, which can be ideal at off-peak times of year, give your outlet useful publicity and make a growing clientele appreciate that you do take an appropriate interest in wines.

3. Making wines and spirits available for off sale:
If a wine or spirit has been enjoyed, capitalise on that success by offering it at an appropriate discount for sale off the premises, such as by the unbroken dozen bottles. Some outlets do this to advantage with hall cabinet displays and others by bedroom and reception stand leaflets: in addition, a note at the foot of a meal invoice will attract attention to this service. Orders can either be satisfied immediately from existing stock or despatched to the customer's home or office address. A customer's own label (for both wines and spirits, like Scotch whisky) can fit this category.

4. By following up customers:
Mail details of your special wine and spirit functions to interested wine clientele and at the time that you introduce a new wine list. Ensure that you foster all first customers, in order that they may become regulars.

When offering wines, spirits, beers and other alcoholic beverages, consider the type of function, and use product knowledge to advantage – do not embarrass through over-sophistication – but give reassurance and look for the repeat sale. This means that the wine list should be offered at an early stage, ideally when the customers are in the bar area prior to entering the restaurant proper. At the same time, a request as to whether they would like an apéritif should be made. The earlier the order for wines, the more time you have to serve it correctly. Mention the apéritif choices you have available as few customers will ask; check how and when customers would like their wines served and ensure the method of service is adopted as explained in Chapter 2. Enquire if wines for other courses will be ordered now or, if there is uncertainty, return during the meal, while other staff have ensured frequent topping up. It is appropriate to have close liaison with the reception in order to anticipate customers' requirements, such as offering a sparkling wine on a birthday or anniversary celebration, which may not have occurred to the customer.

If the customer is particularly unknowledgeable on wines – today this has no bearing on their age – enquire as to their taste preferences. Frequently this is for a sweeter style, despite the fact that they may well enjoy relatively dry beers and other beverages with a low or nil sugar content. Once the degree of dryness/sweetness and colour preference has been indicated or suggested, it may be useful to proceed on grape varietal lines, if not by name, then by inference. Thus, if a preference for a red has been made, try to elicit whether the drier style of Cabernet is preferred or the softer fruit of Pinot Noir or hearty richness of Syrah or Grenache or the lightness of Gamay and thereby the choices available. It may help to have a section of the list under a 'grape variety' heading; a custom which is popular in the U.S.A. and Japan and is relatively easily understood.

Profitability

It is vital to appreciate the profitability of each sector and, within it, each line. Excess profit in one field of catering, alcoholic beverages, is likely to rebound in not bringing further drinks orders and in obtaining fewer repeat visits. Modest profit levels, in line with other catering provisions, and accompanied by knowledgeable and attentive wine and spirit service are much more likely to lead to both higher sales turnover and increased overall profitability to the outlet. In particular, few caterers realise the full potential of selling wine by the glass. The variety of wines that may be served in this way, either separately or in addition to carafe or bottled measures, is enormous; the basic restriction is one of final consumer price and partially unused stock.

There is no legal designation of a glass size for wine and several caterers in the public house field who have tried wines by the glass have met with disappointment. This is a reflection on the generally poor quality of such

Table 1: Wine purchased in bottles and sold at six glasses per bottle

Cost per 12 bottles (exc. VAT)	27p per glass		30p per glass		35p per glass		40p per glass		45p per glass	
£	%	£	%	£	%	£	%	£	%	£
12·50	35·2	5·06	50·2	7·22	75·2	10·82	100·3	14·42	125·3	18·02
13·75	23·0	3·63	36·6	5·79	59·4	9·39	82·2	12·99	104·9	16·59
15·00	12·7	2·19	25·2	4·35	46·1	7·95	67·0	11·55	87·8	15·15
16·00	5·7	1·04	17·4	3·20	37·0	6·80	56·5	10·40	76·1	14·00
17·00		Loss	10·5	2·05	28·9	5·65	47·3	9·25	65·7	12·85
18·00		Loss	4·3	0·90	21·7	4·50	39·1	8·10	56·5	11·70

Table 2: Wine purchased in litres and sold at eight glasses per litre

Cost per 12 litres (exc. VAT)	25p per glass		27p per glass		30p per glass		33p per glass		35p per glass		40p per glass	
£	%	£	%	£	%	£	%	£	%	£	%	£
14·50	43·9	7·32	55·4	9·24	72·7	12·12	89·9	15·00	101·4	16·92	130·2	21·72
15·00	39·1	6·75	50·3	8·67	67·0	11·55	83·7	14·43	94·8	16·35	122·6	21·15
15·50	34·6	6·17	45·4	8·09	61·5	10·97	77·7	13·85	88·5	15·77	115·4	20·57
16·00	30·4	5·60	40·9	7·52	56·5	10·40	72·2	13·28	82·6	15·20	108·7	20·00
16·50	26·5	5·02	36·6	6·94	51·7	9·82	66·9	12·70	77·0	14·62	102·3	19·42
17·00	22·8	4·45	32·6	6·37	47·3	9·25	62·0	12·13	71·9	14·05	96·4	18·85
17·50	19·2	3·87	28·8	5·79	43·1	8·67	57·4	11·55	66·9	13·47	90·8	18·27

Table 3: Sparkling wine purchased in bottles and sold at six glasses per bottle

Cost per 12 bottles (exc. VAT) £	40p per glass %	40p per glass £	45p per glass %	45p per glass £	50p per glass %	50p per glass £	55p per glass %	55p per glass £	60p per glass %	60p per glass £
16·50	51·7	9·82	70·7	13·42	89·7	17·02	108·6	20·62	127·6	24·22
18·50	35·3	7·52	52·3	11·12	69·2	14·72	86·1	18·32	103·0	21·92
21·00	19·3	4·65	34·2	8·25	49·1	11·85	64·0	15·45	78·9	19·05
25·00	0·2	0·05	12·7	3·65	25·2	7·25	37·7	10·85	50·3	14·45
30·00	Loss		Loss		4·3	1·50	14·8	5·10	25·2	8·70
34·00	Loss		Loss		Loss		1·3	0·50	10·5	4·10

The three tables above show the percentage and cash per case profits based on the various selling prices (which *include* fifteen per cent Value Added Tax).

wines offered and the lack of effective marketing, rather than on the concept. The quick food outlet has an immediate opportunity and a simple blackboard can act as the wine list. Hotels, theatre and other pre-meal bars can offer crisp, dry whites and sparkling choices. Restaurants can offer wines by the glass for different stages of a meal as well as in place of, or in competition with, the traditional spirit-based after-drinks trolley. Use chilling cabinets, ice buckets or similar which use no ice and special wine-dispensing cabinets to ensure eye-catching aids for wine and vermouth sales by the glass.

The profit chart (pp. 76–7) is based on a modest eight glasses per 1·8 pints (1 litre) and six per 1·2 pints (70 centilitres) bottle, which is modest: many barmen could achieve nine and seven or even more respectively. The profit levels shown therefore are the most conservative that can be obtained. If you have a particular clientele, such as a small dining club that meets regularly, adapt the charts to allow for special circumstances, such as Champagne by the tankard.

In the event that any complaints about the alcoholic beverages you serve are received, deal with the customer with tact and take appropriate early action. The faults described in Chapter 2 should be considered seriously, because effective marketing of your outlet can be enhanced by the customer satisfaction that results from a speedy solution to such an area of concern. Product knowledge needs to be kept up to date and regular staff training, both in the outlet and on courses as well as visits to shippers, will improve your expertise as well as making your purchasing and sales staff more conscious of new developments. These can be successfully exploited to make your outlet truly effective in the drinks field.

4. Licensing and Labelling Law

'Says Simple Simon to the pieman,
"Let me taste your ware" ', Anon.

It is important to have a working knowledge of the many and varied Regulations which control the alcoholic beverage trade and its service in Britain. While wines and spirits have a long history of taxation, beer was first taxed in 1643. The main source of revenue stemmed from the 1697 tax on malt; this lasted until 1880 with a tax on hops additionally applied from 1711.

Controls operate in two basic ways: through British law and through foreign law. The British Government operates through a number of appropriate Ministries (such as the Home Office and the Department of Health and Social Security) and sees to the implementation of E.F.T.A. and E.E.C. Regulations. British law operates through enabling Acts and Statutory Orders with considerable case law in detail. Examples are the Food and Drugs Acts and the Labelling of Food Regulations. The foreign laws, to which imported wines, spirits and other alcoholic beverages are subject, cover such aspects as the D.O.C. laws of Italy, the West German wine legislation of 1971, or the French laws of Appellation d'Origine Contrôlée.

Reasons for Control

While the consumption of wines, spirits and beers has a very long tradition (see Chapter 1), it has required social and other controls. Spirit consumption has only been significant in the last three centuries and many prints of eighteenth-century scenes remind one today of the bar sign: 'Drunk for a penny – dead drunk for two pence; clean straw free'. The Gladstone

Administration tried to regulate the situation, while the U.S.A. had a period of total prohibition earlier this century. In more recent times, drivers have seen the further social control placed on alcoholic consumption by the breathalyser. Four basic areas of control factor may be identified:

1. Financial:
The British Government relies heavily on income derived from the sale of alcoholic beverages. This work is largely undertaken by H.M. Customs and Excise; they have specialist divisions, such as that for the collection of Value Added Tax.

2. Economic:
The Government has Import Regulations to control the shipment of wines, spirits and other alcoholic items, such as beer.

3. Social:
The licensing and other laws aim to keep the sale and consumption of alcoholic beverages regulated to meet reasonable social demands. There was, is and could well always be a conflict between interests here as to the flexibility of control.

4. Protective:
Controls for consumer protection take such forms as the Labelling Regulations and the Weights and Measures Acts.

TYPES OF LICENCE

With few exceptions, a licence is required at all stages from manufacture (if undertaken in the U.K.) to the point of sale. In England and Wales, there are five basic types of licence:

1. Residential Licence
Permits the sale of alcoholic beverages only to hotel residents and their friends. Many private hotels fulfil the condition for this licence; i.e. the premises are used (or intended to be used) for the *bona fide* purpose of providing for reward, board and lodging, including breakfast and at least one of the other customary main meals. Under this licence, drinks can be

sold or supplied at any time because there are no stipulated licensing hours. The magistrates, when granting this type of licence, will usually impose a condition that at least one other room is provided where drinking is not permitted for the benefit of children and non-drinkers.

2. Restaurant Licence

Permits the sale of alcoholic beverages to those taking substantial meals on the premises. This is for premises which are structurally built or adapted and used or intended to be used for the *bona fide* habitual provision of the main midday and/or the main evening meal. Service should be at a table or a structure, such as a counter, which acts as a table. Non-alcoholic drinks should be available in addition, but the diner can purchase alcoholic beverages before or after the meal, even in another room. They need not be served at the same table, even though they must be ancillary to a meal.

3. Residential and Restaurant Licence

A combination of the first two licences; an example would be a private hotel with a public dining-room attached. Residents could be provided with alcoholic beverages in their own bar; while the public could visit the premises for a meal in the dining-room at which such drinks could be served. When granting a combined licence, the magistrates may impose a condition that the alcoholic drinks are not supplied to the public in the dining-room outside the permitted hours normally allowed for that locality, although this restriction would not apply to residents. The conditions applying to the other two licences also apply to this combined one.

The above three licences are known as Part IV since the provisions relating to them are contained in Part IV of the Licensing Act, 1964. The main meeting of the licensing justices is held once per year during the first fortnight of February and is popularly termed the Brewster Sessions. The magistrates must also hold between four and eight further meetings spaced at regular intervals throughout the year. The licensing year ends on 4 April and licences date from the time of granting to the end of the licensing year, unless granted in the last quarter of the licensing year when they end on 4 April of the following year. When a new licence is granted, no confirmation is necessary and, if refused, an appeal to the Crown Court may be made. Anyone may object to the granting of a new licence without giving prior notice.

The justices may revoke or refuse to grant these three licences if they consider that the premises are not used or intended to be used for the purpose stipulated in the licence application. If the licensee or applicant is considered an unsuitable person, or if there is a fire risk with the premises, the licence can be refused or revoked. If the customary main meals are not being habitually served, or if the premises are being used mainly by unaccompanied persons who are under 18 years of age, a licence may again be revoked.

4. On-licence

Permits the sale of alcoholic beverages for consumption both on and off the premises; it is usually applied for by hoteliers and public house proprietors.

5. Occasional Licences

The holder of an On-licence is entitled to apply for an Occasional Licence, which is required for a beer tent at a village fair or at a race meeting or an outside wedding reception that a caterer might undertake. For the duration of the event, such premises become 'licensed' which gives the police a right of entry during the function to check for the usual offences, like under-age drinking or gambling. When the Occasional Licence expires, the premises cease to qualify as licensed premises and revert to their former use. Should a licensee continue to sell drinks after the expiry of the Occasional Licence, he would become liable for 'selling intoxicants without a justices' licence'. A justices' licence may be either an On- or Off-licence; the term 'intoxicants' covers spirits, wine, beer, cider and 'British wine' – the latter is any liquor made from fruit and sugar, or from fruit or sugar mixed with any other substance, which has undergone a process of fermentation during manufacture (see Chapter 1). It also includes cider and perry at or above 15° proof and honey-based mead and metheglin.

An Occasional Licence is granted by a magistrates' court. Postal applications are accepted if sent in duplicate a minimum of one month before the date to the magistrates' clerk; the clerk will forward one copy to the police to see if they have any objections. If the police do object, they they must send their reasons in duplicate within 7 days to the magistrates' clerk, and he will send one of these to the applicant. Alternatively an applicant may appear in court, provided 24 hours' notice has been given to the local chief police officer. With the court's permission, an Occasional Licence may last up to 3 weeks, such as for a major exhibition. Upon granting the Occasional Licence, the magistrates will specify the hours when alcoholic beverages may lawfully be served. A court will often require an undertaking to be given by the applicant that he will not abuse this privilege.

6. Off-licence

Permits the sale of alcoholic beverages for consumption only off (i.e. away from) the premises.

The first three types of licence were created in the Licensing Act, 1961, and must be granted irrespective of public need, unlike On- and Off-licences, provided certain basic requirements are met. If an application for a full On-licence is refused, the licencing justices can allow the applicant to request one of the first three types of licence instead; if this is refused, the justices must state their reasons in writing.

Growth in Licences

There has been a noticeable upward movement in the total number of licences since the Second World War. This growth has been substantially in the off-licence and club sectors as shown below:

Calendar Year	Full On-licences	Restricted On-licences	Off-licences	Clubs	Total
1946	81,445	N/A	24,265	17,322	123,032
1955	79,669	N/A	26,094	22,355	128,118
1960	77,767	N/A	26,382	25,218	129,367
1965	75,439	6,313	29,900	25,316	136,968
1970	73,690	10,898	31,776	28,205	144,569
1975	73,656	15,798	35,990	30,513	155,957
1977	74,484	17,766	38,405	31,807	162,462

Sale of Alcoholic Beverages

With the exception of a very small number of free vintners, those who sell alcoholic beverages require one or both of the following to comply:

1. Excise Dealer's Licence

This is for the wine and spirit wholesaler or any caterer or other person who wishes to sell in quantities *not less than* 2 gallons (9 litres) of wine and spirits or 4·5 gallons (20 litres) for cider and beer. For example, a mail-order catering firm which only sells in case quantities (approximately 2 gallons/9 litres) would use this licence which does not specify that all the wines need to be the same and therefore can be used for mixed case orders. This licence is granted upon payment of a fee to H.M. Customs and Excise.

2. Justices' Licence

This is for the sale of alcoholic beverages below the quantities given immediately above. Social restrictions are placed by defining the ages which may not be served and the hours when sale is permitted. The justices' licence may be either On- or Off-licence as described earlier.

Under Age: Possible Changes

The control of licensed premises has tended to alter relatively slowly, but a social demand is gaining momentum for a relaxation in the permitted hours and for the admission of young persons to licensed premises, which reflects the Erroll Report.

The general rule is that young people are not permitted in a bar unless they are 14 years of age or more and cannot purchase or consume alcohol in a bar until they are 18. There are exceptions, such as where drinks are purchased ancillary to a meal in certain parts of licensed accommodation. The licensee is responsible even if his staff fail to observe the rules. The regulations were ameliorated in Goodwin v. Baldwin in 1974, which adopted a more commonsense approach to the word 'knowingly' in the context of the supply of alcoholic beverages to youngsters and, more recently, by amendments to Section 169 of the Licensing Act, 1964, contained in the Criminal Law Act, 1977. The licensee still faces a problem over determining the precise age of a young customer. The Erroll Committee recommended that, in the case of young persons, the old 18-years rule should be reduced to 17 years and that children under 14 years should be permitted where a licensee applied to the justices for a certificate which allowed children into the whole or limited parts of the licensed premises.

It is legal to sell to a person of 16 years and upwards beer, porter, cider and perry for consumption at a meal in that part of the premises usually set apart for the service of meals. A caterer or other licensee cannot employ any one under 18 years of age, not even one's own family (except as a messenger), in a bar at any time when it is open for the sale – or even consumption – of alcoholic beverages.

Procedural aspects of licensing are overdue for revision, but caterers should be aware of the dangers of alcoholism, which is recognised by the licensed trade. The balance between the supply of alcoholic beverages in a controlled situation with greater flexibility and control to reduce the worst effects of alcohol should be the aim of forthcoming legislation in this field.

Licensing Laws in Scotland

There are five types of licensed certificate available to applicants in Scotland:

1. Hotel Licence:
Permits sales of alcoholic beverages to both residents and non-residents for consumption both on and off the premises.

2. Restaurant Licence:
Permits sales only to those taking table meals.

3. Restricted Hotel Licence:
Permits sales of alcoholic beverages to residents and their friends and also to non-residents who consume a meal.

4. Public House Licence:
Permits the sale of alcoholic beverages for consumption both on and off the premises.

5. Off-sale Licence:
Permits the sale of alcoholic beverages only for consumption off the premises.

The licensing courts in Scotland meet only twice a year: in March and October. Certificates granted at the March court are current from 28 May to 27 May; certificates granted at the October court are current from 28 November to 27 May. There is no appeal against refusal of a new certificate and the granting of a new certificate requires confirmation by the Appeal Court. Owners and occupiers of property in the neighbourhood may object by giving notice in writing within 5 days.

The English licensing system is more flexible than the Scottish in that more licensing meetings are held, applicants have the right of appeal, no confirmation is necessary, and applicants have a mandatory right to certain types of licence.

There are a number of different types of On-licence in England and Wales, such as the Club Licence. Brewers, distillers and compounders require licences too. In this way all stages of manufacture, up to the point of sale, are controlled when undertaken in Britain.

CONSUMER PROTECTION

There has been a marked shift towards protection of the consumer in the last decade and this applies equally to alcoholic beverages as to other areas. Any literature – such as wine lists, display boards near cocktail bars or tent cards – as well as the specific labels or your wines, spirits, beers and ciders must conform to the appropriate legislation. This may be briefly summarised into four main areas.

1. The Food and Drugs Acts

Alcoholic beverages, like other foods, are subject to the general provisions of the Acts and the Regulations made under them which are concerned with the safety and wholesomeness of food and with the proper protection of the consumer. Regulation 16 of the Labelling of Food Regulations, 1970 (as amended)* requires that alcoholic beverages shall be labelled with an appropriate designation, which is 'a name or description or a name and description sufficiently specific, in each case, to indicate to an intending purchaser the true nature of the food to which it is applied'. This must include, or be accompanied by, a reference to the beverage's country or countries of origin.

Regulation 5(I) exempts alcoholic beverages from the requirement to list the ingredients on the label when sold prepacked.

2. Weights and Measures Acts

These cover various aspects of alcoholic beverages, such as the require-

*England and Wales SI, 1970, No. 400 as amended by SI, 1972, No. 1510 and SI, 1976, No. 859; Scotland SI, 1970, No. 1127 (S91) as amended by SI, 1972, No. 1790 (SI41) and SI, 1976, No. 1176 (S102); Northern Ireland S.R, and 0, 1970, No. 80 as amended by S.R and O, 1972, No. 318 and S.R, 1976, No. 212.

ment in Part VI, Schedule 4 of the 1963 Act (as amended by the Weights & Measures (Exemption) (Beer and Cider) Order, 1966) that non-prepacked beer shall be sold only quantities of $\frac{1}{3}$ or $\frac{1}{2}$ pint (190 or 280 millilitres) or in multiples of $\frac{1}{2}$ pint (280 millilitres).

3. Trade Descriptions Acts, 1968 and 1972

A trader is prohibited from applying a false trade description to goods: in this case, alcoholic beverages. The 1972 Act provided that goods that originate outside the U.K. but to which are applied a British name or mark, should be prohibited unless they bear a conspicuous indication of their true origin.

All descriptions in your wine and spirit literature must be accurate. This means adequate staff training to ensure that they use the correct names and do not mislead customers in such areas as the country or countries of origin of drinks. For example, a non-Appellation d'Origine Contrôlée wine, although possibly bottled in or near an A.C. district and with a similar shaped bottle and label to that same A.C. wine or district, must not be passed off as the same. This can be done inadvertently while updating a wine list when a shipper retains the former brand name to describe a *Tafelwein* or *vin de table*.

Table wines bottled recently need to state their contents but this does not apply to fortified or sparkling wines to date. The enterprising caterer will give those contents levels for table wines on the list. Remember that, since 1 January 1977, carafes may only be offered in the following sizes, which should be detailed on the wine list or other literature:

Imperial: 10 fluid ounces (280 millilitres); 20 fluid ounces (560 millilitres)
Metric: 250; 500; 750; 1000 millilitres

The only exception is where the carafe choice is a sealed container, such as a normal fully-corked bottle, when the size is not designated. While the contents of table wines have to be stated, no Regulation governs what constitutes a bottle or its liquid contents. However a caterer who wishes to have a fair reputation will not resort to listing those smaller-sized bottles which have appeared during the time while the E.E.C. decides on overall bottle capacities.

There is, to date, no Regulation on what constitutes a 'glass' or glass measure, or on such additional terms as schooner.

The E.E.C. Regulation on bottle label printing states that the nominal volume of contents should be quoted; the former situation of not less than a given level has thereby been replaced. This allows for any errors in automatic bottling and periodic checks are made on the results kept by bottlers by the appropriate local authority trading standards officers. It would appear that France would like 26 fluid ounces (750 millilitres) to be the normal contents, except for Alsace (25 fluid ounces/720 millilitres) and Champagne and other sparkling wines (28 fluid ounces/800 millilitres). It seems likely that no size below the half bottle (13 fluid ounces/370 millilitres) will shortly be permitted. Above that level, apart from the bottle, there is likely to be the pint (20 fluid ounces/570 millilitres) and litre (35 fluid ounces). Caterers may find the larger size 53 fluid ounces (1·5 litres) and 70 fluid ounces (2 litres) bottles useful; they should also be familiar with these terms for other large bottles, although they are becoming increasingly produced only for special occasions, such as a firm's centenary:

Magnum	2 bottles	Equivalents
Double Magnum (Bordeaux) or	4 bottles	
Jeroboam (Champagne)	4 bottles	
Jeroboam (Bordeaux)	5 bottles	
Rehoboam	6 bottles	
Methuselah or Imperial	8 bottles	
Salmanazar	12 bottles	
Balthazar	16 bottles	
Nebuchadnezzar	20 bottles	

4. The Customs and Excise Management Act 1979 and Alcoholic Liquor Duties Act 1979

See Chapter 1.

Other Acts

Apart from these four main areas, caterers need to understand the major statutory law and judicial decisions that affect the sale of alcoholic beverages. In the statutory field, the Anglo-Portuguese Commercial Treaty Acts, 1914–16, are important for they restrict the use of the terms 'port' and 'Madeira' to wines certified as being entitled to those names by the Portuguese authorities. Thus it is illegal to describe an Australian tawny in Britain as port, even if prefaced by the national adjective, 'Australian'.

A reference to style or colour (like ruby or tawny) has not been considered illegal to date and may be used if it is considered an adequate description. Whisky and Scotch whisky are defined in the Finance Act, 1969; spirits not conforming with that definition may not be described or labelled as Whisky or Scotch whisky.

Two judicial judgments are important in the wine labelling and listing field. By a 1967 judgment, the term 'Sherry' refers to the delimited region of south-west Spain, even excluding Montilla (see Chapter 6) but allowed as as exception compound titles (such as South African sherry) provided that the national origin is placed in adjectival form next to the word 'Sherry'. Apart from the South African example, this was permitted for Australian sherry, British sherry, Cyprus sherry, Empire sherry and English sherry. Thus it is illegal to describe on a list or label as 'South African cream sherry'; it must be in an alternative form in order that 'South Africa' comes next to 'Sherry'. Descriptive Spanish terms, like *fino* and *oloroso*, are not even to be placed with Montilla by a British agreement, even though they are legally used in Spain for Montilla! Thus Sherry is further protected.

Champagne is the other wine significantly singled out. It is a term which, by a judgment against the Costa Brava Wine Co. in 1960, may only be applied to fully sparkling wines produced by the Appellation d'Origine Contrôlée regulations governing the delimited region of north-east France of the same name.* Therefore, by British law, terms like 'Italian Champagne' are illegal and have to be described as 'Italian sparkling wine'. This is not to be confused with *méthode champenoise* (see Chapter 5) which is a process by which sparkling wines may be made and is not confined to one region or country.

LABELLING

Labelling Wines

Table wines require five basic items to be incorporated in their labels:

1. A statement of the country of origin.
2. A statement of fluid content.

*With the exception of certain cider and perry products that have undergone a secondary fermentation process.

3. An appropriate designation (i.e. an indication to the purchaser of the specific contents of the bottle).
4. The name and address of the responsible bottler. (If the wine is bottled outside the E.E.C., the name and address of the importer with an indication of his relationship to the wine, such as 'Shipped by' or 'Shipped for'.)
5. The term 'table wine' for an E.E.C. produced non-quality wine or the term 'wine' for a non-quality wine made outside the E.E.C. Quality E.E.C. wines have to be termed 'quality wine produced in a specified region' or 'quality wine psr' on the label, unless one of the traditional national quality expressions is used. These cover such terms as *Appellation d'Origine Contrôlée* (A.O.C.) in France, *Marque Nationale* in Luxembourg, *Qualitätswein* in West Germany, or *Denominazione di Origine Controllata* (D.O.C.) in Italy.

In order that wines may circulate without documentary hindrance through the E.E.C., the closure needs to have the bottler's code number or registered name and address applied. The accompanying documentation when the wines enter Britain must match the label description to be given compulsorily. The legal restrictions in each country are those imposed by the separate national organisations (with the D.O.C. and D.O.C.G. regulations in Italy and A.O.C. and V.D.Q.S., for example, in France see Chapter 5) and prohibit the use elsewhere of such names. Dry whites from Spain used to be labelled and listed in Britain as 'Spanish Chablis'; this is now illegal as Chablis is a defined A.O.C. region of France and the term may only be applied to the defined A.O.C. produce of that region. A brand name and other material may be additionally applied to a label, but it must not contravene labelling Regulations or be untrue and the minimal five statements must be included. Fortified and sparkling wines also require the above essential statements except the reference to contents.

Labelling Spirits

Spirits need the same five essential statements on labels as table wines, but in addition one of the following:

6. A statement of alcoholic strength, such as

70° PROOF

If the strength is below 65° on gin, vodka, rum, whisky or brandy (other than brandy which has lost strength through maturation in wood), the appropriate designation would be either:

DILUTED (OR UNDERSTRENGTH) GIN

with the strength indicated in this type of form:

DILUTED WITH WATER TO NOT LESS THAN . . . PER CENT PROOF SPIRIT

or

UNDERSTRENGTH NOT LESS THAN . . . PER CENT PROOF SPIRIT

7. For spirits, other than the five named above, a shortened declaration may appear where the strength is at or above 40° proof; for example:

60·5° PROOF

If it is below 40° proof, the statement must be in this form:

NOT LESS THAN . . . PER CENT PROOF SPIRIT

If you offer any spirits below 65° proof, it is advisable to mention the fact orally and to issue a notice that is clearly visible; here is an example:

NOTICE Spirits sold here show the proof spirit strength on the label. Your attention is drawn to the fact that some of them may be less than 65° proof

E.E.C. Blends

The development of blends of table wines which originate in more than one E.E.C. country has led to confusion in both trade and consumer minds. Some clarification has come from the need for labels of such wines to declare 'Wines from different countries of the European Community' in the language of the E.E.C. member state where it will be offered for consumption. If therefore your shipper declares on the label a brand name (which is optional), followed by a non-British language expression, such as *Tafelweisswein aus Ländern der E.W.G.*, it needs to have the extra information if it is to be sold in Britain or Eire; an abbreviation, such as 'Produce of the E.E.C., bottled in . . .', may suffice.

Wines for Religious Uses

Wine may only be recommended for use for religious purposes if obtained in accordance with the special rules laid down by the religious authorities concerned. With the exception of the terms: 'Kosher wine', 'Passover Kosher wine' and 'Kosher wine for Passover', such recommendations may only be used in trade with the religious authorities concerned.

Optional Labelling Information

Emphasis has been placed on the necessary wine and spirit information that must appear on labels. Additional optional information may be placed, provided it is accurate and conforms with the Labelling Regulations. The expressions most frequently permitted for table wines (i.e. not covering sparkling or fortified wines) are for E.E.C. table wines with geographical origin:

1. White, rosé, red.
2. Brand name.
3. Name and address of shipper, or retailer, or distributor.
4. Actual or total alcoholic strength.
5. Wine citation.
6. Recommendation as to the wine's use.
7. Descriptions for taste, such as dry, medium, sweet and sweet.
8. A traditional expression, such as *landwein, vin de pays* and *vino tipico.*
9. The geographical location (according to agreed limits and expressions).
10. Certain vine varieties.
11. The vintage.
12. Vineyard name.
13. Bottling terms.
14. For quality wines, the term 'quality wine produced in a specified region' or 'quality wine psr'.
15. History of the wine and/or bottler.

For E.E.C. table wines without geographical origin: the first seven items designated above.

Additional colour and type expressions are permitted for both types above in respect of certain wines. For example, French wines may use terms like *vin nouveau, fruite, pelure d'oignon* or *vin gris*; Italian wines may use such terms as *vino novello*, *rubino, granato, rosa,* and *chiaretto.* Terms that refer to the degree of sweetness may be in different languages – dry could be *sec, trocken, secco* or *ascuitto*; medium dry could be *demi-sec, halbtrocken, abboccato*; medium sweet could be *moelleux, lieblich* or *amabile*; sweet could be *doux, suss* or *dolce* – and are given exact chemical meanings, rather than subjective comments on wines. For example, a wine described as 'dry' (or its equivalent) would be one where the residual sugar content is no more than 0·14 ounces (4 grams) per 35 fluid ounces (1 litre), or 0·32 ounces (9 grams) per litre where the level of total acidity (expressed as tartaric acid) does not fall more than 0·07 ounces (2 grams) per litre below the residual sugar content.

Quality wines are permitted a wide variety of extra label qualifications, ranging from the property where the grapes are grown or harvested or where the wine is made (such as *castello* or *schloss* or *château*) to qualities (such as *riserva, superiore* or *classico* for certain Italian wines) or classification levels (such as *vin classé* or *premier cru* or *grand premier cru* for Luxembourg or *cru classé* or *cru bourgeois* for French).

For non-E.E.C. table wines with geographical origin (non-E.E.C. may be referred to as 'Third Country'):

1. Statement that it is wine.
2. White, rosé, red.
3. Smaller geographical unit.
4. Brand name.
5. Wine citation.
6. Actual or total alcoholic strength.
7. Recommendation as to the wine's use.
8. Name and address of distributor.
9. Description of taste in terms of dryness/sweetness.
10. The vintage.
11. Certain vine varieties.
12. Superior quality description.
13. History.

14. Vineyard name.
15. Quality control number.
16. Bottling undertaken on certain premises.
17. Wine award.

For non-E.E.C. table wines without geographical origin:

1. White, rosé, red.
2. Actual or total alcoholic strength.
3. Wine citation.
4. Brand name.
5. Name and address of distributor.
6. Recommendation as to the wine's use.
7. History.
8. Description of taste in terms of dryness/sweetness.

Own Labels

When you are using your own label for table wines or asking a merchant to provide them for a special line, such as your 'house choice' on the wine list, ensure that the essential information is contained on the main label (i.e. not spread over front, back and even neck labels) and that the lettering is clear, legible, indelible and shows clearly against the background, which should ideally be in a light, contrasting colour.

Remember that a coded closure is required; otherwise the name and address of the responsible bottler (or distributor if a non-E.E.C. wine) should be on the closure. This may be by means of a number stamped on the side of the cork or embossed into the capsule that surrounds the cork.

Inspection

The majority of consumer complaints on authenticity or other aspects of wine labelling tend to be directed initially to the Trading Standards Department of the local authority (the former Weights and Measures). They will usually ask the regional inspector of the Wine Standards Board to investigate and to report back. The Wine Standards Board was established by the Vintners' Company, with Government approval, to control the documentation on wines. The Board keeps a register of bottling numbers for coded closures among other information and liaises with overseas inspectorates to police the system. However, it does not itself initiate legal proceedings; this is placed back with the appropriate Trading

Standards Department of the local authority, unless it is undertaken by central government.

PERMITTED HOURS

The general licensing hours for On-licensed premises are:

Excluding London: 11.00 a.m. to 3.00 p.m.; 5.30 p.m. to 10.30 p.m.; a total of 9 hours.

In the 'Metropolis': (which is the Inner London area defined in the Administration of Justice Act, 1964, and the City of London)
11.00 a.m. to 3.00 p.m.; 5.30 p.m. to 11.00 p.m.; a total of $9\frac{1}{2}$ hours.

The licensing justices may vary these hours, depending upon local conditions; they could allow opening from 10.00 a.m. and vary the timing of the afternoon break (provided there is a minimum two hours). They can also increase the hours outside the 'Metropolis' to $9\frac{1}{2}$ hours. These variations can be for different weekdays and for separate periods, but not less than eight consecutive weeks with the hours for the whole year fixed at the Annual Licensing Meeting.

Sunday opening (except for Monmouthshire) in England is 12.00 noon to 2.00 p.m. and 7.00 p.m. to 10.30 p.m.: this includes Christmas Day and Good Friday. Where electors in Wales and Monmouthshire have indicated that they want Sunday opening, the above hours also apply there, as also for Christmas Day and Good Friday.

A licensee is not obliged to open at all unless either the licence stipulates the observance of full hours, or a tenancy agreement exists between the tenant and the owner (usually a brewer) of the premises that it shall remain open for the full permitted hours.

Where the afternoon break occurs before 3.00 p.m., alcoholic beverages may be supplied with meals up to 3.00 p.m. and drinking up allowed for a further 30 minutes to 3.30 p.m. This is for the section of the licensed premises normally allocated for the service of table meals. This facility is automatic in the cases of Restaurant Licences and combined Residential and Restaurant Licences, but in other instances an application must be made.

The permitted hours for Off-licences are 8.30 a.m. to the evening closing hour for that licensing district without any afternoon break. The same conditions for Sunday opening applies as for On-licences.

Extended Hours

1. Supper Hour Certificate:
This is the allowance of an extra hour beyond the normal evening closing hour for the sale of alcoholic beverages to be consumed during a table meal in that section of the licensed premises normally set aside for the provision of table meals.

2. Extended Hours Order:
Weekday permitted hours may be extended until 1.00 a.m. while meals are served and entertainment provided on premises which, beyond normally supplying substantial meals, also undertake entertainment provision. The magistrates may make the time earlier than 1.00 a.m. and restrict the operation of the Order further by limiting it to particular days or times in the year. Such an Order does not extend beyond midnight on Maundy Thursday or Easter Eve and does not apply to Good Friday.

3. Special Hours Certificate:
This grants an extension until 3.00 a.m. in certain parts of London and elsewhere up to 2.00 a.m. for weekdays. This includes Saturdays and Christmas Day, when not a Sunday, but excludes Good Friday with the restriction that permitted hours close at midnight on Maundy Thursday and Easter Eve. Music and dancing as well as the provision of meals is required and the justices will then set specific hours in place of the general licensing hours. This will normally mean 12.30 p.m. to 3.00 p.m. and from 6.30 p.m. to 2.00 a.m. or 3.00 a.m., depending upon the locality as explained above.

4. Special Order of Exemption:
This extends permitted hours for a specific occasion and is not for regular use. It may be a wedding reception, sale or darts match. A Bank Holiday or other day associated with a public holiday, may be regarded in particular areas as a 'special occasion' for this purpose, but in such an event, each licensee must apply for his own Order.

There are certain other licences which apply in particular circumstances.

One such example is the Six-Day Licence which is a form of On-licence where Sunday trading is not required; the public must be informed of the restriction by a notice on the signboard. It may be helpful to clarify that residents may purchase and consume alcoholic beverages at any hour. A *bona fide* friend of a resident may also be served with alcoholic beverages, at the resident's expense, at any hour.

Measures

There is currently no legislation on a wine glass measure, but spirits may be sold for consumption on the premises only in quantities of $\frac{1}{4}$, $\frac{1}{5}$ or $\frac{1}{6}$ of a gill* (35, 28 or 24 millilitres) or multiples of those quantities. A notice must be prominently displayed showing which of these quantities will be used for the service of spirits. These restrictions do not apply to the consumer who specifies his own quantity of spirit(s), or where three or more liquids are mixed together for a drink.

Draught beer and cider may only be sold, according to the Weights and Measures Act, 1963, in quantities of $\frac{1}{3}$ or $\frac{1}{2}$ pint (185 or 280 millilitres) and multiples of $\frac{1}{2}$ pint and must be served in a capacity measure of the same quantity as the alcoholic beverage. This restriction does not apply to mixed drinks, like shandy. With bottled beers, any convenient glass may be used. It is not necessary to use Government-stamped glasses if the draught beer comes through a Government-stamped automatic metering dispenser. If the customer has his own tankard or special glass, it can only be filled directly with draught beer from a stamped meter; otherwise, serve the beer in a normal glass and transfer it to the tankard upon the customer's request.

*A gill equals 5 fluid ounces or 140 millilitres.

5. Table and Sparkling Wines

'Taste is the feminine of genius', E. Fitzgerald.

Within the definition of wine (see Chapter 1), three basic types can be classified:

1. Table: Meaning a still wine that has not had the addition of spirit.
2. Sparkling: Meaning a wine with sufficient carbon dioxide to make it fully effervescent.
3. Fortified: Meaning a wine which has received a spirit additive. Fortified wines are the subject of Chapter 6.

PRODUCTION OF TABLE WINE

The Site

Most wine is made within latitudes 30° to 50° north or south of the equator. The zone within the 30° latitude is too hot and beyond the 50° latitudes it is too cold. This is a generalisation and there are a few exceptions, such as the English vineyards. Threequarters of the world's wine comes from Europe (if one includes the U.S.S.R.) and a very high proportion of good quality wines. Italy and France compete to make the largest volume annually – around 1,400,000,000 Imperial gallons (64,000,000 hectolitres) – ahead of the U.S.S.R., Spain, Argentina, the U.S.A., Portugal, Algeria, Rumania and West Germany in order of volume. Quality wines for consistent production need both a moderately cool winter, when the vine can rest, and adequate hours of sun. The main limiting factors are:

1. Soil:
Experimentation over many years has shown that certain soils are better suited to vine cultivation than others. Rich soil gives quantity but poor quality; poor soil is often ideal for the vine. The mineral elements present contribute to the separate flavours evident through different vines. The grower aims to prune to confine growth and concentrate the mineral absorption. The predominant soils for some typical regions are:

Schist (like slate)	Douro region for port
Chalk	Champagne
Slate and limestone	West Germany
Chalk and some clay	Jerez region for Sherry
Gravel over clay, limestone or chalk	Bordeaux

2. Location:
Most vineyard districts are sited in river valleys both for good drainage and to aid transportation. They are best sited in a warm aspect, which means facing south-east in Europe; away from forest masses which would otherwise allow excessive humidity; and normally away from hill tops where crops can be damaged by bad weather. An annual average temperature of 57 to 59°F (14 to 15°C) is best with a summer limit of 72°F (22°C), a winter limit of 37°F (3°C) and at flowering time of 59°F (15°C). Vines need some six to seven hours of sunshine on average daily from March to late September or, if the harvest is later, into October. Frost in winter is useful to kill disease and rain necessary in spring for growth. Warm and still weather is best during the main flowering month of June with some rain in August to swell the fruit. Good heat is needed in the last six weeks before picking to ripen the bunches.

Although machines have made the cycle easier, they have not taken the worries off the grower. He has to study biology and plant protection in order to choose the right time, as well as the correct method, to combat pests; against natural disasters like frost, hail and drought, he is still largely helpless. In many areas growers provide heating, sprinkle water or disperse hail clouds with shot to avoid the worse damage. The general decline in the climate of Europe is outside the scope of this book, but published material* may throw light on viticultural problems now appearing.

*See Bibliography, Climate.

3. The Vine:
The basic vine species, from which the various individual ones best suited to each region have come, is the *vitis vinifera*.* Unfortunately it is not resistant to the aphid, *Phylloxera Vastatrix*, which largely attacks the roots of vines and kills them. *Phylloxera* was first discovered in Europe in 1863 but was not noticed in French vineyards until about 1866–7. It devastated the vineyards of Europe, save only a few places such as the southern half of the Peloponnese, Crete, the U.S.S.R. and Colares in Portugal. Eventually growers decided that the only practical way to combat the problem was to graft on to resistant American *vitis riparia*; this continues today.

The choice of vine depends upon the location. The main grapes and their best-known regions are:

Sauvignon (W)	White Bordeaux, upper Loire
Sémillon (W)	White Bordeaux
Riesling (W)	West Germany, Alsace, Yugoslavia
Chardonnay (W)	White Burgundy, Champagne
Cabernet Sauvignon (R)	Red Bordeaux
Cabernet Franc (R)	Red Bordeaux, Loire
Pinot Noir (R)	Red Burgundy, Champagne
Gamay (R)	Beaujolais (Red Burgundy), Loire
Chénin (W)	Loire
Müller-Thurgau (W)	West Germany
Palomino (W)	Sherry
Grenache (R)	Rhône

It is the grower's decision as to which grape he grows and the colour of wine made, but this is subject to whether he wishes to sell the product as a quality wine. In this event, he is subject to the rules and regulations as defined by the appropriate authority as with the I.N.A.O. for Appellation d'Origine Contrôlée (A.O.C.) in France. The D.O.C., A.O.C. and other regulations specify not only the vine variety and varieties that may be grown, but such items as their density, pruning, and wine-making (vinification).

In winter the ground is ploughed, the supports (wire and/or stakes) are adjusted and the ground fertilised when appropriate. The vines are

*Named *Vitis Vinifera Sativa* L. by Linnaeus, derived from *Vitis Sezannensis*, now found only as a fossil.

positioned to suit the angle of the slope and the direction of the sun's rays. While the ploughing – usually to a depth of 2 feet (60 cm) – and fertiliser work is largely undertaken using machines today, it is normal to undertake the planting by hand as well as any pole or wire installation. Today a grower in, say, West Germany will invest 32,000–40,000DM per 2·47 acres (1 hectare) in labour and materials. Amortisation of such a sum can only start, in West Germany, with the first harvest, usually three years later. In spring, pruning takes place, followed by another ploughing to aerate the soil; excess buds and suckers below the graft are removed. In summer, the shoots are tied to the wire supports and trimmed; spraying is regularly undertaken and further ploughing to remove weeds. In autumn, about 100 days after flowering, the harvest is held, followed by ploughing and then banking up of the soil around the vine root to protect it for several months against frost damage. In addition, the vintage equipment is cleaned.

Red, Rosé and White Table Wines

1. Red Table Wine:
Red grapes are picked, crushed and sometimes have their stalks removed. They are then placed into an open vat with their skins in order that both colour and tannin* may be extracted. This process usually lasts from five to twelve days when the 'must', or grape juice, is removed and the skins separated. The skins and residue are pressed to produce a dark and almost unpalatable liquid, which is then distilled into a local brandy (called *marc* in France or *grappa* in Italy). The intensity of colour will depend upon the length of time the grape skins have been in contact with the juice and the efficiency with which the skins have been kept in contact, although the grapes will in turn be dependent upon the weather before the harvest.

2. Rosé Table Wine:
Rosé, or pink-coloured, wine is usually made from red grapes, which are crushed and sometimes have their stalks removed. The juice ferments with the skins until sufficient colour has been extracted. The fermenting must is then run off. The residue is pressed and turned into a spirit through distillation; meanwhile the fermentation continues in another vat, but

*An important astringent component which gives longevity to wine.

without the skins. The colour of rosé wines varies from district to district and even within a year depending on the intensity of colour of the grapes used and the length of time that the wine-maker has left the skins and fermenting must together.

3. White Table Wine:
Either red or white grapes (or a combination of both) may be picked for white table wine, which is then crushed and de-stalked. It is pressed and then the skins are removed prior to fermentation. If a drier style is required, the must is left fermenting until it is complete; for a sweet wine, the must is removed before all the sugar is coverted into alcohol (and carbon dioxide).

Traditional wine-makers disagree with the more modern approach over both pressing and fermentation vats. Initially grapes were trodden with bare feet. When they had reached pulp stage, they were placed in a sack and the juice squeezed out. The Emperor Charlemagne forbade this method on hygienic grounds and hand presses were introduced. The older style is to use a screw-down press (or even foot-treading) which can cause bruising and excess harshness. The modern method is to use a horizontal press which allows the juice to be extracted without excessive damage to the skins, hence it avoids imparting harsh flavours to the must. It also reduces oxidation.

With the old hydraulic presses, the grape must absorbed increasing quantities of oxygen during the 4 to 6 hours of pressing, which then had to be reduced by a higher input of sulphur dioxide. In addition, the high pressure (up to 200 atmospheric pressure above normal) brought bitterness. Modern presses avoid these drawbacks with a pressure of only 6 to 15 atmospheres above normal and a 1 hour pressing time.

Fermentation

Older methods include the use of wood for the initial and some of the subsequent fermentation, whereas better temperature control can be obtained by using stainless steel vats.

Fermentation is the conversion of sugar into ethyl alcohol, carbon dioxide and other components. It is best held at 68 to 86°F (20 to 30°C); this avoids the need for yeast cultures below this temperature and prevents bacterial spoilage at the higher temperatures. Most of the carbon dioxide escapes during fermentation with yeasts providing the enzymes which cause the chain reaction known as fermentation.* Among the important side products produced during the process are acids like citric, tartaric and lactic, as well as higher alcohols, minerals and colour pigments.

It is frequently necessary to give the fermenting must a sulphur dioxide addition to control the yeast cultures and to prevent premature oxidation. A sugar solution may be added to the must to build up its alcoholic content; this is known as 'chaptalisation'. If this is done with care, it can be beneficial, but too high a sugaring can result in an unbalanced wine with either too sweet a final taste or too high an alcoholic reading. It is normal for table wines to undergo a secondary fermentation or 'malo-lactic fermentation' where the malic acid is converted to lactic acid. This has nothing to do with the production of a sparkling wine where a residual sparkle is induced (see below).

If a wine is bottled before the malo-lactic fermentation, it will often have a freshness for the months immediately after bottling and a prickle on the palate, such as Beaujolais Nouveau and the other forms of Nouveau or Primeur. It is, however, likely that in due course the wine will pass through this secondary fermentation. This can result in a cloudiness and excessively *pétillant* quality at that moment. This is one of the reasons why merchants encourage the early consumption of Nouveau.

In simple chemical terms, omitting the many other components produced during fermentation, the conversion of the sugar in grape must into alcohol and carbon dioxide may be expressed as:

$$\underset{\text{(sugar)}}{C_6H_{12}O_6} \xrightarrow{\text{enzymes}} \underset{\text{(ethyl alcohol)}}{2C_2H_6O} + \underset{\text{(carbon dioxide)}}{2CO_2}$$

Post Fermentation

After fermentation, wine is 'fined'; this means that a substance is added to cause the particles in suspension in the wine to coagulate in order to produce a clear, star-bright wine. Additives include white of egg; bentonite (a buff-coloured powder which is useful against protein; isinglass (a white fluffy substance, like down in a dry state, which comes from the swim bladder of the sturgeon); gelatine (to remove actual tannins); ox blood (particularly useful on fine reds); and polyvinyl pyrrolidine (a

*In the process called *carbonique maceration*, now in use outside Bordeaux and in southern France, the carbon dioxide is trapped and used commercially.

white, free-flowing powder which protects against a haze formation). After fining, the wine is racked. This entails pumping off the lees (sediment including the particles that have been coagulated) and putting the wine into a clean sterilised vat or cask.

The length of time in the cask or vat will vary upon the style of wine being made, the quality aimed at, the circumstances of the year (in terms of depth of colour and balance of acidity and tannin), and the physical constraints on the producer – such as having to use swimming pools in one recent abundant vintage in West Germany! Once ready for bottling, the wine will be bottled within the region or will be shipped in bulk and follow the sequence advised in Chapter 2.

The main wines shipped to Britain are assessed below. Minor variations in viticultural and vinification procedures occur from district to district and even within districts that space precludes discussing, but the sources suggested in the bibliography should assist where a particular wine is of greater interest to the reader. Since wine is very much an art and dependent upon nature, variations are frequent and add to the charm (and sometimes the frustration) of anyone studying this absorbing subject.

Sparkling wines are considered after table wines and not within each national heading.

WEST GERMANY

The vine was probably first planted by the Romans and was then encouraged by the Frankish nobility. The Church also needed wine for religious purposes and set a high standard, for which they are noted to this day. Britain has been a regular shipper of German wines, only interrupted by warfare. Viticulture was controlled by a series of wine laws which were codified in 1930. The present legislative framework dates from 1971.

Classification of Wines

The 1971 law reduced vineyard names and defined quality terms with an exactitude which was formerly missing. Practically all individual names for a vineyard smaller than 12 acres (5 hectares) were eliminated and, where necessary, old vineyards were regrouped as a new vineyard, taking one of the former site names for the whole group. The classification is:

1. Table (i.e. non-quality) Wine:
   i. Deutscher Tafelwein (which is entirely West German in origin).
   ii. Tafelwein (which is a blend of wines originating in both West Germany and in other E.E.C. states).
2. Quality wine (called *Qualitätswein* in Germany):
   i. Qualitätswein bestimmer Anbaugebiete (QbA).
   ii. Qualitätswein mit Prädikat (QmP) with such added terms as Kabinett, Spätlese, Auslese, Beerenauslese, Trockenbeerenauslese, Eiswein.

Quality wines must indicate from which of the eleven wine-producing regions (called *anbaugebiete*) they originate. These are the Ahr, Hessische Bergstrasse, Baden, Rheinpfalz (called Palatinate often in English), Württemberg, Franken, Rheinhessen, Rheingau, Nahe, Mittelrhein, and Mosel-Saar-Ruwer. The names of these regions cannot describe Deutscher Tafelwein. Each of these regions is subdivided into one or more districts (each called a *bereich*), so arranged that the vineyards within any *bereich* make wines of equivalent quality. The name of a *bereich* may be used for Deutscher Tafelwein, QbA or QmP.

Each *bereich* is divided into a number of villages, each of which is composed of single sites (*lage* or *einzellage*). To allow for blending and marketing, the term *grosslage* is applied to a collection of vineyards in a composite area, all of which produce a sufficiently similar quality of wine.

If 85 per cent or more of one vintage is bottled, the label may state that year. Vine varieties, if named, are in descending order of quantity; if a single variety is named, a minimum 85 per cent of the wine must originate from that vine and be characteristic of the style. A single vineyard description must contain not less than 75 per cent of wine from that estate.

QmP wines must originate within a single *bereich* and each part of any QmP blend must be of QmP status. Thus, it is allowed for a kabinett and a spätlese from the same *bereich* to be blended together and a kabinett (which is the lower quality) so labelled. QbA must originate from a single *anbaugebiete*. Unlike French law, only items expressly permitted by law may appear on the label of a West German wine.

Liebfraumilch, which used to be a wine from the Rheinhessen, is today a generic term for a medium to medium-sweet white style, made in any one of four *anbaugebiete*: Nahe, Rheingau, Rheinhessen and Rheinpfalz.

Unlike the French Appellation d'Origine Contrôlée system, which relies substantially on limited production from a given area, the West German system is not to restrict production in this way, but to control the overall quality, tested by both tasting and analysis. If approved, a wine is given a *prüfungsnummer* (examination number) which appears on the label as evidence that the required standard has been reached.

The five grades for QmP wine each carry a different, traditional meaning, but must conform with the 1971 wine law in terms of the must weight (the grape's original sugar content) for that term within the *anbaugebiete*. No sugaring (see below) is allowed for any QmP wines. The 'traditional' meanings are:

Kabinett:	Elegant, fully matured, harvested at the normal time of the harvest, which is usually October. It used to mean the wine regarded by the grower as his best of the year.
Spätlese:	Rich, full taste, made usually from grapes gathered after the general harvest, frequently about 14 days later.
Auslese:	Made from fully ripe grapes which are separated and pressed away from other grapes. Particularly elegant and balanced.
Beerenauslese:	Selected overripe grapes, separated by hand, yielding a mature, fruity, full style with distinct nose and taste.

Trockenbeerenauslese: Selected shrivelled grapes of the highest taste concentration. Rare, very fine style.

Apart from the above five grades for QmP, the term *eiswein* may, if appropriate, be additionally applied. It means a wine that has been produced from grapes which were frozen into ice. They were then picked, still in that state, and pressed frozen. The concentration leads to a lovely sweet elegance.

The Vines

A wide range of vines is approved for German wines:

1. Riesling:

Accounts for about 26 per cent. Small bunches, late ripening with good style, noted for fruity acidity that gives longevity. Grown particularly in the best districts.

2. Sylvaner:

Accounts for some 35 per cent. Higher yield than Riesling and less frost resistant. Softer style suited particularly to Rheinhessen and Rheinpfalz.

3. Müller-Thurgau:

Probably a cross between Riesling and Sylvaner. Early ripener with large yield. Light but flowery style without excess acidity.

4. Scheurebe:

Ripens up to a fortnight before Riesling; like Müller-Thurgau, a crossing of grapes and fairly frost resistant. Good muscat fruit on taste.

5. Morio-Muscat:

A cross of Sylvaner and Pinot Blanc, yielding large crop of flowery-nosed wine.

6. Spätburgunder:

Soft, fruity red; the same vine as the Pinot Noir of Burgundy.

7. Portugieser:

Yields fairly ordinary reds, particularly in Rheinhessen and Rheinpfalz. *Not* from Portugal.

The last two vines are red and the others white. The late ripening Bukett-Riesling, a little Traminer in Rheinpfalz, light Elbling on the Mosel, and light red Trollinger are vines also cultivated.

Geography and Climate

The vineyards of West Germany are the most northerly commercial ones in Europe (apart from the few in England and Wales that sometimes produce a commercial vintage) with Mainz on the same latitude as Cornwall. About 109,987,500 gallons (5,000,000 hectolitres) are usually made per annum, much of which is quality wine. The two main rivers are the Rhine (or Rhein in German) and Mosel (often spelt Moselle in English-speaking countries); the Mosel joins the Rhine at Koblenz. There is often a lack of summer heat, but the country has adequate rainfall and humidity (owing to the rivers Rhine, Mosel, Main, Neckar and Nahe, and Lake Constance) and has essentially a temperate climate. In view of the overall position of her vineyards, West Germany has one of the latest harvests, often not beginning until early October and continuing through to December.

West German Wine Regions

1. Rheingau:

Lies on the river Rhine, protected by the Taunus hills. The best sites lie near the water where they can enjoy not only the direct effect of the sun but also the reflection of the sun from the Rhine. Produces the greatest proportion of fine wines, although the smallest region, noted for their balance and longevity. 79 per cent Riesling, 11 per cent Müller-Thurgau, 6 per cent Sylvaner, 2 per cent Spätburgunder. Region stretches from Lorch to the Rhine gorge through the red wine district of Assmannshausen to Rüdesheim, Geisenheim, Johannisberg, Oestrich, Hattenheim, Erbach, Eltville, Kiedrich, Rauenthal and Hochheim. Hochheim gave the name 'hock' to Rhine wines in general. They are distinguished by being bottled in brown glass: Mosel wines are bottled in green glass.

2. Rheinhessen:

Lies across the river in rolling country between Bingen and Worms. 34 per cent Sylvaner, 37 per cent Müller-Thurgau, 6 per cent Riesling, 5 per cent Portugieser. Light fruity wines from a heavier soil than the

The Wine Districts of the RHINE & the NAHE
RHEINGAU
KOBLENZ
FRANKFURT
WIESBADEN
WÜRZBURG
60 miles
[inset]
River Rhine
Rauenthal
Hallgarten
Steinberg
Schloss Vollrads
Johannisberg
Rüdesheim
Erbach
Martinsthal
Oestrich
Winkel
Mittelheim
Hattenheim
Eltville
Hochheim
R. Main
Assmannshausen
Geisenheim
BINGEN
MAINZ
Laubenheim
Bodenheim
Nackenheim
Nierstein
Oppenheim
Dienheim
Guntersblum
Alsheim
Mettenheim
NAHE
Rüdesheim
Schloss Böckelheim
Bad-Kreuznach
Bad-Münster
R. Nahe
River Nahe
Niederhausen
R. Glan
River Alsene
RHEINHESSEN
DARMSTADT
Thüngersheim
Veitshöchheim
R. Main
WÜRZBURG
FRANCONIA
WORMS
PALATINATE [PFALZ]
MANNHEIM
LUDWIGSHAFEN
R. Neckar
HEIDELBERG
Kallstadt
Ungstein
Dürkheim
KAISERSLAUTERN
Wachenheim
Forst
Deidesheim
Ruppertsberg
Gimmeldingen
Haardt
Mussbach
Neustadt
Hambach
SPEYER
Over 3,281 feet
GERMANY
FRANCE
MILES
0 5 10 15 20
KARLSRUHE

The Wine Districts of the MOSEL the SAAR & the RUWER
BELGIUM
LUXEMBOURG
FRANCE
Over 3,281 feet
KOBLENZ
River Moselle
Kanlen
Kochem
River Rhine
RHEINGAU
WIESBADEN
MAINZ
BINGEN
NAHE
River Nahe
R. Simmer
River Glan
R. Lieser
River Kyle
MOSEL
Zell
Enkirch
Truben
Trarbach
Uerzig
Erden
Zeltingen
Wehlen
Graach
BERNKASTEL
Piesport
Brauneberg
Wintrich
Dhron
Klüsserath
Detzem
Ruwer
Eitelsbach
Longuich
Maximin Grunhaus
Kasel
Sommerau
RUWER
R. Ruwer
TRIER
Wiltingen
Ober-Emmel
Kanzem
Scharzberg
Ayl
Ockfen
SAARBURG
Serrig
SAAR
R. Saar
R. Moselle
MILES
0
5
10
15
20

Rheingau; with earlier ripening than Rheingau. Includes Nierstein and Oppenheim.

3. Nahe:
Between Rhine and Mosel with some terracing. 33 per cent Sylvaner, 29 per cent Müller-Thurgau, 25 per cent Riesling. Fragrant, fruity wines, often noted for a slight spiciness. Includes Bad Kreuznach, Rüdesheim (not to be confused with the Rüdesheim in the Rheingau) and Schloss Böckelheim.

4. Rheinpfalz or Palatinate:
Lies south of Rheinhessen on eastern slopes of Haardt mountains. Fine fruity whites with fairly high sugar content; some red also produced. 28 per cent Sylvaner, 24 per cent Müller-Thurgau, 14 per cent Riesling, 13 per cent Portugieser. Includes Kallstadt, Ungstein and Dürkheim in the north and Forst, Deidesheim, Ruppertsberg and Wachenheim to the south. Heavier soil.

5. Mosel-Saar-Ruwer:
Large number of small properties on steep slaty soil. Saar and Ruwer and tributaries of the river Mosel. 69 per cent Riesling, 17 per cent Müller-Thurgau, 10 per cent Elbling. Fresh, delicate wines with high natural acidity but in balance. The best area is the middle Mosel, such as Lieser, Trittenheim, Piesport, Bernkastel, Graach, Zeltingen, Wehlen and Erden; wines from the upper Mosel above Trier and lower Mosel near Koblenz are of poorer quality.

Steely, austere wines are characteristic for the Saar-Ruwer; Wiltingen, Ockfen, Serrig and Ayl are fine Saar wines to look for, while Kasel, Eitelsbach and Waldrach are noteworthy on the Ruwer.

6. Baden:
Lying in the south-west along the shore of Lake Constance, fringing the Black Forest and running parallel across the Rhine to Alsace (in France). 33 per cent Müller-Thurgau, 20 per cent Spätburgunder, 15 per cent Rülander, 10 per cent Gutedel, 7 per cent Riesling, 5 per cent Sylvaner. Both fruity whites, which are likely to become better known on the U.K. market, and light reds are found. Kaiserstuhl, Buehl and Ortenau are worth looking for.

7. Franconia:
Lying upstream on the river Main, based on the city of Würzburg. Flinty, dry wines mainly, which are bottled in a flagon-shaped *bocksbeutel.* 44 per cent Müller-Thurgau, 41 per cent Sylvaner, 4 per cent Riesling. Kitzingen, Sulzfeld, Winterhausen and Eibelstadt are worth looking for.

8. Ahr:
The most northerly of all the 11 regions, noted primarily for soft, fruity reds. The Lower Ahr on the Eifel slopes is one of the largest districts. 30 per cent Portugieser, 25 per cent Spätburgunder, 24 per cent Riesling, 17 per cent Müller-Thurgau.

9. Mittelrhein:
Lying south of the Ahr but north of the Mosel on the river Rhine. Fresh, fruity whites, mainly from the Riesling. Largely terraced on the Rhine's right bank from the mouth of the Nahe to the Siebengebirge. 82 per cent Riesling, 10 per cent Müller-Thurgau, 4 per cent Sylvaner. Lorch, Bacharach, Steeg, Oberdiebach, Linz and Koenigswinter are districts.

10. Württemberg:
Lying south-east of the Rhine, noted for full whites and several fruity reds. Schiller (a blend of red and white) is locally popular. 25 per cent Trollinger, 22 per cent Riesling, 9 per cent Portugieser, 9 per cent Sylvaner, 7 per cent Müller-Thurgau. Villages include Enztal, Jagsttal, Remstal, Kochertal.

11. Hessische Bergstrasse:
Lying between Rheinhessen and Franconia, a small region noted for fruity wines with a 'tangy' quality. 53 per cent Riesling, 18 per cent Müller-Thurgau, 18 per cent Sylvaner. Villages include Auerbach, Bensheim, Heppenheim and Zwingenberg.

Oechsle

Oechsle, named after a chemist of that name, is the term applied to the specific gravity of grape must (i.e. after pressing but before fermentation). It is defined as the number of grams (28 grams = 1 ounce) by which 1·75 pints (1 litre) of must is heavier than 1·75 pints (1 litre) of water: sugar is heavier than water. If the specific gravity of a must is 1080, it represents 80 Oechsle degrees; on conversion, such a must has a 17 per cent sugar content. After fermentation, such a must would make a wine with about 3 ounces (80 grams) of pure alcohol per 1·75 pints (1 litre).

In an average year, West German wines achieve a must weight of 70 to 80° Oechsle. Each QmP quality (Spätlese, Auslese, etc.) has a minimum Oechsle for its region. In three or four years of each decade, the grapes are insufficiently ripe and sugaring is necessary; this is called chaptalisation in France or *verbesserung* in Germany. This is the process of adding sugar in solution to the must at pre-fermentation stage to raise the alcoholic strength to the normal level. All wines except QmP can be enriched in this way, provided it is a poor vintage.

Süss-reserve is either unfermented or partially fermented must with, therefore, a high degree of sugar. It is used to mask a high degree of acidity. The term *naturrein* was stopped by the 1971 law; it meant a wine to which no sugaring had been undertaken. It is permissible to de-acidify in poor years.

Hot Bottling

West Germany, more than probably any other country, has made hot bottling, called *warm-abfüllung* in German, a part of its sterile approach to bottling. This is particularly so for the lower priced wines since the nose and taste can be said to lose some of their quality by this process and because it speeds maturation. The process consists of passing hot water through a closed circuit into a heat-exchanger (which resembles a stainless steel radiator). The wine is filtered through EK sheets, pumped into a container, and then around the heat-exchanger to raise its temperature to about 131°F (55°C). It next passes into another container and then into the filler, dropping 7–9°F (4–5°C) by the time of bottling. The 'ullage', or difference between the end of the cork and the wine, may be rather too great once the wine has cooled down and this is frequently taken into account by using longer capsules! Hot bottling is a technique which is likely to be seen increasingly on non-quality table wines and on everyday wines from Spain, Greece and central Europe.

Bottling Terms

A wine bottled by the producer is described on the label as *Erzeuger-abfüllung* or, if from his own site, *Aus eigenem lesegut*. These terms are not restricted to individuals and, provided the grapes were grown by the bottler, can apply to a co-operative, too. If a bottler has purchased the wine from a grower, with the latter's permission, the label may term it as coming 'from the vintner's own vineyard' (*Aus dem lesegut des winzers*).

FRANCE

Wine Law

France designates four table wine divisions:

1. Vin de Table:
This was formerly called *vin de consommation courante* or *vin ordinaire* and is an everyday wine without delimited status. Most carafe wine originating from France is of this category and is sold by its alcoholic degree.

2. Vin de Pays:
Literally country wine, this describes certain regional wines, conforming to particular vine varieties, a minimum alcoholic level and sometimes a tasting test. Examples are Hérault and Tarn.

3. Vin Délimité de Qualité Supérieure (V.D.Q.S.):
This is better than *vin de pays* but of lesser quality than A.O.C. It is a class, formed in 1949, which sets geographical limits, permitted vines, minimum alcoholic strength and usually approval through a tasting panel. Sound wines. Examples include Cheverny in the Loire, Tursan in the South-West and Côteaux de St Christol in Languedoc-Roussillon. Labels carry a V.D.Q.S. postage stamp style of insignia in one corner.

4. Appellation d'Origine Contrôlée (A.O.C.):
This is designated for best quality districts with higher A.O.C. categories, often within outer A.O.C. ones. The regulations specify the density of vines, the vine varieties and proportions that may be grown, how the vines may be trained, chaptalisation (sugaring of the must), as well as the minimum alcoholic strength and other aspects of control.

The last two categories are accepted in both French and E.E.C. terms as quality wines and the first two as non-quality. The average for French annual production for the harvests in 1972–6 inclusive was:

	Hectolitres	Gallons
A.O.C.	11,925,000	262,350,000
V.D.Q.S.	3,019,000	66,418,000
Vin de pays	5,419,000	119,218,000
Vin de table	42,225,000	928,950,000
Wines for Cognac	9,942,000	218,724,000

(1 hectolitre equals 100 litres, equals 22 imperial gallons.)

BORDEAUX

Bordeaux has enjoyed long shipping contacts with the U.K. which have survived many wars. The region was first planted in Roman times and the English connection was established in 1152 with the marriage of the future Henry II to Eleanor of Aquitaine. This brought Gascony under the rule of the Kings of England, who thus acquired hereditary title to Aquitaine. England lost the territory after the Battle of Castillon in 1453, at the end of the Hundred Years War, but trading continued despite this.

The region was the first to classify its wines; in 1885 a classification was made of 62 of the leading Médoc wines (and one red Graves). Although many wines in this classification deserve higher status and many which are not included deserve recognition, it remains a useful historical guide. Nearly one-third of France's A.O.C. wines come from Bordeaux with over 2,000 châteaux in the Médoc district alone. The Graves district was classified in August 1953, and St Emilion in October 1954. The 1855 classification, as amended, now lists five estates as First Growth status: Châteaux Lafite from Pauillac, Latour from Pauillac, Margaux from Margaux, Mouton-Rothschild* from Pauillac and Haut-Brion from Graves. The same classification listed 14 estates in the 2nd Growth, 14 in the 3rd Growth, 10 in the 4th and 17 in the 5th Growth or class. In St Emilion, 12 are rated *Premier Grand Cru Classé* (or First Great Classified Growth) and 70 as the next tier, *Grand Cru Classé*. Pomerol has no official classification, but the better wines are referred to as *Grand Cru*. Classed growths overall represent about one-tenth of all Bordeaux estates, but set a level of quality that makes them important, quite apart from their investment potential. The A.O.C. laws lay down alcoholic levels for each district; overall Bordeaux Rouge is at least 10° G.L. with production set at a maximum 1,100 gallons (50 hectolitres) to 2·47 acres (1 hectare), while Bordeaux Supérieur is 10·5° G.L. minimum and 880 gallons (40 hectolitres) per hectare.

Climate and Soil

Bordeaux enjoys a mild climate with influence from the Atlantic, since the region lies in the south-west between the rivers Garonne and Dor-

*Ch. Mouton-Rothschild was elevated from 2nd to 1st Growth status on 22 June 1973.

dogne, and among pine forests. Late warm summers are followed by temperate winters. Hailstorms can do damage to crops. In the Haut-Médoc, the soil is quartz and gravel on a subsoil of limestone and clay with admixtures of iron. There is more gravelly soil in the Graves district, mainly limestone in St Emilion, and clay with silica in Entre-Deux-Mers.

Grapes and Viticulture

The main grapes for red wine are Cabernet Sauvignon, Merlot, Cabernet Franc, Malbec and Petit Verdot within the Médoc and Graves. In St Emilion and Pomerol the main grapes are Merlot, Bouchett the name used in these two districts for the Cabernet Sauvignon), Cabernet Franc and Malbec (occasionally known as Noir de Pressac in these districts).

For white wines, the dry and medium-dry styles are made from the Sauvignon Blanc, Sémillon and Muscadelle* vines; for the sweet whites the Sémillon, Sauvignon and Muscadelle are used in that order. The normal method of vine-training is to spread an arm or branch from each side of the vine, known as Double Guyot. In certain districts, such as Entre-Deux-Mers, wider spacing of rows is taking place to allow tractor movement. This is called Lenz Moser, after the late Austrian of the same name, who pioneered this method.

Grapes in Bordeaux (and other regions) are protected against the following main viticulture problems:

1. *Oidium Tuckeri* (powdery mildew), treated with sulphur.
2. *Peronospora* (downy mildrew), treated with zinc or copper based sprays.
3. Anthracnose.
4. Chlorosis (iron deficiency), treated with ferrous sulphate.
5. Black Rot, treated with zinc or copper based sprays.

The Districts of Bordeaux

1. Médoc:

Lies north of the city of Bordeaux and is noted for its fine red wine (called Claret throughout Bordeaux). Sub-divided into:

i. Bas-Médoc: Northerly sector, ordinary wines.
ii. Haut-Médoc: Finest district between Blanquefort and St Seurin

*A type of Muscat grape.

with four well-known parishes or communes.

1. St Estèphe: Noted for tannic reds that need many years to mature. Includes Châteaux Cos d'Estournel, Montrose and Calon-Ségur.

2. Pauillac: Noted for clarets with cedarwood taste. Elegant, slow to mature. Includes Châteaux Latour and Lafite-Rothschild.

3. Margaux: Noted for fruity clarets. Includes Châteaux Margaux and Giscours.

4. St Julien: Noted for well-balanced clarets. Includes Châteaux Léoville-Lascases and Gruaud Larose.

2. Graves:

Two-thirds are white, dry and medium-dry and not usually expensive. The reds have fruit and body and include Châteaux Haut-Brion and La Mission Haut Brion, as well as Pape Clément. Tasters frequently describe the nose of Graves reds as akin to tobacco.

3. Entre-Deux-Mers:

This is the district between the rivers Dordogne and Garonne; light reds and predominantly dry whites. Usually good value.

4. Graves de Vayres:

A small district which lies north of Entre-Deux-Mers, noted for whites of elegance and fair body.

5. Sauternes:

Noted dessert white district, best in years when the 'noble rot' (*botrytis cinerea*) has developed on the grapes, thereby concentrating the available sweetness in the grape. Best known châteaux include d'Yquem, Climens, Coutet and Doisy-Daëne.

6. St Croix du Mont and Loupiac:

Noted for cheaper-priced sweet whites than Sauternes; these two districts lie across the river Garonne from Sauternes.

7. St Emilion and Pomerol:

Two noted red districts to the east of Bordeaux on the north bank of the

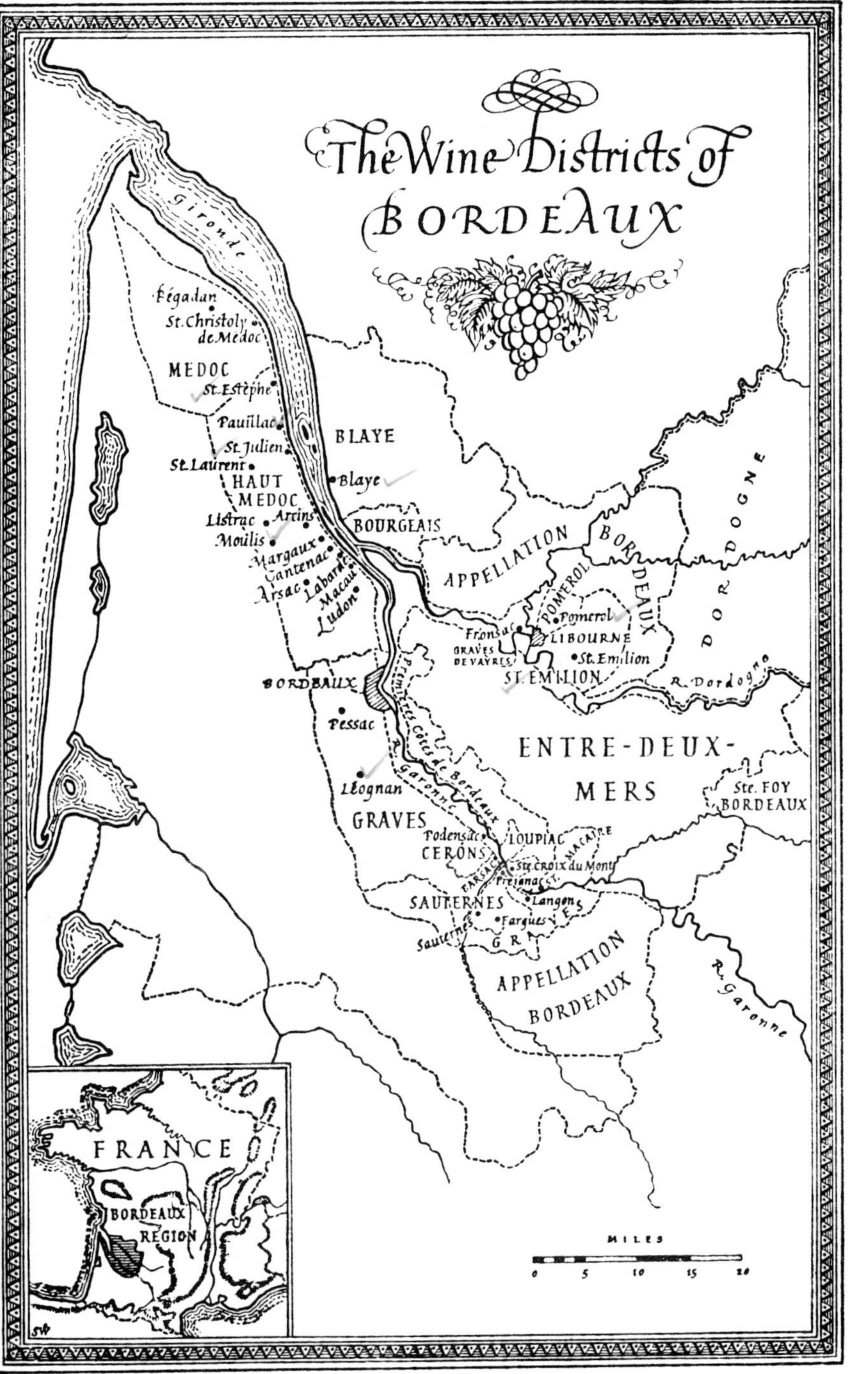

The Wine Districts of
BORDEAUX
Gironde
Bégadan
St. Christoly de Medoc
MEDOC
St. Estèphe
Pauillac
St. Julien
St. Laurent
HAUT MEDOC
Listrac
Arcins
Moulis
Margaux
Cantenac
Arsac
Labarde
Macau
Ludon
BLAYE
Blaye
BOURGEAIS
APPELLATION BORDEAUX
POMEROL
Pomerol
Fronsac
LIBOURNE
GRAVES DE VAYRES
St. Emilion
ST. EMILION
R. Dordogne
DORDOGNE
BORDEAUX
Pessac
Premières Côtes de Bordeaux
R. Garonne
ENTRE-DEUX-MERS
Léognan
GRAVES
Ste. FOY BORDEAUX
Podensac
CERONS
LOUPIAC
ST. MACAIRE
Ste. Croix du Mont
BARSAC
Preignac
SAUTERNES
Langon
Fargues
Sauternes
GRAVES
APPELLATION BORDEAUX
R. Garonne
FRANCE
BORDEAUX REGION
MILES
0 5 10 15 20

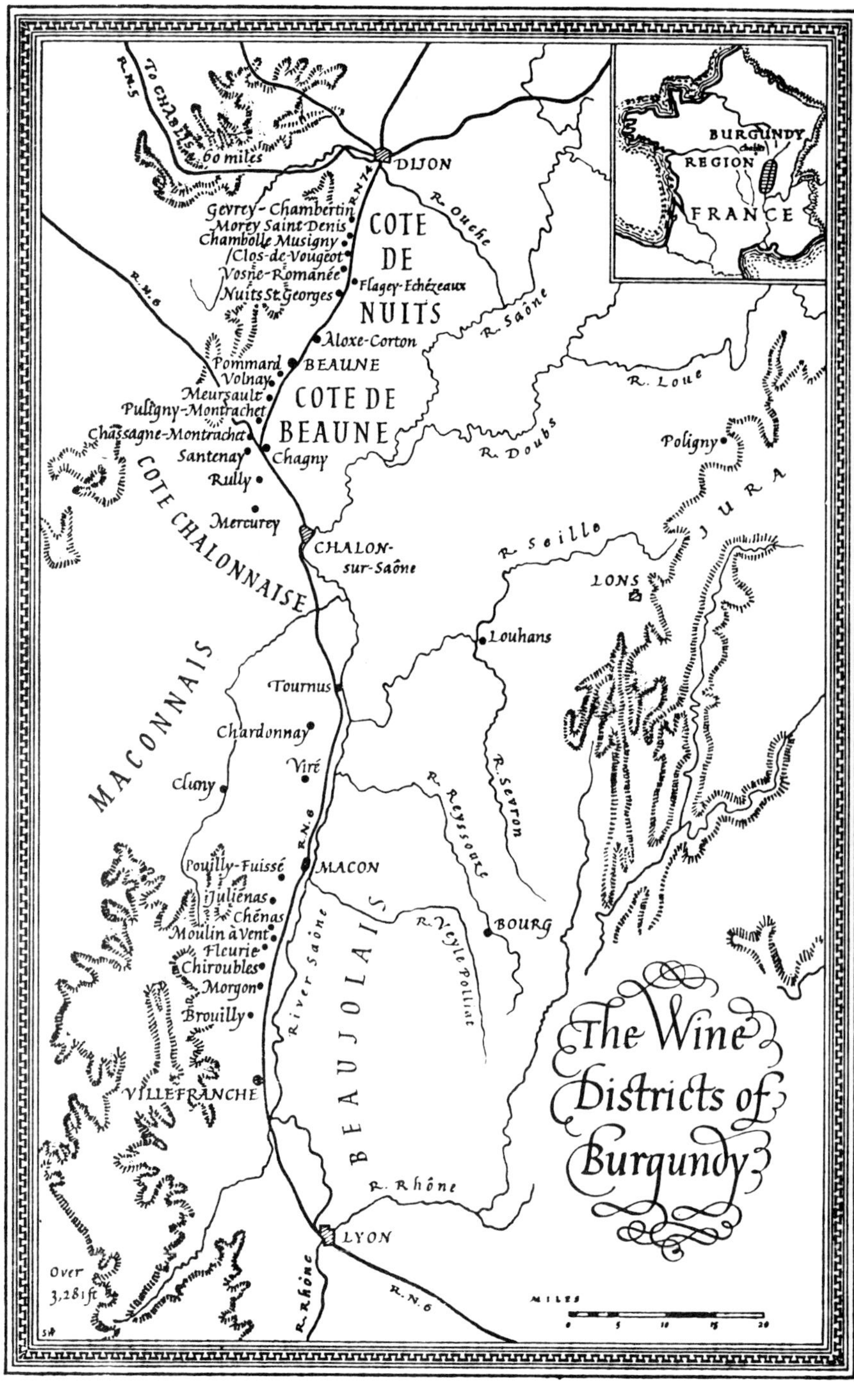
The Wine Districts of Burgundy
DIJON
COTE DE NUITS
Gevrey-Chambertin
Morey Saint-Denis
Chambolle Musigny
Clos-de-Vougeot
Vosne-Romanée
Nuits St. Georges
Flagey-Echézeaux
Aloxe-Corton
BEAUNE
Pommard
Volnay
Meursault
Puligny-Montrachet
Chassagne-Montrachet
COTE DE BEAUNE
Santenay
Chagny
Rully
Mercurey
COTE CHALONNAISE
CHALON-sur-Saône
MACONNAIS
Tournus
Chardonnay
Viré
Cluny
MACON
Pouilly-Fuissé
Juliénas
Chénas
Moulin à Vent
Fleurie
Chiroubles
Morgon
Brouilly
VILLEFRANCHE
BEAUJOLAIS
River Saône
LYON
R. Rhône
R.N.6
R.N.5
R.N.74
To CHABLIS 60 miles
R. Ouche
R. Saône
R. Loue
R. Doubs
Poligny
JURA
R. Seille
LONS
Louhans
R. Seyron
R. Reyssouze
R. Veyle
Pollias
BOURG
Over 3,281 ft
MILES
0 5 10 15 20
BURGUNDY
REGION
FRANCE

Dordogne. Tendency to be richer and fuller than Médoc reds. Châteaux Cheval Blanc (definitely a red wine despite the name), Ausone well-known in St Emilion; and Pétrus in Pomerol.

8. Fronsac, Blaye and Bourg:
Red wine districts on the north bank of the river Dordogne; normally early maturing and fair value. Slightly coarse style.

BURGUNDY

Roman legions first introduced the vine to Burgundy, but major developments did not occur until the Middle Ages with the Church playing a major part in land ownership. This altered at the Revolution of 1789 which in time led to piecemeal compartments. Individual vineyards are known in the region as *climats*. Today most blends, in order to be successfully marketed in any volume, are formed from the produce of many separate vineyards, often widely spaced.

Location and Climate

Burgundy lies in central France with a continental climate: hot summers and cold winters.

Grapes

For the reds, the main vines are the Pinot Noir in the Côte d'Or and Côte Chalonnaise. In the Mâconnais, both Pinot Noir and Gamay are grown; while Gamay is grown extensively in Beaujolais. For the whites, Pinot Chardonnay is the main grape, but some Aligoté is cultivated for a cheaper style.

The Pinot Noir yields a full, fruity style of elegance, a softness often missing in Bordeaux. Gamay shows a light, very inviting youthfulness, while Chardonnay has a dry fruity quality; Aligoté tends to give a dull, slightly coarse edge.

The Districts of Burgundy

1. Chablis:
Lies north-west of the rest of Burgundy. It is a white wine area, noted for

its dry style using the Chardonnay grapes. It is centred on the town of Chablis, about 100 miles (160 kilometres) south-east of Paris. Limestone and clay (called kimmeridge clay) predominate. Classified as Grand Cru (7 sites), Premier Cru (21 sites), Chablis and Petit Chablis.

2. Côte de Nuits:
Northern part of Côte d'Or; it runs from Dijon to south of the village of Nuits-Saint-Georges. Fine, fruity reds such as Fixin, Gevrey-Chambertin, Morey-Saint-Denis, Chambolle-Musigny, Vosne-Romanée and Nuits-Saint-Georges. Traditionally these northern reds keep well and have good length.

3. Côte de Beaune:
Southern part of Côte d'Or from Pernand Vergelesses to Santenay and includes such red wine parishes (or communes) as Aloxe-Corton, Beaune, Pommard and Volnay. It is also known for the fruity dry whites of Meursault and various Montrachet (such as Bâtard-Montrachet and Puligny-Montrachet) sites, made from Chardonnay grapes.

4. Côte Chalonnaise:
Light fruity reds and fair value whites based on the town of Chalon. Parishes include Rully, Givry, Montagny and Mercurey.

5. Mâconnais:
Based on Mâcon, a large district in the south noted for good value reds and whites. Pouilly Fuissé is the best known crisp white of the district.

6. Beaujolais:
Predominantly red, using the Gamay, and a little white from the St Véran district. The better style is Beaujolais-Villages with individual village names of even finer style. Villages are referred to as *crus* and include Brouilly, Saint-Amour, Chénas, Juliénas, Fleurie, Morgon, Chiroubles and Moulin-à-Vent. Youthful Beaujolais, that has not normally undergone its secondary (malo-lactic) fermentation in vat, can be bottled and sold as *Nouveau* or *Primeur*. It is sold usually between 15 November and 14 December; after that, it becomes *vin de l'année*.

Passe-Tout-Grains is a blend of Pinot Noir and Gamay, yielding a fruity red, usually ready for early consumption.

It is usual in Burgundy for the best site or *climat* names to be affixed to the commune name on the label. There are few châteaux, but the estates are referred to as *domaines*. Bottling at the domaine is quite common but in view of the fragmented land ownership, *négoçiants* play a key role in locating adequate stocks, blending them as necessary and having sufficient stocks for sale, whether for the French or export markets. It is legal only to blend within an Appellation unless one is going for the general one of A.O.C. Bourgogne (i.e. the whole Burgundy wine field). Individual characteristics are evident, not only because of height variations, but also because of soil variations. The Côte d'Or is mainly sandy limestone, the Chalonnaise is pebbly limestone, the Mâconnais is limestone and granite, and the Beaujolais is granite.

THE FRENCH RHÔNE

The Rhône enjoys a history stretching back over 5,000 years. With Greek and later Roman influence, it is evident that the Syrah vine has been cultivated in the Rhône valley for 2,500 years, having originated probably in Shiraz, Persia.

The French Rhône runs from Lyons in the north to Avignon in the south and is divided into two sections: the Northern Rhône has a Continental climate and the Southern Rhône a Mediterranean climate. The vines are planted in a bush-like shape to allow the mistral to pass through and round them. Stony soil is characteristic and absorbs the heat during the day, releasing it at night. In general, the reds are full-bodied with good depth of colour and taste texture, almost having a 'roasted' nose. The whites are dry largely and, again, full-bodied.

The Districts of the Northern Rhône

1. Côte Rôtie:
Fruity heavy reds using 80 per cent Syrah and some Viognier vine. Two well-known slopes are the Côte Blonde with limestone and the Côte Brune with iron oxide content.

2. Condrieu:
Fruity dry white, using the Viognier vine.

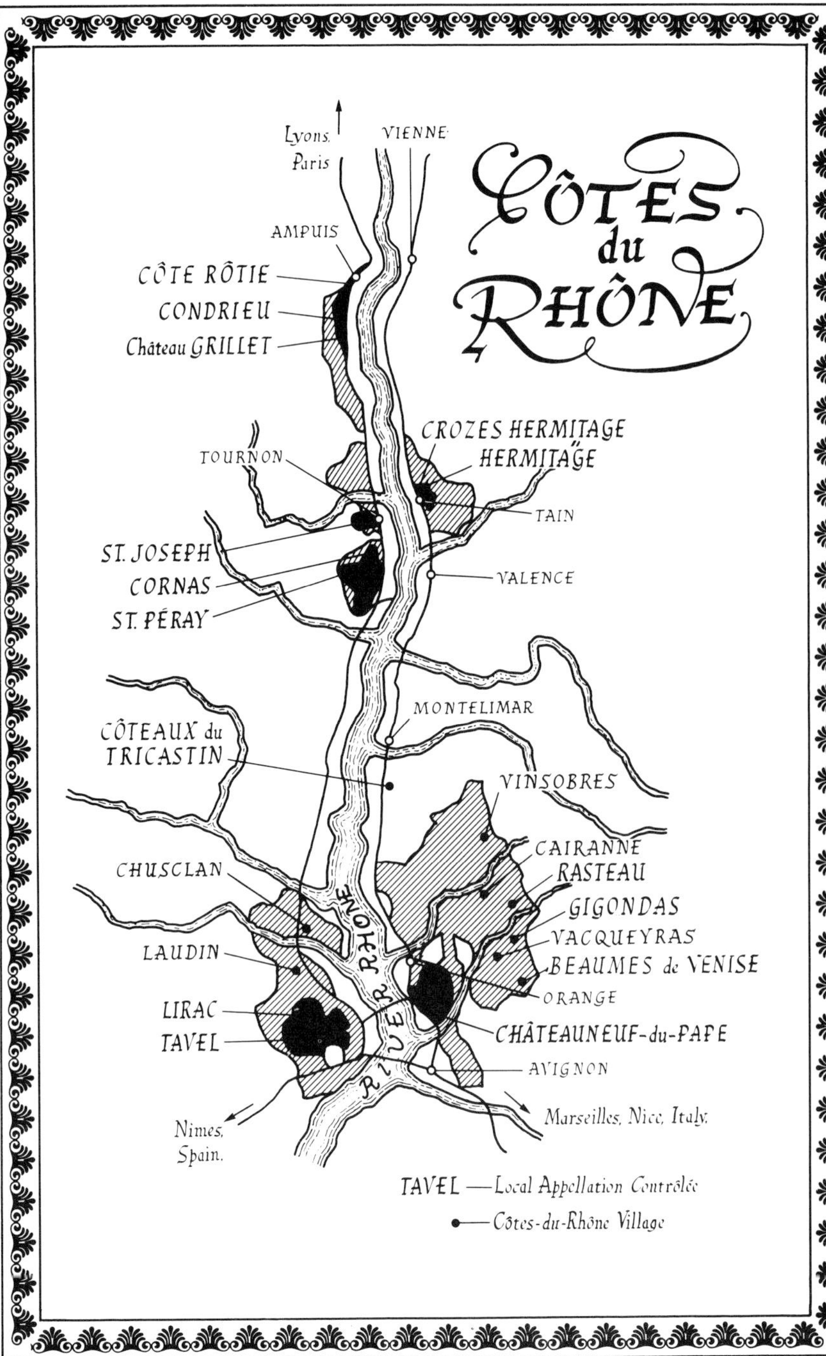

CÔTES du RHÔNE
Lyons, Paris
VIENNE
AMPUIS
CÔTE RÔTIE
CONDRIEU
Château GRILLET
CROZES HERMITAGE
HERMITAGE
TOURNON
TAIN
ST. JOSEPH
CORNAS
ST. PÉRAY
VALENCE
MONTELIMAR
CÔTEAUX du TRICASTIN
VINSOBRES
CAIRANNE
RASTEAU
CHUSCLAN
GIGONDAS
VACQUEYRAS
LAUDIN
BEAUMES de VENISE
ORANGE
LIRAC
TAVEL
CHÂTEAUNEUF-du-PAPE
RIVER RHONE
AVIGNON
Nimes, Spain.
Marseilles, Nice, Italy.
TAVEL — Local Appellation Contrôlée
Côtes-du-Rhône Village

3. Château Grillet:
The only A.O.C. in France composed of a single vineyard. Dry, violet-scented wines of longevity. Like Condrieu, the Viognier vine is used.

4. Hermitage and Crozes-Hermitage:
The latter is a lesser outlying district. Syrah with up to 15 per cent white grapes. Good depth of colour and fruit. A little white Hermitage is made of dry style from the Marsanne and Roussanne vines.

5. St Joseph:
Both reds and whites, ideal for winter.

6. Cornas:
Full-bodied red from Syrah vine.

7. St Péray:
Can be still white or sparkling; dry fruity style from the Roussanne and Marsanne vines.

The Districts of the Southern Rhône

1. Châteauneuf du Pape:
Mainly fruity red of high alcoholic strength using a mixture of vines which include Cinsault, Syrah and Grenache. The district enforces an arrangement whereby any grower exceeding his crop quota, forfeits the right to call even the lower quantity 'Châteauneuf'. A little dry white is made. Les Reflets is the name of the leading group of growers who share a common cellar and organisation.

2. Tavel and Lirac:
Both pink or rosé wines using 65 per cent Grenache and 15 per cent Cinsault vines. Tendency to be dry, pale pinky-orange in colour, called onion-skin pink. Grown on sandy soil. Lirac is cheaper than Tavel owing to the substantial export demand for Tavel.

3. Gigondas:
Elevated from Côtes du Rhône A.O.C. status; light fruity reds.

There is the general area covered by both Côtes du Rhône and Côtes du

Rhône Villages, much of which is made in the village co-operatives. The southern Rhône is increasingly experimenting with carbonic maceration, which involves the storage of grapes under carbon dioxide pressure for a few days prior to fermentation. During this time, the skin cells die and the colour (anthocyanin pigment) diffuses out. This process results in light table wines with little tannin, which are ready for consumption earlier than by traditional methods.

THE LOIRE VALLEY

The Loire was occupied by the Romans with the Church responsible for the selection of most of today's vineyard districts. In fact, in 344 A.D., St Martin (Bishop of Tours, an important middle Loire market town) introduced a more efficient method of pruning, which shows the interest taken by the Church in viticulture. Much of the cultivation was later taken over by the nobility, who endowed the vineyards with graceful buildings. The region is predominantly flat with slight elevation. The soil varies but chalk is particularly noteworthy. Most vineyards lie on the hillsides of the main Loire river or its tributaries, such as the Loir and Layon. This is because the growers wanted good drainage and transport using water travel. The Loire enjoys a mainly mild climate.

The Districts of the Loire

France's longest river may be divided into four main districts, running from the source to the estuary:

1. Upper Loire or Central Vineyards:
Nivernais, Berry and Orléanais. The Sauvignon is grown mainly at Sancerre, Pouilly (for Pouilly Blanc Fumé), which is said to have a gun-flint aroma), Quincy, Reuilly and Ménetou-Salon; while the Chasselas is used for the lesser Pouilly-sur-Loire. A few other vines are grown, such as a little Gamay to make a thin red and a rather acidic, tannic rosé. The Sauvignon yields a crisp, dry white of class, ideal both as an apéritif and to accompany poultry, fish and light meats.

2. Touraine:
Yields dry, medium and sweet whites, such as Vouvray and Montlouis

Wine Districts of the Loire Valley
MILES
0 5 10 20 30 40
CHATEAUX
Vannes
Redon
Châteaubriant
Segré
LE MANS
La Flèche
ANJOU
Beaugency
Talcy
Ménars
BLOIS
Chambord
Beauregard
Cheverny
Fougères
Château-Renault
Château-la Vallière
Baugé
ANGERS
COTEAUX de la LOIRE
MUSCADET
VOUVRAY
TOURS
Vouvray
Chaumont
Amboise
Montlouis
Luynes
Langeais
Villandry
Chenonceaux
Romorantin
ST NAZAIRE
Ancenis
R. Loire
NANTES
Le Loroux-Botteroux
Vertou
Vallet
Maisdon
Brissac
Gennes
Chalonnes
R. Layon
Chanceaux
SAUMUR
Martigné-Briand
COTEAUX du LAYON
les Verchers
Bourgueil
Ussé
Azay-le-Rideau
Chinon
Fontevrault
Valançay
Loches
R. Indre
Cholet
Loudin
Châtillon
Thouars
Bressuire
Challans
CHATELLERAULT
R. Vienne
CHATEAUROUX
LA ROCHE
Chantonnay
Parthenay
Le Blanc
POITIERS
Chauvigny
FONTENAY
Montmorillon
NIORT
Melle
Civray
LA ROCHELLE
Over 3,281 ft
To TOURS 100 miles
Cosné
Sancerre
Pouilly
La Loire
NEVERS

(both still and sparkling) from the Chenin vine, some red at Bourgueil and Chinon mainly, and also some rosé. The Cabernet Franc or Breton vine is mainly used for the red and rosé.

3. Anjou and Saumur:
District famed for its rosés, made either from the Cabernet Franc (and sometimes Cabernet Sauvignon) or a mixture, including the Cot and Groslot. If the label simply states 'Anjou Rosé', it means the latter and should be cheaper. Usually medium-sweet but can be medium-dry. Whites and reds and some sparkling are also made using such other vines as the Chenin Blanc, Malbec and Furmint. The dessert Côteaux du Layon on the Layon tributary includes the fine Quart de Chaume that combines fruit, acidity and some sweetness, using the Chenin Blanc.

4. Muscadet:
The Muscadet or Melon de Bourgogne vine predominates for a light, dry white. This wine is made around Nantes and also called Muscadet. The finest sub-district is known as Sèvre et Maine, but Muscadet is also made in the A.O.C. Coteaux de la Loire. Some V.D.Q.S. is also made including Gros Plant, a 'poor man's Muscadet'.

Most Loire wines are best served when fairly young. The exceptions are certain of the finer dessert whites, like Quarts de Chaume, and a few of the reds. Wines bottled without fining are called *sur lie* and are common in the Muscadet district.

ALSACE

The Alsatian region became French in 1743 under Louis XV. Until the Revolution, the Church and aristocratic influence predominated; but after the Franco-Prussian War of 1870, the region was used by the Germans simply for everyday wine production. The Chasselas vine was cultivated, virtually exclusively from the end of the Franco-Prussian War until the region reverted to France after the First World War. The Alsatian growers then made a decision to grow quality vines and to sell their wines under their grape names – unlike practically anywhere else in France – rather than under district or site names.

The main revival in Alsatian wines has been since World War II with the growth of the Riesling and Traminer vines. Alsace has long cold winters that delay the growth of the vine but hot summers. Rain falls by condensation on the western side of the Vosges mountains, leaving the eastern side – where the vineyards are – relatively dry. The vines are pruned high to protect against frost damage on the Double Guyot system. The picking on this limestone and granite soil is usually late.

Today the area is largely planted with fruity Riesling, the Tokay or Pinot Gris, the light Sylvaner, and the more heavily scented Muscat and Traminer. Each of these grape names is the same name given to the wine except the Traminer. Traminer used to be used for two wines: a straightforward lightly spicy white called Traminer and a spicier one that used the selected clones, called Gewürztraminer. In time, all wine from the Alsatian Traminer has become called Gewürztraminer. The term *edelzwicker* is used for a blend of 'noble' grapes. There are now several higher quality Alsatian wines which are entitled to the designation Grand Cru. Some sparkling wine is made, mainly by the *méthode champenoise*.

Although a little red and rosé is made – often rather light in colour and with a tendency to be on the acidic side – most Alsatian wine is white. Unlike the wines of West Germany that lie just across the frontier, Alsatian wines are fermented right out; they are drier and have a slightly higher strength than West German wines. Serve Alsatian whites, which are traditionally bottled in green-coloured 'flütes', lightly chilled; they accompany poultry, light meats and fish dishes well. The fine Gewürztraminer is traditionally the wine to serve with *pâté de foie gras*.

LESSER-KNOWN FRENCH REGIONS

Space precludes adequate coverage on all other French wines (apart from Champagne, which comes under 'Sparkling' later in this chapter and French Fortified in Chapter 6). The wines of the central and eastern frontier of Savoie and Jura yield light, fruity wines; those of the Savoie are mainly crisp, dry and fairly acidic, making good first course choices. The Jura has a wide range including the rare Château Chalon, one of the few wines outside the Sherry region to grow *flor* (see Chapter 6). The southern coastal strip of Languedoc-Roussillon is producing wines of growing importance on the U.K. market. The dessert Monbazillac of the Dordogne and the fruity styles from Gaillac deserve consideration, too.

SPAIN

One of the largest volume producers in the world, her wine-makers are noted for their art in blending. Spain has a continental climate with very hot summers and cold winters. The main districts are:

1. Rioja:
Named after the river Oja, a tributary of the river Ebro. Mainly fruity dry reds, using the Tempranillo and Garnacha vines, but some dry white from the Malvasia, Viura and other vines, plus a few dry rosés. Much of the maturation and racking procedures owe their origins to Bordeaux, for many Bordeaux families sent part of their families to the Rioja in the hope of purchasing land there after the aphid, *Phylloxera*, struck Bordeaux. The Rioja has one of the world's oldest trademarks, dating from 1560. Vines are of low bush style, pruned to three shoots. The sub-districts are:

i. Alta or Upper Rioja: Based on Haro. The most westerly district on sandstone and limestone. Fair quality.
ii. Baja or Lower Rioja: In the east, based on Logrono. Wines not quite as good as the Alta.
iii. Alavesa: Small district north of the river Ebro near Haro, noted for top quality.

2. Catalonia:
District on Spain's eastern seaboard that lies north and south of Barcelona. It is often divided into coastal, central and upland zones with the rosés and reds made mainly on the coastal strip. In the north lies the mountainous Alella district, noted for its dry and medium whites and pale rosés. The chalky soil of part of the next district, Panadés, is ideal for whites and particularly for sparkling wines. Tarragona lies further south and is made largely in the village co-operatives; today it is little sought after by comparison with the turn of this century when different duty bands operated. Tarragona is a sweet, raisiny style mainly but some finer qualities are made in the delimited smaller zone of Priorato.

3. La Mancha:
This is a vast central area of Spain where much of the first fermentation and subsequent ageing is undertaken in large earthenware vessels, known as *tinajas*. The wines tend to be earthy reds and full-bodied whites.

4. Levante:
Further south along Spain's coast from Catalonia, where ordinary whites are made at Alicante and a wide range at Murcia and Valencia.

Among other Spanish regions should be mentioned the dry, almost *vinho verde* style of north-west Galicia; the fruity dessert Málaga wines of southern Spain near Gibraltar: the lighter-than-Sherry wines of Montilla and Moriles, which are frequently not fortified; and the sweet wines of Aragon, based on the town of Cariñena.

PORTUGAL

Portugal has exported her wines to England for longer than any other country. They achieved great popularity in the Napoleonic Wars and today Portugal produces the best selling branded rosé in Britain. While the legal controls in Spain are under the Consejo Regulador, in Portugal the demarcated areas (as delimited regions are known) are controlled by the Junta Nacional do Vinho. In addition, exporters need to belong to the Gremio dos Exportação to obtain export certificates of authenticity, etc. The main districts, from the north to just south of Lisbon, are:

1. Minho (Green Wine District):
Mountainous region from the Spanish border in the north to south of Oporto. The soil is a type of granite, called schist, where both red (about 75 to 80 per cent) and white wines are made. This is *vinho verde*, a dry, almost austere wine made from grapes that do not fully ripen as they are trained up pergolas of 8 to 12 feet (2·4 to 3·7 metres). This is done to avoid the heat of the ground and to allow other cash crops to be grown below, such as cabbages or maize. The Azal vine is popular for the white. The high malic acid present in the wine ensures that it is *pétillant* in the glass because it is bottled within the region before the malo-lactic fermentation (where the malic acid is converted to lactic acid) takes place.

2. Douro:
Apart from port, the Douro valley makes much table wine. This is mostly *pétillant* rosé, but a sweet white is made at Alijo on the mountain top from grapes which have been attacked by *Botrytis cinerea*.

3. Dão:
A broad, upland plain that is centred on the old city of Viseu. Fruity, slightly tannic reds and dry whites are predominant.

4. Estremadura:
Comprises many smaller districts, such as Colares (mainly red where the vine grows from a clay soil through sand where the *Phylloxera* cannot penetrate); sweet Bucelas made on heavy clay; and the dessert Moscatel de Setúbal, made the Tagus estuary south of Lisbon. Although modern presses are coming in, it is still possible to see foot-treading in *lagares*.

ITALY

Italy has enjoyed a long tradition of wine-making, dating probably to 900 B.C. The cultured vine was brought to Italy by the Greeks about 750 B.C. and flourished during the Roman era. The Mediterranean climate ensured consistency of style; and the wine regions take their names from the old Italian provinces. Control is by the 1963 Denominazione d'Origine Controllata (D.O.C.) with three broad categories:

1. Vino da Pasto: The ordinary table wine. Non-quality.
2. D.O.C.: Quality wine from a defined district, conforming to the appropriate restrictions.
3. D.O.C.G.: D.O.C., but in addition *Garantia* whereby the Italian Government authenticates the bottling. Few wines are, as yet, in this category.

The Major Regions

1. Piedmont:
In the upper reaches of the river Po. The white Moscato d'Asti and sparkling Asti Spumante are well known; as are the fruity Barbera, Barbaresco (from the Nebbiolo vine) and heavy Barolo, all of which are reds. Gattinara is a lighter red, maturing ahead of Barolo.

2. Alto Adige or Trentino:
This is a light white and fruity red wine district of north-eastern Italy. The Riesling grows well here and the soft Lago di Caldaro is worth looking for.

3. Veneto:
Yields the dry and medium white Soave from 80 per cent Garganega and 20 per cent Trebbiano vines. The raspberry red Valpolicella and light Bardolino, from the shore of Lake Garda, also come from this area.

4. Emilia Romagna:
This region is noted for the dry sparkling red, Lambrusco.

5. Tuscany:
Is centred on Florence and Siena and is particularly noted for Chianti

with a heartland, called Classico, which describes the traditional area of production. Chianti should be predominantly made from 70 per cent Sangiovese, 20 per cent Canaiolo Negro and 10 per cent Trebbiano and Malvasia together. A youthful wine for drinking early is made by a system known as the *governo*. This entails adding the fermenting juice of late-maturing grapes to the wine after it is made. White wine in this district cannot be called Chianti; it is Tuscan Bianco.

6. Marshes and other Regions:
In the Marches, the dry white Verdicchio is well known. In Lazio (Latium), the medium dry to dry Frascati near Rome and the medium sweet Est! Est!! Est!!! – also white – is made. In Umbria, Orvieto is made which can vary on taste from *secco* (dry) to *abboccato* (medium-sweet). In southern Italy, Campania yields the white Lachryma Christi (or Lacrima) from volcanic soil. Several wines come from Sicily, the best known of which is the fortified wine, Marsala (see Chapter 6).

OTHER TABLE WINES

Small quantities of table wines are shipped to the U.K. from the U.S.A. (California), South America (mainly Argentina and Chile), the U.S.S.R. (Georgia), Australia, South Africa, New Zealand, northern Africa and central and eastern Europe. At present only a small range of Swiss and Greek wines are shipped to Britain, coming mainly from Lavaux, Neuchâtel and Valais in the case of Switzerland where light, fruity, dry whites predominate; and from Attica, Samos, Crete and the Peloponnese in the case of Greece. If Greece joins the E.E.C. as a full member (for she has associated status already), it is likely her wines will be seen more widely within the Community. The most distinctive Greek style is *retsina*, which means a wine to which pine resin has been added. Many of these come from Attica, a district which lies to the west of Athens. Most of the central and eastern European wines are sold as branded wines with a grape name, except the dessert Tokay of northern Hungary which is particularly special.

Although the first South African plantings date from 1655, when the first Dutch settlement was made at the Cape of Good Hope, it was the French Huguenot influence in the last decade of the seventeenth century that saw the potential. Over-production in the early twentieth century led to the formation of a central growers' body in 1918, known today as the K.W.V. Wine production was limited in the Western Cape in 1957 and further in 1972 by the introduction of a system of area delimitation, known as 'Wines of Origin'. At the present time, these consist of Brede, River Valley, Caledon, Constantia, Boberg, Durbanville, Klein Karoo, Swartland, Paarl, Olifantsriver, Piquetberg, Robertson, Stellenbosch, Swellendam, Tulbagh, Worcester and Malmesbury.

The quality seal applied to the bottle neck is certified and approved by the South African government-appointed Wine and Spirit Board for each contents so labelled. The blue-coloured band certifies the origin, the red-coloured band the vintage as stated on the bottle, while the green-coloured band shows that the grape variety (or cultivar) complies with the label and those permitted. *Superior* indicates a high quality wine, and *estate* (or *landgoed*) marks a wine originating from a recognised approved estate; these are extra terms. The serial number on each such seal indicates Board control through the processing, fermentation and bottling stages.

Australia makes a range of wines, many of which are noted for their

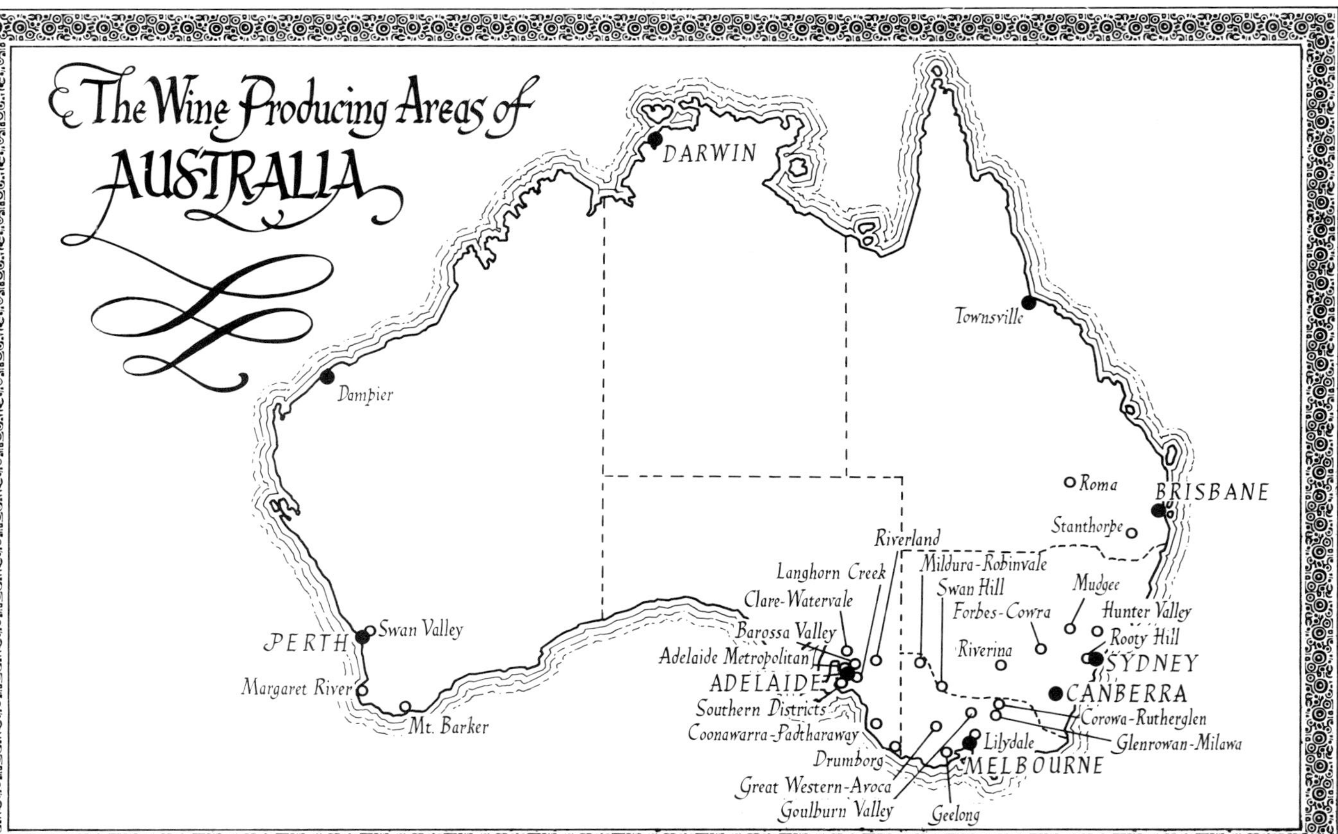

The Wine Producing Areas of
AUSTRALIA
DARWIN
Townsville
Dampier
Roma
BRISBANE
Stanthorpe
Riverland
Langhorn Creek
Mildura-Robinvale
Mudgee
Swan Hill
Clare-Watervale
Forbes-Cowra
Hunter Valley
Barossa Valley
Rooty Hill
Riverina
SYDNEY
Adelaide Metropolitan
ADELAIDE
CANBERRA
Southern Districts
Corowa-Rutherglen
Coonawarra-Padtharaway
Lilydale
Glenrowan-Milawa
Drumborg
MELBOURNE
Great Western-Avoca
Goulburn Valley
Geelong
PERTH
Swan Valley
Margaret River
Mt. Barker

fine quality. They can trace their origin to the vines planted in the late eighteenth century by Captain Arthur Phillip. The major regions today are in New South Wales (which includes the famous Hunter River Valley, north of Newcastle), Victoria and South Australia. Irrigation has been introduced to advantage as can be seen from such districts as the Murray Irrigation Area (sometimes known as the Murray River Valley) in South Australia, and Mildura in Victoria.

SPARKLING WINES

A sparkling wine is one that retains 3 or more atmospheres of carbon dioxide. The main methods of production are as follows.

1. Direct Impregnation:
Carbon dioxide is pumped into a still table wine. The bead (or bubble) dissipates quickly upon opening. Not satisfactory.

2. Tank or *Charmat* or *Cuve Close*:
Here a series of inter-linking, closed vats are used. A still table wine is taken, to which is added a sugar solution and yeast culture. This is then allowed a secondary fermentation within the vat. The wine is then transferred, while still within the vat system, to another vat and filtered between the two. It has a dosage or sugar element in old wine added to make it a *brut* (dry style), *demi-sec* (sweet), etc. This is a better method than direct impregnation and is regularly used for most West German sparkling wines. It can give rather a chemical taste and large bead size.

3. Transfer:
In this process, the secondary fermentation takes place in bottle (as described in 4. below) but is then transferred (hence the name) to a vat under pressure. The wine is clarified, receives its addition of sugar solution to determine its degree of final dryness or sweetness, and is then bottled.

4. *Méthode Champenoise*:
A still table wine is bottled and given an injection of sugar solution and a yeast culture, which induces a secondary fermentation in the bottle. The deposit is usually brought to the neck of the bottle by twisting the bottles over several weeks. This is called *remuage* in French, although parts of Spain and France are now undertaking this by machine. The temporary cork is removed, the deposit removed and a sugar solution in old wine added to determine the final dryness or sweetness of the wine. Unlike transfer, in this method, the wine stays in the bottle throughout. It achieves less uniformity than the *cuve close*, but produces an elegance and small bead size that cannot be achieved by any other means.

Champagne

Although the producers of Blanquette de Limoux in south-west France claim they originated the process, the Champagne region can claim to have made sparkling wine their strength. Champagne has to be made by *méthode Champenoise*, although a little still is sold under the A.O.C. of Coteaux Champenois (which replaced *vin nature de Champagne*). It is centred on Reims, Epernay and Ay, and on the three districts of the Mountain of Reims, the Valley of the Marne and the Côte des Blancs. The white Chardonnay and Pinot Noir are the main grapes with a little Meunier and Arbanne.

Expansion is likely to be mainly in the southerly Aube which forms part of the Champagne A.O.C. The region is graded into districts of quality, ranging from 77 per cent as the lowest (like the Aisne and Aube) to 100 per cent for the highest (like Ambonnay, Avize, Bouzy and Sillery among others), which affects the grape price. Although the major grape used is black or red, most Champagne is white. This means the grape skins., etc., are removed from the must immediately after pressing.

Crémant

Crémant has two meanings: a lighter atmospheric pressure for Champagne – around 3·5 or 4 atmospheres – to the normal 5 to 6; or a *méthode Champenoise* A.O.C., not necessarily Champagne. Examples include Crémant d'Alsace and Crémant de Loire. It is not to be confused with the name of a village of Champagne called Cramant.

Other Sparkling Wines

Outside Champagne, good quality sparkling wines are made within France at Blanquette de Limoux, Loire (particularly Vouvray and around St Hilaire St Florent), Alsace, and the Rhône (St Péray and Clairette de Die, for example). The best known, non-French, sparkling wines are, in the U.K., those from Italy (particularly Asti Spumante from the sweet Muscat grape); Spain, from the Panadés district of Catalonia; and West Germany, where the quality descriptions from lowest to best are *schaumwein, sekt* and *prädikatssekt*.* Small quantities also come from England,† Austria, Hungary, Australia, South Africa and Israel.

**Schaumwein* is the West German term for a sparkling wine with the method of production unspecified; in practice, it is used for the sparkling *Tafelwein*. Although a E.E.C. Court ruling made the term, *Sekt*, not specifically West German, no other state

Sparkling Wine Terms

Blanc de Blancs means a wine produced exclusively from white grapes.
Brut means dry style.
Sec means dryish.
Demi-Sec and *Demi-Doux* both mean sweetish.
Rich or *Doux* mean sweet.
Dégorgement is the process whereby the temporary cork is removed and the deposit, which has been brought to the neck of the bottle through the *remuage* shaking process in *méthode Champenoise*, is ejected. This can be done either by hand or – more often – automatically.
Dosage or *liqueur d'expédition* is the mixture of old wine in which sugar has been dissolved. This is added after *dégorgement* to ensure the final style to be made.

Uses

Apart from being the natural wine of celebration – from baptisms to wedding breakfast – sparkling wines make ideal apéritif choices. The special stoppers which retain the *mousse* (effervescent bead) are helpful here. Champagne may be served throughout a meal as well. More specifically, the drier styles will accompany fish and poultry courses well, also lighter meats like lamb. The sweeter styles, like Champagne Rich and Asti Spumante, are attractive with desserts, particularly fresh soft fruit like raspberries and strawberries.

---

has taken up the term to date. In West Germany, *Sekt* (or *Qualitätsschaumwein*) can be made by any of the methods except direct impregnation. *Prädikatssekt* – which by the same E.E.C. Court ruling of March 1975 is not necessarily West German – must have a minimum 60 per cent grapes originating in West Germany. If a district or regional name is applied to either of the last two wines, a minimum 75 per cent of the grapes must originate in that district or region.

†Experiments are taking place on *méthode Champenoise* wines produced from naturally-made English vineyard wines, such as in Felsted, Essex, and Somerset. These are in no way to be compared with an unnatural reconstituted British sparkling wine that uses one or more concentrates.

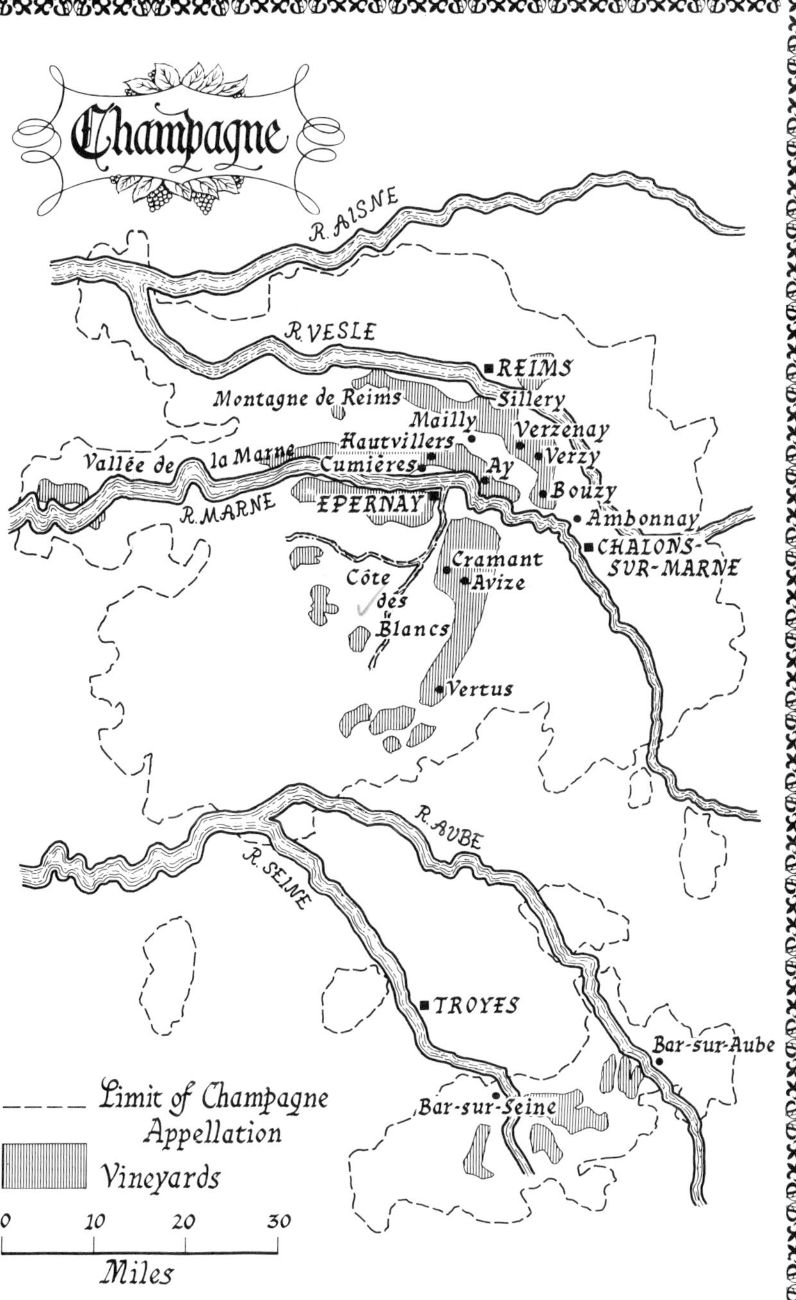
Champagne
R. AISNE
R. VESLE
REIMS
Montagne de Reims
Sillery
Mailly
Verzenay
Hautvillers
Verzy
Vallée de la Marne
Cumières
Ay
Bouzy
R. MARNE
EPERNAY
Ambonnay
CHALONS-SUR-MARNE
Cramant
Avize
Côte des Blancs
Vertus
R. AUBE
R. SEINE
TROYES
Bar-sur-Aube
Bar-sur-Seine
Limit of Champagne Appellation
Vineyards
0
10
20
30
Miles

6. Fortified Wines

'The wild vicissitudes of taste', Samuel Johnson.

Fortified wines are wines to which a spirit has been added, thereby increasing the alcoholic level. While table wines often have an alcoholic level around 10° G.L., fortified wines are frequently in the 18 to 24° G.L. zone. Port has its fermentation arrested by the addition of a spirit, while Sherry* has spirit added after fermentation. Thus the timing as to the spirit fortification varies.

SHERRY

Sherry, without qualifying the name by any country of origin, comes from a relatively small area of south-western Spain in the province of Cadiz. It is estimated that vineyard cultivation began some 3,000 years ago. The Greeks called the principal town of the area Xera. The Romans renamed the town Ceret during their occupation from 133 B.C. to A.D. 409. It became Seret under the Visigoths who stayed until the Moors invaded from north Africa in A.D. 711, calling the town Sheris in pronunciation. The Moors were finally driven out in 1264 by Alfonso X, known as the Wise.

Shakespearean England called the wine Sheris, Sack, which eventually evolved into 'Sherry'. During the same period, the Spanish referred to the town as Xeres, and then Jerez (its present name). Jerez de la Frontera

*A capital 'S' denotes Spanish Sherry, made within the delimited area of S.W. Spain. All imitations of it are given with a small 's'.

was so named because it lay at the frontier between the Christian and Moslem religions. Sherry became a popular drink in England as the port of Cadiz was conveniently situated for passing merchant ships.

Geography and Climate

The Jerez delimited area is a triangular shape between the Guadalete and Guadalquivir rivers and the Atlantic. It lies approximately at latitude 36·5° N. and includes the towns of Jerez de la Frontera, Sanlúcar de Barrameda and Puerto de Santa Maria. The landscape shows few trees across the low rolling hills.

The Jerez area has a regular climate with an average annual 294 days of sunshine and 71 days of rain. It has an annual average temperature of 72°F (22°C) with a 32 to 104°F (0 to 40°C) total variation. Some 22 inches (55·9 centimetres) of rain fall on average annually or 121 gallons (550 litres) per square metre. Forty per cent of the rain falls during the last three months of the year. Moist southerly and westerly winds blow from the sea, but the drying easterly and north-easterly Levante wind can break the flowers on the vine. With so little rain, the vineyards are dependent upon the irrigation of the Guadalquivir and other rivers which carry the melted snows down from the Sierra Nevada.

Soil

The Jerez area is graded basically on the proportion of chalk (calcium carbonate) that it contains:

1. Albariza: The finest quality which contains approximately 40 per cent chalk; it is able to absorb large quantities of water. When wet, it has a paste-like consistency, but it dries to a fine, brilliant white tilth which reflects heat and protects the moist ground below. Albariza gives wines a higher alcoholic balanced acidity and a typical Sherry character.
2. Barros: Contains up to 10 per cent chalk, but is mainly a dark mud clay with some iron. Yields coarser and heavier wines than those on the Albariza, and some 20 per cent greater in volume.
3. Arenas: Sandy soil containing up to 10 per cent chalk with a similar yield to Barros. Much lower grape quality but good for dessert vines like Pedro Ximenez and Moscatel.

Much of the coastal belt is Barros or Arenas.

Vines

Palomino de Jerez is grown mainly in the Albariza.

Pedro Ximenez (often referred to as P.X.) is grown at the bottom of slopes in the Barros and Arenas soil districts.

Moscatel is grown in small quantities in the Barros and Arenas, particularly at Rota and Chipiona.

Viticultural Year

October/November:

Foliage falls at the end of October. Fertiliser is applied every fourth or fifth year as otherwise production increases but quality diminishes. Long wedge-shaped troughs are also made between vine rows to collect the rainfall and prevent erosion; this is called *la serpia.*

December/January:

Pruning and planting: one long branch with buds is left to bear the fruit of the year as well as one short stub which in the following year will bear the crop. In turn, the long branch is pruned short. When planting, a 39 inch (1 metre) deep hole is dug, fertilised and American root stock planted with its roots 12 to 18 inches (30 to 46 centimetres) deep, projecting about 5 inches (13 centimetres) above ground. Grafting is done the following year if adequately developed. A six foot six inch (two metres) space is allowed between rows to facilitate tractor movement.

February:

Grafting in new vineyards; weeding continues. The vine will be producing three years after grafting (i.e. six years after planting).

March:

Spraying against mildew as buds start to grow in mid March. Spraying today is largely by helicopter until the vines are about 20 inches (50 centimetres) tall and until flowering starts. Later in the season, spraying is by tractor to cover the undersides of the leaves.

April:

The vines are either attached to wires for training (the new method) or tied to a stick. Small new buds are removed to prevent unnecessary growth.

May:
Flowering is at the end of May, lasting 3 to 4 days.

June:
Land is rotavated and rolled flat to prevent undue cracking, because the rain ends in mid to late May. Weeding is done by a special machine which does not damage the vine.

July:
Light spraying if rain occurs. The press house equipment is prepared for the harvest.

August:
Any area where vine roots were taken out after the last harvest, is given a further deep ploughing, prior to sugar beet or cereal cultivation for up to five years before a new vine is planted.

September:
The Sherry harvest, usually commencing in the first week, continues for about 20 days. The P.X. are picked first. Older vines ripen earlier than young ones; vines on south-facing and higher levels also ripen earlier.

Vinification

In the old system, Palomino grapes were left to dry in the sun for up to 24 hours. Most modern producers only give such a treatment today to the P.X. vine to help it to concentrate the sugar. Under the former system, the grapes were pressed by boots with angled nails, which prevented the crushing of pips and stalks, in wooden *lagares* (square troughs on wooden supports with a central screw). Today modern presses are largely used, although gypsum is still added to increase acidity.

The first fermentation starts some 12 to 24 hours later and is violent, taking only 36 to 50 hours to convert the sugar present in the grape juice to alcohol largely. The fermentation then slows down to a pace which lasts for about 45 to 50 days. Unlike port, Sherry ferments until it is dry. The wine begins to clarify naturally when the weather turns cold.

The first classification takes place before the development of *flor*, which is a film-forming yeast *Saccharomyces Ellipsoideus*. Three broad categories are taken:

1. Likely to develop *flor* and become a 'fino' or 'amontillado';
2. Not yet developed sufficiently to tell; and
3. Coarser ones where *flor* will not grow.

The *flor* first category is known as 'Palmas' and the non-*flor* third category as 'Rayas'. A light fortification is given, to 15·5° G.L., for the first two categories and to 18° G.L. for the third style, which will be matured into the 'oloroso' type. By raising the oloroso to 18° G.L., the risk of refermentation and of *flor* development is removed.

In June, the first two categories are retasted. It is then easier to determine their progress as the wines will have been clarified (or racked) and *flor* development will be evident. The *flor* forms a yellow-white film on top of the wine, not unlike talcum powder sprinkled on water. *Flor* likes spring temperatures and feeds on air, glycerine, some alcohol and other properties present. This is the *anada* stage and is the point when the vintage wines are decided upon. The wines are called by the year of their harvest and usually also have the name of the vineyard. Olorosos do not require further classification and are frequently placed to stand in the sun for one or two years. This process encourages the particularly characteristic nose and taste associated with this style. The shippers experience a higher loss by such sunning as the evaporation rate increases from an annual 4 per cent within the *bodega* (Sherry store) to 15 per cent. At the June classification, any Sherry designated as oloroso will receive the addition of grape brandy to fortify it to the same level as the earlier olorosos.

The wines develop in a series of casks, known as the *criadera*. Fino is characterised by the growth of *flor* up to its final fortification to 17 or 18° G.L. (*flor* cannot grow above 16·4° G.L.). The *flor* development imparts a distinct nose and taste to the fino. Amontillado has a greyish-white *flor* present, thinner than on fino, which lives for two to three years and then dies, falling to the cask floor. Often amontillado is referred to as an 'old fino'; this is because finos can be converted to amontillados by the addition of grape spirit. Without refreshment, the *flor* will slowly die. Classification is to be seen in a *bodega* by the markings on a cask.

The wines are now ready for entry into the *solera* system of ageing. Since old wine can be 'refreshed' by the addition of a younger wine, the system has been devised to ensure some of the character of the older wine is passed on to the younger one. Although physically the *bodega* may not look like housing a series of pyramid casks, it may be easier to understand the *solera* system that way. When a consignment of Sherry is required, up to one-third of a butt (the name in the Sherry area for a cask holding 108 imperial gallons/490·68 litres) may be drawn out. Most shippers, however, would not take more than one-quarter annually per butt. The space left in the butt is filled with wine from the row above (first *criadera*); this in turn, is filled or refreshed with Sherry from the row above that (second *criadera*). This continues until there is space for new wine, whereupon the Sherry of approximately three harvests before enters the *solera* system. The date of a *solera* is the year in which the series of butts were first created for that blend, not the date of all the wine within it! Frequently famous people lend their names to particular *soleras* or shippers call them after events. A dated *solera* therefore implies that careful treatment over many years has been given to the wines in the blend and that a small quantity remains from its original establishment. More vitally, it also implies that the original wine has passed on its characteristics to the later vintages that were introduced. Replacement stock to a *solera* must be of similar style, but not so youthful as to upset the balance.

The wines are blended prior to shipment. A good fino, for instance, might be composed from up to fourteen selections. The final alcoholic level is usually raised for export to 18·5–18·7° G.L. The sweetness present in Sherry comes from the addition of P.X. and Moscatel since spirit is added to them immediately after pressing to prevent fermentation. They are not aged in the sun, like olorosos, but kept at *anada* stage for two to seven years before entering their own *criaderas* and a *solera*. The tawny hue of many olorosos derives from the addition of *color* wine; this is made from boiled fresh must, which is reduced in volume by some 70 per cent when it caramelises and is non-alcoholic. At this stage, more fresh must is added and the mixture is allowed to ferment for a short time.

Fining with egg white or gelatine and, additionally, bentonite is undertaken to refrigeration to (18°F/ – 8°C) for eight days which precipitates excess tartrates. Shipping is in butts of American oak or safrap containers, or by ships' tank. By Spanish law, Sherry cannot be exported by road and this usually means the ports of Puerto de Santa Maria and Cadiz are used.

Types of Sherry

1. Finos:
Are pale straw in appearance, light and dry on nose and taste, with a delicate and refreshing quality. They make apt apéritif choices and to accompany fish and soup dishes.

2. Manzanilla:
Is a Sherry, usually fino, which is matured by the sea at Sanlúcar de Barrameda. It has a salty flavour and, like all genuine fino, is bone dry.

3. Amontillados:
Are wines of the original fino class which have acquired an amber appearance with age and a dry, nutty flavour. Many are sweetened to suit the English palate. Serve as above.

4. Olorosos:
Dark gold or deep amber in appearance with a distinct and heavy nose from the Raya strain. Soft and with more body often than amontillado. Usually medium-sweet, but are additionally sweetened for the U.K. market to become 'Golden' ,'Brown' or 'Cream' where P.X. and some Moscatel have been added. They may be enjoyed at the end of a meal.

5. Palo Cortado:
Is a rare type of oloroso with an attractive deep-amber hue, but a dry nuttyness on the taste, that fits it between a normal oloroso and an amontillado in style.

The drier Sherry styles benefit from chilling lightly. Serve all Sherries in *copitas*, the elongated tulip-shaped glass that has a narrower top than its base and which allows one to appreciate the nose and appearance fully.

Sherry plays an important part in Britain, accounting for one quarter of fortified wine sales by volume and 29 per cent by value in 1977.* Britain imports more Sherry than any other country and, over the past twenty years, U.K. consumption of Sherry has quadrupled. To meet the growing demand, the delimited area of Sherry has expanded its acreage under vine from 26,000 acres (10,521 hectares) in 1971 to 48,500 acres

*Source: H.M. Customs and Excise clearances and estimates from John Harvey & Sons Ltd of Bristol.

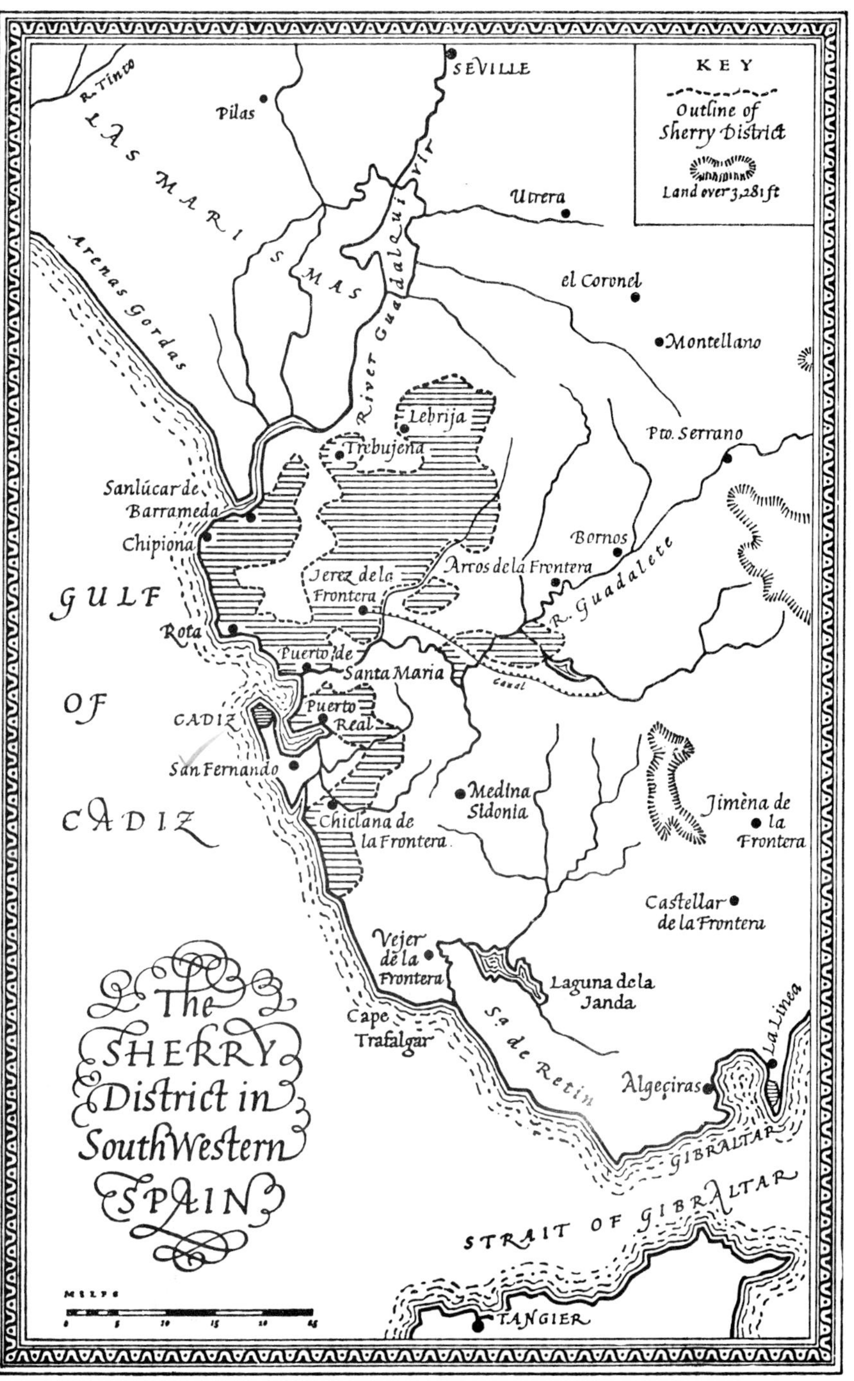

KEY
Outline of Sherry District
Land over 3,281 ft
SEVILLE
R. Tinto
Pilas
LAS MARISMAS
Utrera
Arenas Gordas
River Guadalquivir
el Coronel
Montellano
Lebrija
Trebujena
Pto. Serrano
Sanlúcar de Barrameda
Chipiona
Bornos
R. Guadalete
Arcos de la Frontera
Jerez de la Frontera
GULF OF CADIZ
Rota
Puerto de Santa Maria
Canal
CADIZ
Puerto Real
San Fernando
Medina Sidonia
Jimèna de la Frontera
Chiclana de la Frontera
Castellar de la Frontera
Vejer de la Frontera
Laguna de la Janda
Cape Trafalgar
Sa. de Retin
La Linea
Algeçiras
GIBRALTAR
The SHERRY District in South Western SPAIN
STRAIT OF GIBRALTAR
MILES
0 5 10 15 20 25
TANGIER

(19,627 hectares) by 1977, an increase of 86·5 per cent. Some 360,000 butts annually is the production capability estimated in the Sherry area by 1980.

MONTILLA

In considering Montilla and other 'Sherry style' wines made outside the delimited Spanish area, it is important to consider the overall fortified wine market. Consumer sales in 1977 over the previous year suggest a Sherry increase of 2·3 per cent and a Cyprus sherry drop of 8 per cent. In volume terms, non-Sherry styles take 12 per cent of the market in volume and 8 per cent on value.

Montilla lies only about 120 miles (192 kilometres) north-east of Jerez in southern Spain and includes the towns of Montilla, Moriles, Aguilar de la Frontera, Lucena, Cabra, Cordoba and Puente Genil. It is effectively in the heart of Andalusia, covering in delimited vineyard terms some 49,422 acres (20,000 hectares) which are being increased by some 25 per cent per year in the mid 1970s. Total expansion can be up to about four times that of the present area under cultivation. The Consejo Regulador controls the method of cultivation and production.

In Montilla, the root stock is cut back in January to allow five stems to grow from each root in Goblet style with two buds or shoots on each stem. This differs from Jerez where only one stem is allowed to grow with all shoots on the one stem. For the first tumultuous fermentation, Montilla uses large 'Ali Baba' pots, which stand some 20 foot (6·1 metres) high and hold 1,760 to 2,200 gallons (8,000 to 10,000 litres), unlike wood used in Jerez; these pots are called *tinajas*. After the full fermentation, the wine is pumped from the *tinajas* into oak casks for development, prior to placement in the Montilla *solera* scheme. Like Jerez, Montilla does not sun-dry its grapes before pressing – other than the Pedro Ximenez P.X. – and is usually not fortified, unlike Sherry. However, much exported Montilla does have a small addition of grape spirit to stabilise it.

By an agreed settlement in late 1976, terms ascribed to both Sherry and Montilla hitherto, such as fino and amontillado, will in future not appear on Montilla labels or promotional literature. This is the likely result of the Judgment by Consent given in the case brought between Sandeman, Valdespino and Duff Gordon (for the Sherry shippers) and Western Licensed Supplies Ltd and Avon Licensed Supplies Ltd (as Montilla distributors); although technically the actual judgment was between these particular parties. Instead Montilla styles are now described in English as 'crisp dry', 'medium-sweet', or such other variations as Montilla distributors prefer. With the lightness of body and delicacy of nose and palate, Montilla has a distinct appeal.

AUSTRALIAN SHERRY

The first commercial shipment of Australian wine to Britain was in 1854. Today sherry-style examples account for a small, but significant, part. Techniques involving the introduction of *flor* and ageing on *solera* lines, have resulted in a high standard. In the drier field, the Palomino, Temperano and Albillo vines have been grown with particularly good results in South Australia. The medium and dessert styles of several New South Wales and South Australia wineries make for interesting comparative tasting; although the high cost of freight to Britain may mean that they will be unlikely volume contenders against Spain.

CYPRUS SHERRY

The island of Cyprus at the eastern end of the Mediterranean exports a fair volume of her grape crop to Britain as a 'sherry style' wine. For the drier style, a specially selected white wine is placed in American oak casks into which a cultured *flor* yeast is introduced. In Jerez, the *flor* grows naturally on the fino. Up to half the contents per cask is removed for blending and export. Several sweeter styles are also made, including a 'cream' type, which are aged in all weathers in wood for two to three years. A small proportion of Cyprus sherry is bottled on the island, but most is shipped in bulk to Britain.

The Cyprus market emerged in 1961, largely as a result of skilful brand marketing and the appeal of the dessert style to the mass market tastes at a low price. Already the Cyprus wine industry had laid foundations with the establishment of the Vine Products Commission in 1968. This is an independent body, whose main functions are to control new plantings, classify vines, regulate viticultural practices, establish quality zones and appropriate controls, administer Government subsidies, and deal with the overall disposal of each year's crop. The island's main grapes are the black Mavro, white Xynisteri (which are both drought-resistant), white Málaga (sometimes called Muscat of Alexandria), and black Opthalmo.

Cyprus has never suffered *Phylloxera* and is accordingly taking great care with new plantings. They have introduced a substantial number of vines from South Australia, which is also *Phylloxera*-free. The island's wine industry employs approximately one in four of the population. The main vineyards are in the Limassol and Paphos districts and in the volcanic soil of the southern foothills of the Troodos mountains.

SOUTH AFRICAN SHERRY

Imitation 'sherry style' wines were first made about 1932 in South Africa with the attempt to age on *solera* lines starting about 1942. Paarl, centre of the South African wine-making industry, lies on a similar latitude to Jerez, capital of the Sherry region. *Flor* does not grow naturally in South Africa and, after an initial classification into *flor* and oloroso potential types, a cultured yeast is injected into those wines which show a delicate quality and low tannin; tannin inhibits *flor* growth. On average the wines spend seven years in the Cape *soleras*.

Five vines are cultivated for this use:* Steen, Palomino (*sic*), Sémillon, Pedro and Colombard. A variety of different styles are shipped to the U.K., but none achieve the balance and elegance of Sherry to date.

*South African Act No. 25 of 1957 on Pale Liqueur wine.

MADEIRA

Madeira is the fortified wine of the island of the same name, Portuguese in nationality, which is only 35 by 14 miles (57 by 22 kilometres) in size and some 500 miles (800 kilometres) south-west of Portugal. This island, only slightly larger than the Isle of Wight, has a warm climate suitable for vine cultivation on account of its mid-Atlantic position, just to the north of the Tropics. Its temperate climate shows an average 61°F (16°C) in winter and 70°F (21°C) in summer.

The soil is rich and volcanic in origin. It was discovered in 1419 by two Portuguese mariners whose early successors were said to have burnt down a few trees to make a clearing and, in the process, to have started a fire which lasted seven years. The wood ash deposits that resulted have increased the soil's fertility still further. In fact, the word *madeira* is Portuguese for 'timber'.

Historical Background

The Malvasia vine was first planted in 1427, having been brought from Crete. Madeira was extremely popular in the sixteenth and seventeenth centuries in Britain. In fact, Charles II was offered the island as part of his dowry when he married Portugal's Catherine of Braganza but he took Bombay and Tangier instead. By 1680 there was a thriving wine trade with Britain supplying 10 of the 26 Madeira shippers.

Towards the end of the seventeenth century, fortification commenced which allowed Madeira to compete with Sherry and port. After the 1715 and 1745 Jacobite rebellions, many Scots settled in Madeira. English merchants cornered the Madeira market when the Napoleonic Wars reduced supplies of French and other European wines. By the nineteenth century, Madeira became the drink of hospitality. But the aphid, *Phylloxera*, struck about 1873 and, by the time resistant American root-stock had been planted, Madeira had lost its place in the drinks field. Madeira is one of the four wines protected in Britain by the 1914 Treaty with Portugal, not the earlier Methuen Treaty of 1703. Today it is largely appreciated by clubs, livery companies and university common rooms; although there are signs of a slow reawakening of general interest.

Types of Madeira

Four main vines were originally planted, each yielding white grapes, and are still cultivated. There is a natural overlap between the styles of wine, depending upon the shipper and his market. Since few of these wines are composed exclusively of one vine, the E.E.C. is arguing that the grape name cannot be used.

The problem stems from the wild vines introduced from the U.S.A. after the *Phylloxera* plague. They were originally brought with other experimental root stock and did not even produce grapes in their native North American soil. Yet in the rich Madeira soil, these vines flourished; the wine made from them was mixed with the rapidly declining stocks of quality Madeira during this critical period. Since these vines did not need grafting in order to survive, they were easier work for the growers and, since there were then no incentives to replant with the better 'noble' varieties, the farmers retained them. This poses a real problem today when in an average annual vintage, only some 593,900 gallons (2,700,000 litres) from the total 2,419,650 to 2,639,600 gallons (11,000,000 to 12,000,000 litres) harvest comes from grafted vinifera vines. About 1,539,800 gallons (7,000,000 litres) is consumed locally as table wine and only the balance is fortified into Madeira.

Only after the E.E.C. was established, did the Madeira wine trade initiate a system of encouraging the replanting of grafted vines. The Portuguese Government runs a comprehensive subsidy scheme on the island aimed both at replacing the non-grafted vines and at improving viticultural practices generally. It is encouraging the planting of new vineyards by grubbing up other crops, such as bananas and sugar cane. The Madeira shippers may in time argue that the four basic types are 'styles', rather than exclusive vines:

1. Sercial:
Originates from the Rhine Riesling; makes a light, dry to medium-dry, pale coloured wine. Blends usually over eight years old.

2. Verdelho:
A cross between the Italian Verdea and Spanish Pedro Ximenez; a medium-dry to medium-sweet soft, amber to golden coloured wine with a dry finish.

3. Bual (sometimes spelt Boal):
Originally from Portuguese vines imported during the island's early days

of settlement. A dessert wine: deep gold appearance, medium-sweet to sweet, full-bodied, rich style.

4. Malmsey:
Sometimes referred to as Malvasia, originated in Morea and came via Crete. Dark, rich, soft and full; the longest lived wine in the world. Fine old Malmsey challenges vintage port.

While Malmsey is said to last the longest of the Madeira wines, it enjoys longevity through all its styles (in fortified form). The high acidity from the rich volcanic soil is largely responsible with the volatile acidity of a young wine reaching 1·2 gm/l quickly. The *estufa* system and long maturation in wood helps reduce this harshness, but even a very old, rich concentrated Malmsey has sufficient acidity to cut across the sweetness. Most blenders add some wine from the neighbouring island of Porto Santo, where the soil has a fairly high chalk content, and yields a softer style. For the purpose of the wine regulations, Porto Santo forms part of Madeira.

Little Muscatel is now grown but there have been new plantings recently of Bastardo and Terrantez. A prolific, purple coloured vine known as Negra Molle, which is grafted, is widely found as is the ungrafted Cunningham, a drier style than Verdelho. The latter grape is used for a fifth wine type, Rainwater, which is popular in the U.S.A.

Some ascribe the name 'Rainwater' to the wine made from grapes traditionally grown on the higher land above that watered by the *levadas* (irrigation system) and therefore solely dependent on rain; while other commentators ascribe its name to a merchant in Savannah, Georgia – Mr Habisham – who achieved a pale and limpid blend for his Madeira. A third source states the name originated with half-empty casks left on a beach since it was the custom to float the wine out to sea to the ships awaiting off-shore. Today Rainwater is an attractive medium-dry style, not dissimilar to Verdelho.

Cultivation

The grapes in Madeira are trained some 5 to 7 feet (1·5 to 2·1 metres) high up pergolas, such as were used in ancient Egypt. This is because land is so scarce that other crops, such as potatoes, must be grown beneath the vines. Also the shade created helps in cattle rearing. The grapes are gathered from within the pergolas. Terracing is necessary on the steep, rocky slopes with a yield of 6 to 7 pipes (224 to 260 gallons/1,018 to 1,182 litres) per 2·47 acres (1 hectare). The vineyards are mainly in small patches near the coast.

The harvest is the longest in Europe, commencing in mid August and ending in October in the more mountainous regions. Bual and Verdelho are picked first, followed by Malmsey and then Sercial. Grapes are collected in wicker baskets and carried on the back since the ground is too steep to use animals. Grapes are carried to the *lagares* (see Sherry section). These are elongated on Madeira, often measuring 10 by 3 feet (3·1 by 0·9 metres), which size makes 200 gallons (910 litres). Foot treading is still common, after which the mash is further compressed by a large stone, which is forced down by a central screw. The must is brought to Madeira's capital, Funchal, by goatskin (known as *bottachos*, which contain 10 gallons/145·6 litres per skin), in barrels conveyed on sledges, or by road tankers from local centres.

Vinification

Fermentation starts immediately or on arrival at the lodge (the name of the winery in Funchal). The Sercial and Verdelho ferment slowly throughout the winter. The fermentation of the Bual and Malmsey styles is arrested by the addition of wine brandy, while rectified sugar cane spirit was used formerly as by-product of the island's sugar industry. In view of the high cost of spirit today, early fortification is becoming less and less used and the dessert styles move to the next sequence at an early stage. After clarification, the wines are placed in the *estufa*, or hot house, which simulates the beneficial effects the wines used to enjoy in the eighteenth century when they were shipped from the island to the East Indies. It was found that the voyage removed the austere taste and mellowed the wine.

The *estufa* today is usually a vat, up to 8,800 gallons (40,000 litres) capacity, which is heated by a system of internal pipes through which flows either hot water or steam. Occasionally it is a room in which selected casks have been placed. The temperature is gradually raised to about 115°F (46°C)* over a month to six weeks, held at that temperature for three to four months, and slowly reduced to normal temperature over the

*By Portuguese law, 122°F (50°C) is the maximum allowed with a 9°F (5°C) variation permitted.

remainder of the total usual six months. Those shippers aiming to produce a superior wine, will heat to 86°F (30°C) for about six months with the time reaching and reducing from that temperature extra. For finer wines, pipes are placed in a large store chamber which is centrally heated. During the *estufa* process – which takes a minimum of 90 days – both oxidation and slow caramelisation of sugar take place. The wines then rest for 12 to 18 months – a period known as the *estágio* – before being blended into lots and racked into fresh casks. At this stage, the unfortified drier wines are now treated with spirit, with the exception of a few vintage Madeiras. The wines enter the *solera* system (see Sherry above) which means a slight refreshment of casks.

Madeira rarely has a district location within the island, although Camera de Lobos is the best example. Instead shippers blend to a style for each importer or distributor of size. The sweeter styles are given the addition of *surdo*; a mistella-type of sweetening wine which is made by adding 20 to 25 per cent spirit to fresh grape juice, thereby preventing fermentation and resulting in a very rich product.

Before shipping, the alcoholic level is checked and adjusted upwards to the normal 17·6° G.L. By law, Madeira cannot be exported until at least 13 months after the harvest, but in practice this period is considerably longer. There are independent Madeira shippers, but the majority now have formed the Madeira Wines Association which has a central lodge and can achieve scale economies. There is a little single vintage Madeira shipped, but most is from the *solera* ageing system. Like Sherry, Madeira is now restricted in its shipments to a quota system within the E.E.C., with a reserve stock for later in each year if an importing country requires it. Unlike France, most Madeira consumed in Britain is in the last two months of each year which means the stock additional to the quota cannot realistically be applied for.

Uses for Madeira

Sercial, drier styles of Verdelho, and Rainwater make apt apéritif choices, all enhanced if lightly chilled. Sercial, Verdelho and Rainwater can also be served with melon and soup.

Bual can be served with the dessert or, according to some, with turtle soup; it requires less Madeira than Sherry. The islanders serve Bual with fruit, sweet cakes and biscuits, such as the dark treacle cake *bolo del mel*.

Malmsey may be served with cheese or, like Bual, after a meal; it was once the custom to have glass of Malmsey mid-morning with cake.

All Madeira wines can be used as a base for cocktails. In addition, Madeira is appropriate in the kitchen for sauces especially because it has a strong flavour and is not affected by cold and heat after its long exposure to heat during its life.

Provided the cork is replaced, Madeira will keep for weeks without marked deterioration. The drier the style, the more likely it is to lose its freshness. In value, Madeira today is the most underestimated in the fortified-wine list.

PORT

Port has been known for years as 'the Englishman's wine', which is not surprising when one recalls that the first record of importation to England dates back to 1353. At that stage port was not a fortified wine; it was a heavy, coarse and unreliable red wine. To give the wine stability in later years, grape spirit or brandy was added.

The Methuen Treaty of 1703 provided for the importation into Portugal of English woollens, which had previously been prohibited, in return for a preferential tariff on Portuguese wines. This helped to cement the English enjoyment for port. The term 'port' is protected under the Anglo-Portuguese Commercial Treaty, 1914, which restricts the word to the delimited fortified wine of the Douro region of northern Portugal. Unlike Sherry, no other national prefix may be placed before the term. In 1932 the Casa do Douro was established to regulate the port trade.

Controls

Port is the fortified wine of the Alta Douro district. Although some 170,000 pipes (each pipe* contains 115 gallons/522·48 litres) of wine may be made in the area, only 50,000 to 60,000 pipes (5,750,000 to 6,900,000 gallons/26,140,075 to 31,368,090 litres) are authorised to be made into port. The balance is turned into table wine. The port vineyards have been divided since 1948 into six classes, based on such factors as altitude, productivity, the method of vine training, quality of the grapes, aspect, slope, vine density, and shelter.†

Control is vested in several authorities. The Casa do Douro is the farmers' union, while Government supervision is by the Instituto do Vinho do Porto and by the Ministerio de Economia. The shippers' association is the Gremio dos Exportação de Vinho do Port. No shipment can be dispatched until a sample has been analysed, approved by the Instituto, and a certificate of origin issued for it.

Climate and Soil

Frosts and fog are common during the months of November to February

*This is simply the port term for their type of cask, although it used to also be applied to Tarragona.

†For a fuller explanation of the classification, see Fletcher, W. – *Port: An Introduction to its History and Delights* (1978), pp. 107–14.

with an intensity of summer heat amounting to 104°F (40°C). Most of the 50 inches (127 centimetres) rainfall, which is twice Britain's average, falls in the first quarter of the year.

It is a largely mountainous district, lying some 45 miles (72 kilometres) inland and continuing for 80 miles (128 kilometres) up the Douro river to the Spanish frontier. Schist, which is a slate-like stone, predominates on these steeply terraced hillsides. The soil is naturally deficient in nitrogen, but rich in potassium, and lacks lime.

Viticulture

Some thirty-eight different vine varieties are cultivated. While planting is easier on the plains, better grapes are grown on the steeper, terraced soil. Cultivation can be difficult, with spraying often done by small two-stroke engine sprayers mounted on the back. Recently there has been a move away from the very labour-intensive systems. Very few terraces are now being built. Instead horizontal platforms are being constructed with the use of bulldozers, which avoids the building of walls. The spacing between vine rows has been widened to enable small tractors to work between them.

The best known vines are:

White: Grown in the higher districts and in cooler conditions: Verdelho, Córdega, Malvasia Fina and Malvasia Corado.

Red: Rufete: ripens early with good sugar content.
Roriz: low yielder but heat resistant; good colour and sugar.
Tinto Francisca: low yielder, very sweet grapes of good quality.
Mourisco de Semente: resists heat well.
Sousão: used particularly for its depth of colour. Touriga Nacional, Tourigo Francesca and Bastardo.

The harvest is usually in late September. The grapes are taken down to the press houses which lie in the upper Douro.

Vinification

Two basic systems are used. Firstly some 15 to 18 per cent of the crop is trodden by foot, particularly for the making of the better quality wines, like vintage port. Treading stops once the fermentation begins. It takes forty men four hours to 'cut', or tread in, a 20 pipe (300 gallon/1,364 litre) *lagar*. In the port region, this is a large stone trough. The alternative

The Port Wine District of the River Douro
[as defined by Portuguese Law]
KEY
Outline of Port Wine District
Land over 3,281 ft
MILES
0 5 10 15 20
ATLANTIC OCEAN
SPAIN
GREEN WINE DISTRICT
Viana do Castelo
Braga
Vila do Conde
OPORTO
Vila Nova de Gaia
Espinho
Aveiro
Valonga
Penafiel
Amarante
Chaves
Vila Real
Murça
Mirandela
Alijo
Tua
Vila Flor
Carrazeda
Moncorvo
Régua
Pinhão
S. João de Pesqueira
Vila Nova de Foscoa
Freixo de Numão
Meida
Barca d'Alva
Figueira do Castelo Rodrigo
Guarda
Lamego
Tabuaco
Moimenta da Beira
R. Douro
R. Tamega
R. Corgo
R. Pinhão
R. Tua
R. Sabor
R. Huebra
R. Agueda
R. Coa
R. Tavora
R. Paiva

method is autovinification, which is more effective than the first method in extracting colour once fermentation has begun. It is very useful in hot years, like 1977, when the autovinification plant will keep working throughout the night, which cannot be expected from foot labour. Grapes are crushed and a proportion of the stalks removed.

There are two types of vat. In the circulatory vat, which is usually of stainless steel but sometimes of cement, there is a central column with an Archimedean screw; this is rotated by an electric motor and carries the pulp continuously to the vat floor. The alternative is the siphon vat; here liquid must is forced up, by the fermentation, into an open tank which opens when full and allows the fermenting must to fall back with force upon the pulp, thus removing colour and extracting tannin from the latter. The cycle continues time after time until the colour required has been obtained.

Unlike Sherry, port is not allowed to complete its fermentation. It is pumped off, still in a fermenting state, into vats in which a spirit – traditionally grape brandy – of 77° G.L. has been placed. The port shippers prefer this to be the distillate from central Portuguese wines, rather than the spirit from Douro table wines. Modern methods allow better temperature control and for this operation to be executed with greater hygiene than formerly. The shippers have to purchase the spirit from the Casa de Douro. The effect of the spirit addition is to stop the fermentation immediately and to ensure that the port is sweet. In the spring, the wine is drawn off and taken down the Douro to the lodges at Vila Nova de Gaia from the *quintas* or press houses. At Vila Nova, which lies across the river from Oporto, the port matures and undergoes its blending.

Styles of Port

There are two basic ways of maturing port: in cask and in bottle.

1. Cask or Wood Aged Ports:

   i. Ruby: Young, relatively fresh wine, blended to a commercial standard. Bottled between third and seventh year, usually in fourth or fifth year. Colour is the same as the name.

   ii. Tawny: In appearance the same colour as its name, which is achieved by wood ageing for usually 8 to 10 years. This can take longer, even on occasion up to 40 years. Fine Old Tawny is indeed fine and not to be confused with a blend of young white and red

Ports, or a low quality Ruby, to which a colour fining treatment has been applied.

iii. White: Pale golden in appearance and made from the Douro's white grapes. Little in demand. The style sold in Britain is dry to medium-dry, but sweet in France.

iv. Vintage Character: Good quality, aged Ruby, usually from a single vintage but without bottle age.

v. Late Bottled: Port of almost vintage quality which has been aged in cask and left its deposit there. Minimum age 3 years.

2. Bottle Aged Ports:

i. Crusted: Bottled after 3 to 4 years in cask; forms a deposit or 'crust' in the bottle. An average maturation period in wood and bottle is often a decade.

ii. Vintage: The port of one exceptional year, bottled after 2 or 3 years in cask, which matures mainly in bottle. It can be served between 14 and 30 years or more of age, depending upon the vintage.

By law, port exports must not exceed one-third of a House's stocks. All the cask or wood aged ports should have deposited their lees or crust in the cask; therefore, it should be in order to pour safely to the last glass. Decanting is necessary with both crusted and vintage ports to remove the deposit and refreshen the port by allowing it to come into contact with air. Store bottle-aged ports horizontally; if there is no label, store white-wash splash upwards which ensures the deposit is always on the reverse. Serve white port as an apéritif, lightly chilled, and all other ports at the end of a meal at room temperature. Some people like their tawny port lightly chilled. See Chapter 2 for the maturity of vintage ports.

MARSALA

Italy's best known dessert wine is Marsala. It is made in north-western Sicily, the island to the south of Italy. It was made famous by the Woodhouse brothers of Liverpool, who first added a little grape spirit, sweet wine and some unfermented must that had been slowly heated, to the local white wine in about 1770.

Marsala is made from the Grillo and Catarratto vines, either singly or blended together. In addition, up to 15 per cent from the Inzolia vine is permitted. There are four styles.

1. Marsala Fine or Marsala Italia Particolare (I.P.):
Requires a minimum four months' ageing, varying in style from dry to sweet. Minimum alcoholic level is 17 per cent by volume.

2. Marsala Superiore:
Must be a minimum of 2 years old. Style from dry to sweet on taste. Minimum 18 per cent alcohol by volume. Often referred to as S.O.M. (Superior Old Marsala) or G.D. (Garibaldi Dolce) or O.P. (Old Particular).

3. Marsala Speciali:
These have a variety of flavour addititives, such as almond or egg. They start as Marsala Superiore and therefore have a minimum 18 per cent by volume alcohol.

4. Marsala Vergine:
Is aged for a minimum of 5 years and is at least 18 per cent by volume in alcohol. It is made without the addition of cooked must, is dry, and is aged on *solera* lines. It makes an attractive apéritif, lightly chilled.

The spirit is usually added one year after the harvest. Before the spirit addition, all but the finest is given an infusion of concentrated, non-alcoholic must (*mosto cotto*) which is obtained by heating must in large open vats which contain a serpentine of very hot water pipes. This gives it a taste of caramel. Between 6 to 7 per cent of this viscous liquid is added to the wine three months after the vintage.

The drier styles above the Marsala Vergine are all appropriate as apéritif choices; the balance may be served at the end of a meal. Only 10 to 15 per cent of production is exported from the total 14,298,000 gallons (650,000 hectolitres) annual yield.

OTHER FORTIFIED WINES

There are several other fortified wines produced, such as Málaga from Spain and Moscatel de Setúbal from Portugal, but their sales in the U.K. are small.

Málaga enjoys a long and distinguished history, recorded by Pliny, Virgil and others. It lies east of the Sherry region and south-east from Montilla, covering some 19·3 square miles (5,000 hectares), where sweet Moscatel, Lairén and Pedro Ximenex (P.X.) are the main vines. Although it can be found unfortified, most Málaga has spirit added to 23 per cent alcohol by volume, after ageing in oak. This is usually done in Málaga itself.

Across the Tagus estuary from Lisbon lies the Setúbal roughly pronounced *stewball*) district, whose rich Moscatel did not become known until the last century. The Moscatel de Setúbal is one of Portugal's delimited wines, or demarcated as they prefer to say, where the fermentation is stopped while a high proportion of sugar remains in the must. It is frequently aged for five or more years in wood, achieving a lovely tawny hue and is exceptional value for money. It may become better known if Portugal joins the E.E.C.

The best known French fortified wines, where they are rather misleadingly called *vin doux naturel*, are Muscat de Beaumes de Venise, Muscat de Frontignan and Banyuls. Beaumes lies in the southern Rhône valley, east of Châteauneuf du Pape and was a spa centre in Roman days. The wine became popular when drunk at the Papal court in Avignon, although the dessert Muscat may only have originated in the early nineteenth century. The grapes are picked in mid to late October and given added alcohol during fermentation. Although attractive as a dessert wine, the fresh, raisiny Muscat aroma makes it appealing in melon if lightly chilled, or (in the French way) as an apéritif.

In the late eighteenth and for most of the nineteenth century, Frontignan was one of the most popular wines in Britain. It is still made near the coast, east of the wine port of Sète, not far from Montpellier on the southern French coast. Many French prefer this rich, fruity style – which is found in the Muscat from Frontignan; Mireval which is just to the east; and Lunel, which lies further eastwards toward Nîmes – to port. It is frequently served in a long glass with ice, topped with soda. This makes a refreshing drink, particularly in summer. Banyuls, also noted for its

Muscat, lies on the French side of the frontier with Spain, south of Perpignan.

Rasteau, just north of Beaumes de Venise, yields a fortified style, largely using the Grenache grape. The two districts of Maury and Rivesaltes, north-west and north of Perpignan respectively, are little seen on the export markets. The fortified wine of Cognac is Pineau des Charentes, which is made by adding a young Cognac to a fermenting must that is up to one day old. It tends to be both sweet and spirity; and it has its own A.O.C.

7. Spirits, other than Liqueurs

'Palate, the hutch of tasty lust,
desire not to be rinsed with wine . . .', Gerard Manley Hopkins.

A spirit is the essence of a substance which has been first converted into a vapour and then condensed. It is impractical to obtain a spirit other than through distillation by heat. It has a long tradition, which can be traced back over 2,000 years, although modern recognition stems largely from the 'burnt wine' of the sixteenth century. The best known examples are whisky, gin, vodka, brandy and rum.

The Still

The vessel used to distil is known as a still. The distiller separates water from alcohol, which is possible as alcohol boils at 142°F (78°C) and water at 212°F (100°C). Other substances present, such as fusel oil, can be present in the alcoholic wash and affect the spirit taste. There are two basic types of still: the continuous, or patent, or Coffey still and the pot still. The pot still is used for malt Scotch and Irish whiskies, Cognac and some rums; the continuous still is used for the balance.

1. Patent/Continuous/Coffey Still

This is based on a patent taken out by an Irish Customs officer, Aeneas Coffey, in 1832. It was an improvement on one invented by Robert Stein of Scotland, whose design was patented in 1826. Unlike the pot still, the continuous still need not be stopped, opened, and refilled after each distillation. It consists of two columns (the rectifier and the analyser). The alcoholic wash is heated as it passes through the rectifier; it is then passed slowly through the analyser where it drops downwards, on to and

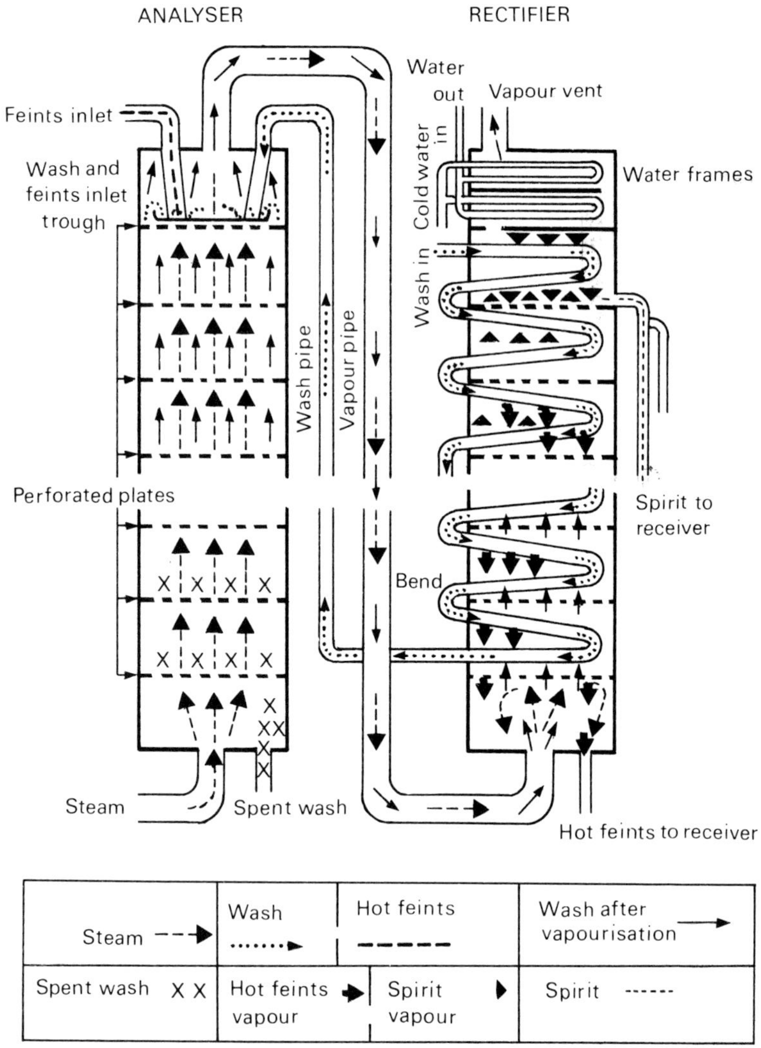

ANALYSER
RECTIFIER
Water out
Vapour vent
Feints inlet
Cold water in
Water frames
Wash and feints inlet trough
Wash in
Wash pipe
Vapour pipe
Perforated plates
Spirit to receiver
Bend
Steam
Spent wash
Hot feints to receiver
Steam
Wash
Hot feints
Wash after vapourisation
Spent wash X X
Hot feints vapour
Spirit vapour
Spirit

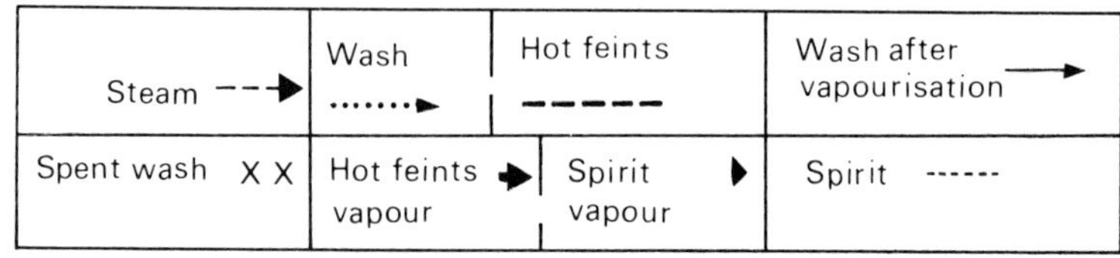

Continuous Coffey or patent still.

through a series of perforated plates. Steam is introduced through the base of the analyser, and rises through the plates to meet the heated alcoholic wash, vaporising the alcohol in it. This, in turn, rises and passes into the rectifier. In the rectifier column, it passes through the perforated plates and condenses as the temperature drops. The balance of the wash goes through the floor of the analyser. The unwanted first sections ('foreshots') and last parts ('feints') of the distillate can be removed because of the time at which they vaporise in relation to the rest of the alcohol.

2. Pot Still

The pot still is a vessel, generally made of copper and shaped like an onion with a spout at the top, in which the alcoholic wash is placed. The still is heated, causing the vapour that is given off from the wash to pass through the head via a tube to a condenser. The condenser cools the vapour, thereby causing it to turn back to a liquid state, which has the effect of separating the alcohol from the water in the initial wash. This is a slow process, unlike the continuous still, because the pot has to be refilled between each distillation with a fresh alcoholic wash. It is normal in Scotch malt whisky production to distil twice through the pot still; some distillers may even distil three times. See page 170.

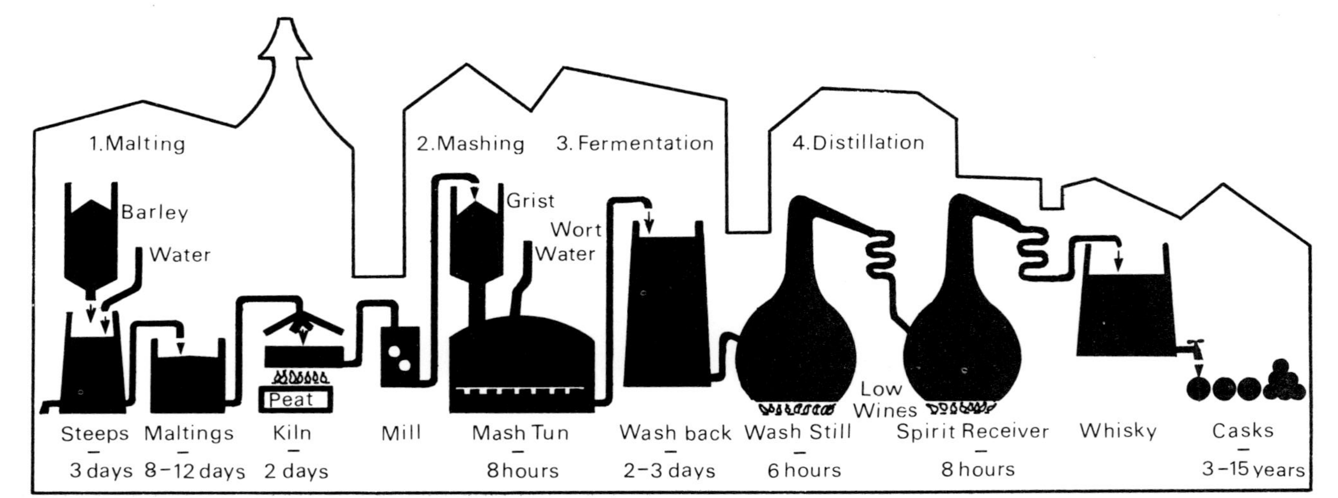

The pot still for Scotch malt whisky production.

SCOTCH WHISKY

By definition, this is a spirit which has been obtained by distillation in Scotland from a mash of cereal grain, saccharified by the diastase of malt, fermented by the action of yeast, and which has matured in cask for a period of not less than 3 years.* 'Saccharified' means sugaring or sugared.

Scotch whisky has had a long history, first on record in 1494 when the Scottish Exchequer Rolls refer to an entry of 'eight bolls of malt to Friar John Cor wherewith to make aquavitae'. The first reference to a distillery in the Acts of the Scottish Parliament was in 1699. Not until 1823 was an Act successful in controlling effectively the legal distilling of Scotch whisky.

Scotch whisky may be divided into malt, grain, blended and de luxe. Grain Scotch whisky is made by the continuous still and differs from pot still malt in four ways:

1. The mash consists of a proportion of unmalted cereals together with malted barley.
2. Any unmalted cereals used are steam pressure-cooked for about 3½ hours during which time the mixture of grain and water is agitated by stirrers inside the cooker. The starch cells in the grain burst and when this liquid is transferred to the mash tun (with the malted barley), the diastase in the latter converts the starch into sugar.
3. The 'wort' (fermenting malt) is collected at a specific gravity lower than in the pot still process.
4. Distillation is effected in a continuous still and the spirit collected is at a considerably higher strength.

The Production of Scotch Malt Whisky

1. Malting:

The barley is screened to remove any alien matter and then soaked for 2 to 3 days in tanks of water (called steeps). After this it is spread out on a concrete floor (the malting floor) where it germinates for 8 to 12 days, depending upon the barley and time of year. During germination, the barley secretes the enzyme, diastase, which makes the starch in the barley

*Customs and Excise Act, 1952, s. 109 (I)., consolidated in the 1979 Act.

soluble, thereby preparing it for conversion into sugar. The barley must be turned throughout this period to control the rate of germination and also the temperature.

Germination is arrested at the correct time by drying the 'green malt', or malted barley, in the malt kiln. Malting may also take place in drum maltings or in Saladin boxes where the process is mechanically controlled. It is more efficient today for the distiller to purchase the malt from a central maltings.

2. Mashing:
The dried malt is ground, thereby becoming 'grist'. It is mixed with hot water in a mash tun (large circular vat) in order that the soluble starch is converted into a wort which is subsequently drawn off from the mash tun. The residue is used for cattle food.

3. Fermentation:
After cooling, the wort is transferred to large vessels where it is fermented by yeast which feeds on the sugar in the wort and converts it into alcohol. Fermentation takes about 2 days and yields a 'wash' (liquid) of low alcoholic strength, plus various minor by-products.

4. Distillation:
Malt Scotch whisky is generally distilled twice. In the first distillation (see the pot still), the alcohol is separated from the fermented liquid. The distillate is known as a 'low wine' at this stage. The central portion of the second distillation is considered satisfactory and is collected in a 'low wines and feints still', known colloquially as a spirit receiver.

Scotch malts are usually divided into four zones:

1. Highland: Made north of a line drawn from Greenock on the west to Dundee on the east with a delicate smoky style and rich flavour.
2. Lowland: Made south of the above line with lighter body and mellow appeal.
3. Islay: From the island of the same name with a penetrating, almost medicinal nose and a rich, fruity flavour.
4. Campbeltown: A town in the Mull of Kintyre with a light and slightly oily quality.

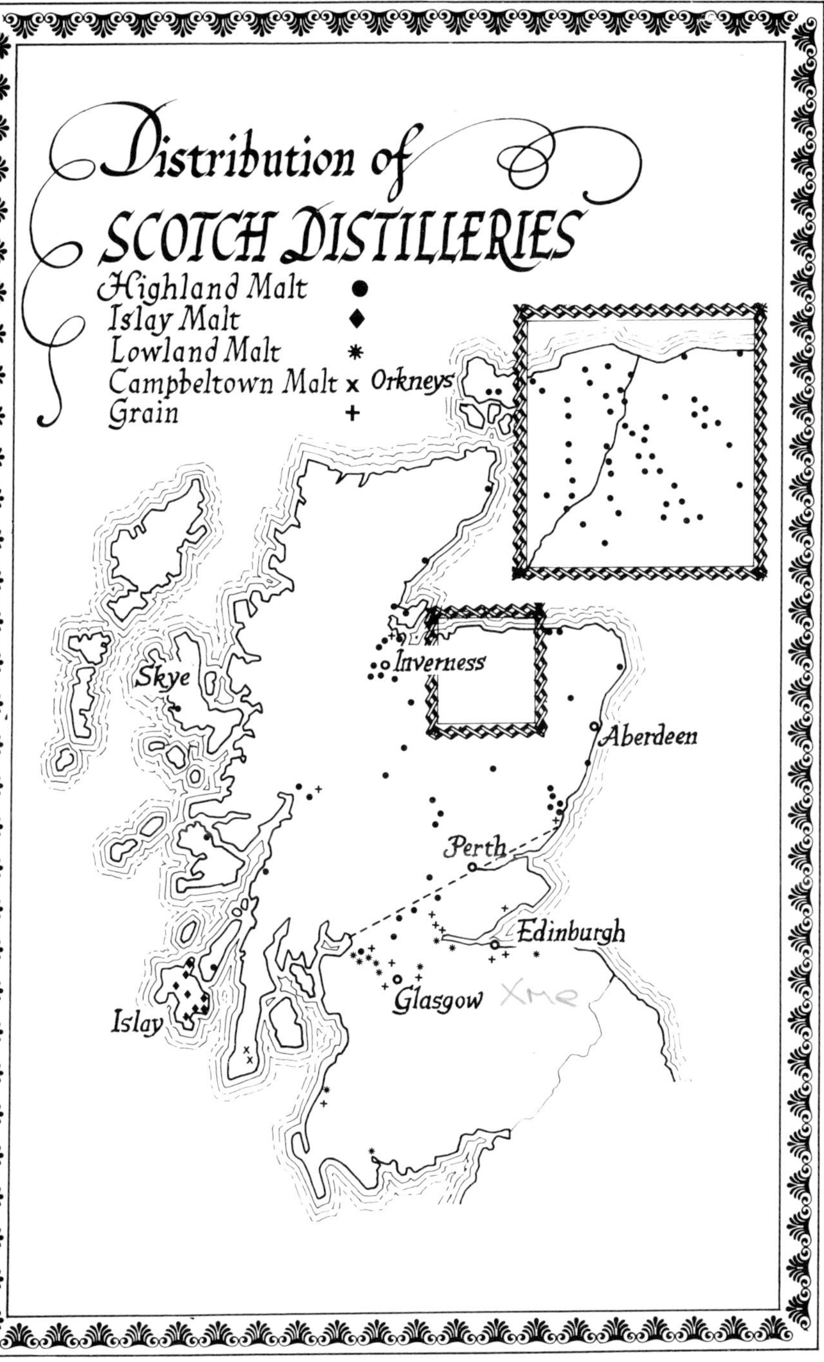
Distribution of
SCOTCH DISTILLERIES
Highland Malt ●
Islay Malt ◆
Lowland Malt ✳
Campbeltown Malt x
Grain +
Orkneys
Skye
Inverness
Aberdeen
Perth
Edinburgh
Glasgow
Islay

Single malts are distillates from one single Scotch malt distillery, unblended with other whiskies, and therefore showing their individual character. There are a wide number of single malts with varying final alcoholic degrees and differing cask ageing periods.

A Blended Malt is simply a blend of two or more – usually several – malts to obtain a better harmony than is possible in one distillate. However much malt Scotch is sold for blending with grain Scotch to make the blends which are so popular. Here the pungent styles of Islay and Campbeltown malts are invaluable; they contribute a small, but important proportion.

The other variations are Vatted, which is a blend of malts which sometimes declare a minimum age; and De luxe, which is a careful blend of usually predominantly malt and a lesser proportion of grain. This blend is aged in cask for a longer period than popular branded blends.

5. Maturation:

After distilling, both malt and grain Scotches are placed in casks of new oak. These are permeable, allowing air to pass in and evaporation to take place. In time, such whisky mellows; malt Scotch needs several years more – up to 15 years in some cases – than grain. Only at the prebottling stage is the spirit reduced by the addition of pure water to the alcoholic level required for the market it is to be sold into. On the British market, it is traditional to sell Scotch whisky at 70° proof. A small caramel addition is given to ensure colour consistency.

A branded blend may consist of up to 40 different distillates, both grain and malt, which are brought together and where the style previously marketed successfully will be copied as exactly as possible. Therefore, with the exception of the final alcoholic strength, a particular brand of Scotch whisky should look, nose and taste the same in South America, Canada, Australia, Japan, Rome and London. Blending was introduced in the early 1860s by Andrew Usher of Edinburgh who helped thereby to make the English appreciate the northern spirit. The greatest concentration of malt distilleries is in Speyside which lies between Inverness and Aberdeen.

OTHER WHISKIES

Irish whiskey (note the addition of an 'e') is pot-still produced. Unlike most Scotch, Irish whiskey is distilled three times. Furthermore, the malted barley is not dried over peat and therefore lacks the 'smoky' taste of Scotch. By Irish law, Irish whiskey has to mature for 5 years, although some is aged for much longer. Apart from distillation in Eire, there is one Ulster distillery which is usually associated in the same style. This is Old Bushmills which holds a distilling licence dating back to the seventeenth century and whose de luxe quality bears the brand name of Black Bush.

Bourbon whiskey was originally the corn whiskey made in Bourbon County, Kentucky, and first made in the late eighteenth century by a local clergyman, Rev. Elija Craig. It is now a generic term applied to the distillate of under 40° over proof. This originates as a mash of at least 51 per cent corn and is aged for a minimum of 2 years in new charred oak casks. Much Bourbon is kept in cask for 4 years.

A separate category is Tennessee whiskey where the spirit is filtered through several feet of charcoal to remove any rough, fiery character and leave it mellow. Jack Daniel's distillery, which is the oldest registered distillery in the United States and opened in 1866, filters through 9 ft (2·75 m) of charcoal. They use a special charcoal made from burning the locally-grown hard sugar maple tree. It is aged for 5 years in new white oak. Many distillers in this area use spring water that has come through limestone.

Rye whiskey must contain a minimum 51 per cent rye with the same maximum alcoholic level as Bourbon. Ageing again is in new charred oak. Canadian rye can only be made from cereal grain. It is noted for its mild quality and ageing in heated rooms, whilst Bourbon is matured in cold warehouses.

Japanese whiskey is now produced in large quantities, but little is exported to date. It relies on bulk Scotch malt whisky to enrich the flavour.

GIN

Gin originated in Holland in 1575 when rye spirit was flavoured with juniper (known as *genièvre*) to make it more palatable. It was known as 'Dutch Courage' by British soldiers in James I's era and first came into England during the following reign of Charles I. Juniper, one of the principal flavourings, was considered good for the kidneys. After the 1688 Revolution, William of Orange's 'gin' supplanted James II's 'brandy' in popularity. It was cheap to make which led to many of the abuses seen during the eighteenth century. It was widely available and the scenes depicted in Hogarth's prints show the background to the inn slogan: 'Drunk for a penny: dead drunk for two pence: straw free.'

In 1736, attempts were made to control gin sales but this created riots. The Temperance Movement was established and, later still, Gladstone tried to control the situation in 1871 by reducing the duties on wine. In the end, gin consumption was controlled by taxation during World War I. The trend in the U.S.A. – to invent cocktails in order to drown the taste of cheap 'bath-tub' gin produced during Prohibition – soon moved across the Atlantic, but required a good gin as the base for a socially acceptable cocktail.

Modern Production

The raw spirit is obtained by distillation using grain or molasses* by the Patent or Continuous or Coffey still. Today cane spirit is not usually used as it gives a harsh character to the gin. The spirit is rectified to 166° proof and then sold to the gin rectifier, or compounder, on a duty-paid basis.

The gin compounder adds water to the spirit to reduce it to around 70° proof and adds herbs, called botanicals, in a powdered form. The exact herbs used and their proportion differ from one compounder to another and are kept secret. However, the most widely used are juniper berries, angelica root, coriander seeds, orange peel, orris root and cardamon seed. In some plants, the essence of the botanicals is prepared by a separate distillation and then added to the lower strength spirit. Alternatively, the botanicals are placed on a mesh in the still head and the spirit is boiled underneath them. The vapour that passes through the botanicals picks up the flavours. As with other forms of distillation, the first and last

*Molasses: a thick syrup, like treacle, which is drained from the raw sugar.

parts (foreshots or 'heads', and feints or 'tails') are removed and re-distilled.

Lower quality gin may be produced by steeping the botanicals in cold high-proof spirit, filtering and then reducing in alcoholic strength to 70° proof.

In view of the pure state of the spirit rectified for gin, which has no or extremely few harmful congenerics, it is legally possible for it to be sold without further maturation.

Gin Styles

1. London Gin:
Despite the adjective, may be made anywhere. May be clear or straw coloured. A clean, all purpose gin.

2. Plymouth Gin:
In style, intermediate between London gin and Dutch gin. It is slightly more distinct in taste. A traditional Royal Navy drink; the only distillery still making it is located at Plymouth. Often enjoyed with a dash of Angostura bitters.

3. Dutch Gin:
Sometimes known as 'Geneva' or 'Hollands' as the former is the Dutch name for juniper. The distillers use a malt wine; there is a hint of almonds on the taste. Usually made in a pot still from a mash of rye, barley and maize. Often marketed in stone crock bottles.

There are several gins which are flavoured, such as lemon gin, orange or sloe gin; most of them are marketed as liqueurs at a lower alcoholic strength. A 'gin sling' is based on gin and is aimed at the market for a longer drink with ice or lemonade additives and garnished with fruit.

The clean taste of gin, like vodka, with its fairly neutral qualities continues to make it a popular choice. It may be served with water, ice, fruit juices, various mixers or as a base for many cocktails. It therefore has great versatility.

VODKA

Vodka has been the major growth spirit of the 1960–78 period and, like gin, is the distillate from a patent, continuous or Coffey still. In Britain, it accounts for 11 per cent of the spirit market. It can be made from several sources, ranging from potatoes to grain or molasses and, sometimes the grape. Like gin, vodka is first distilled and then rectified. The Russian distilled vodka has usually a soft, slightly sweet taste and a distinctly different aroma to its British and American distilled counterparts.

The finer vodkas are passed through fine quartz sand and filtered through beds of activated charcoal, which are traditionally prepared from Siberian birch. This removes any pronounced nose or taste trace. Since activated charcoal is expensive, vodka is frequently marketed at a lower strength (65·5° British proof). Most vodkas sold in Britain and the U.S.A. are distilled in those two countries respectively. In Russia and the Eastern European countries, vodka is often flavoured. For example, Polish zubrowka is flavoured with zubrowka grass, while others use cherries and other fruits.

Traditionally vodka accentuates the taste of food. It is often served with caviar. It is a versatile drink and may be enjoyed with fruit juices, ice, mixers and as a cocktail base. As it is predominantly tasteless – meaning 'little water' in Russian – vodka cannot destroy the flavour of other cocktail ingredients or the food with which it is served. It is frequently poured in a very cold state directly from the refrigerator.

BRANDY

Traditionally the term 'brandy' signifies a spirit obtained from the distillation of fermented fresh grapes. In this chapter it will be used in this context; however fruit-based brandies or *eaux-de-vie* are discussed after liqueurs in the next chapter. Wherever wine is made, brandy is also.

In France, only two A.O.C. areas have been specifically designated for brandy – Cognac and Armagnac. Within these areas, the use of stars and other label attractions is strictly governed. This is not so elsewhere; an extensive number of stars on an Italian brandy (termed *grappa*) or a Spanish, for example, may indicate the reverse of quality! Such brandy is useful for cooking as well as a base for cocktails or with ginger ale or soda.

Marc is the French term applied to the distillate made from the residue after the grape juice has ordinarily been extracted for wine. It may be harsh as it is often derived from the skins, stalks and pips, but can have an appealing, flowery nose. This is evident on such regional *marc* as Bourgogne (Burgundy) and Champagne, which are occasionally exported.

BRANDY–COGNAC

The vine is thought to have been cultivated in the Cognac region of south-west France since pre-Roman days. During the Middle Ages, table wines from the region were exported through the port of La Rochelle to countries including England, which is evidenced by the writings of Chaucer and others. In about 1620, there was a serious surplus combined with substantial taxes. To reduce their tax liability, the farmers started to distil their wines, thereby making an *eau-de-vie*. When merchants came to the Charente to purchase salt and some wine, they agreed to take this 'reduced' wine which would save space on the ships. They could add water or restore it at a later stage.

In time the distillation processes improved; this was greatly aided by maturation in the wood derived from the nearby forest around Limoges, the source of Limousin oak. The Cognac area is now legally designated within the A.O.C. laws and has to be pot distilled twice and then aged.

Soil and Vines

The Cognac region lies north of the rivers Garonne and Dordogne, centred on the old town of Cognac. It enjoys a temperate and rather damp climate with hot summers and good winter rainfall, moderated by the Gulf Stream. It is largely a chalk and limestone region with a high proportion of lime in the finest district, the Grande Champagne.

The three main grapes are the Ugni Blanc (known often as the St Emilion), Folle Blanche and Colombard. Five other vines are grown but are not allowed to make up more than 10 per cent of any blend. Almost 90 per cent of the crop is now St Emilion, yielding an austere wine, which is not well balanced and which makes an ideal base for distillation.

Vinification and Distillation

The grapes are pressed twice, care being taken not to crush the pips or stalks which would give too high a tannin content. The fermentation takes up to 10 days, yielding a light, rather acidic wine. The wine is then distilled in a pot still; the distillate is called *brouillis*. It is then further distilled to gain refinement. The central portion from the second distillation, known as the *bonne chauffe*, is then retained. The spirit after one distillation is about 30° G.L., which rises to about 70° G.L. after the second distillation. It is then matured in Limousin oak from the Tronçais forest, half being placed in new wood and half in old casks to obtain the right degree of tannin overall. Air enters the casks and mellows the initial harshness. Of the 70,000 farmers who grow Cognac vines, some 7,000 distil and age the wine made. This includes about 175 Cognac shippers and a number of co-operatives.

Districts and Blending

Much of the Cognac distiller's art lies in blending the different Cognacs; he must blend Cognacs of various ages and districts and even within districts, to obtain consistency of style. The distiller also needs to add demineralised water to obtain the final strength required for the market. This is often 70° proof in the U.K.

Geographical names rarely appear on labels, but are important since they contribute separate characteristics to a blend. In order of quality, the districts are:

1. Grande Champagne:

Covers 14·65 per cent of the region, noted for great finesse. It is sometimes also referred to as Grande Fine Champagne.

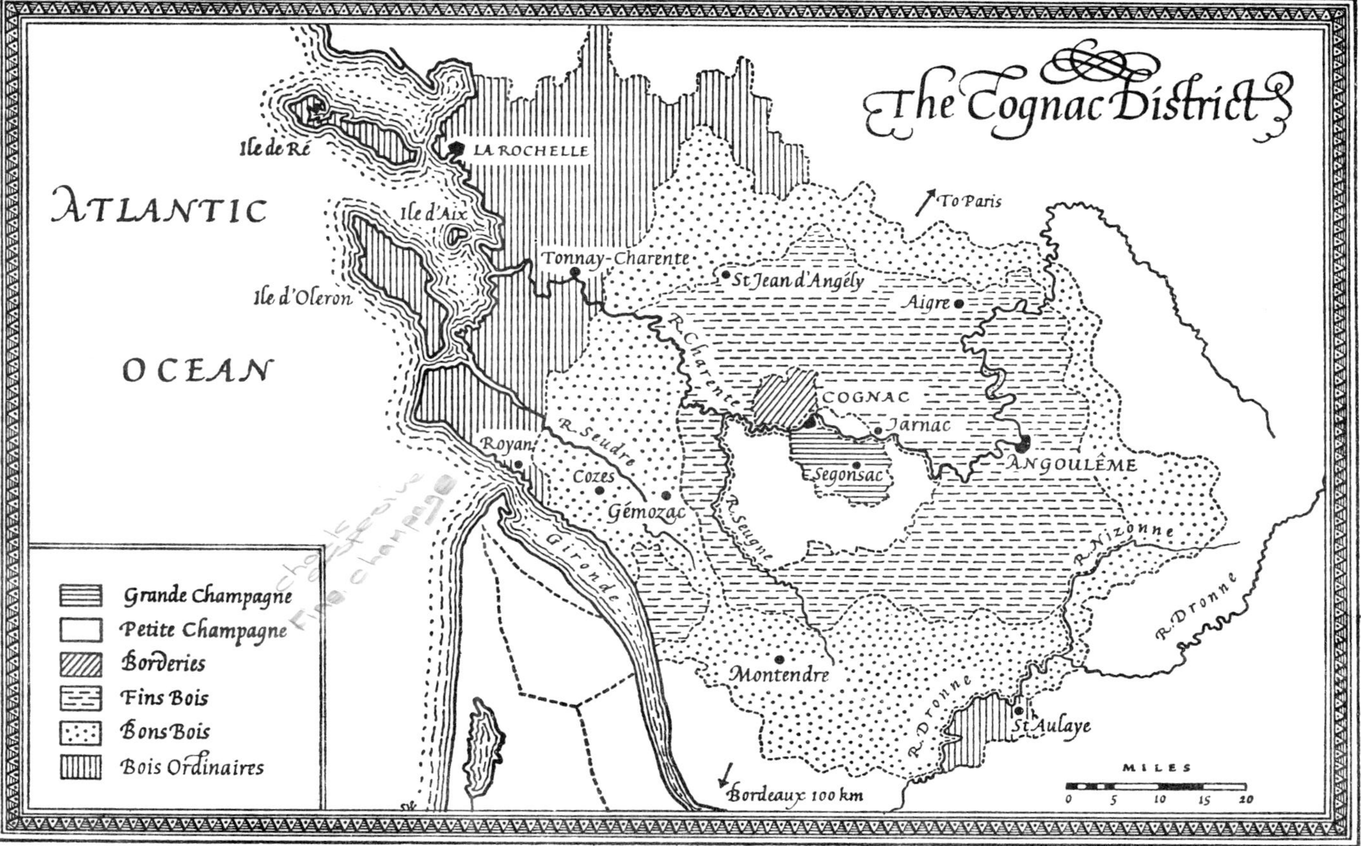
The Cognac District
Ile de Ré
LA ROCHELLE
ATLANTIC
Ile d'Aix
Ile d'Oleron
OCEAN
To Paris
Tonnay-Charente
St Jean d'Angély
Aigre
R. Charente
COGNAC
Jarnac
ANGOULÊME
Segonsac
Royan
R. Seudre
Cozes
Gémozac
R. Seugne
Gironde
R. Nizonne
R. Dronne
Montendre
R. Dronne
St Aulaye
Bordeaux 100 km
MILES
0
5
10
15
20
Grande Champagne
Petite Champagne
Borderies
Fins Bois
Bons Bois
Bois Ordinaires

2. Petite Champagne:
Covers 15·98 per cent of the region; matures slightly more quickly than Grande Champagne. Less chalky soil.

3. Borderies:
Covers 4·53 per cent of the region. It does not border the first two districts but faces them across the river Charente on the north. Noted for giving body.

4. Fins Bois:
Covers 37·82 per cent of the region. A lesser zone.

5. Bons Bois:
Covers 22·19 per cent of the region. Like Fins Bois, a zone of lesser importance.

6. Bois Ordinaires:
Covers 4·83 per cent of the region. A fair proportion of this district lies along the shore, where the sea breezes have a distinct effect.

It is emphasised that the term Champagne in Cognac has no connection with any sparkling wine of the region; it is merely a reference to the chalky nature of the soil, which the Cognac region has in common with parts of the Champagne region of north-eastern France. Grande Champagne and Petite Champagne Cognacs may be blended together and described as 'Fine Champagne', provided such a blend contains a minimum 50 per cent Grande Champagne.

Cognac Types

In France the authorities will not certify any Cognac as more than 5 years of age because of the vast number of small distillers. In Britain, the following types are sold.

1. Three Star:
Must be at least 3 years old by British law. The standard Cognac sold, accounting for about 90 per cent of the market.

2. V.S.O.P.:
This stands for Very Special Old Pale, and is over 4 years of age. It tends

to be a more mellow style of fine quality.

3. Liqueur Cognac:
A term for qualities above Three Star, such as Fine Champagne.

4. Vintage:
A few merchants purchase and age their Cognacs under bond from a particular year. Since the French authorities will not certificate Cognacs over 5 years old, it is likely that this style will become less available in the future. They are sometimes referred to as 'old landed' or 'old London landed' Cognacs and need to be warehoused in damp cellars with a low rate of evaporation.

While there is a brand called 'Napoleon', there is really no such Cognac of this age of real merit. If it was still in wood from the time of Napoleon (1769–1821), it would be too woody to consume; if it was in bottle, it would be of little interest (other than curiosity as to the blending art of that time) since spirits do not mature once bottled.

Service
Serve Cognac and Armagnac (which follows) in large glasses which allow the liquid to be fully rotated and the nose to be properly evaluated. Excessively large balloon-shaped glasses are superfluous. It is unnecessary to artificially warm brandies as the cupping effect of the hand does this quite adequately.

Apart from the better qualities, the Three Star brands may be enjoyed on ice with soda or ginger, or as the base for a cocktail. It makes for a good winter promotion.

BRANDY–ARMAGNAC

While Cognac lies to the north of Bordeaux, the Armagnac region is situated to the south-east of Bordeaux, largely in the department of Gers. In 1909 the region was divided into three main districts:

1. Bas Armagnac: On the west, largely watered by the river Douze, with mainly sandy soil. The main town is Eauze.
2. Haut Armagnac: To the east, watered by the rivers Gers and Sousson, with mainly chalky soil. Auch is the main town.

3. Ténaréze: In the centre of the region, along the river Baise, centred on Condom. The southern part, where the soil is clay, yields lighter and faster maturing brandy.

Usually Armagnac is aged for a longer period than Cognac. It is common for Three Star Armagnac to be 5 years old, V.S.O.P. to be 20 years and for the 'Extra' style to be 40 years old. The main vines are St Emilion, Picpoul (or Folle Blanche), Colombard and Juraçon. By a 1951 law, claims for an age greater than 10 years are not permitted on a label.

Unlike Cognac, Armagnac is distilled by the continuous still and is of lower strength, but is often marketed at the same level. It has a strong fruity nose and flavour, more pungent than the mellow tones of Cognac. For identity, Armagnac is often bottled in a squat flagon-shaped flask called a *basquaise*, which has the advantage of securing greater space on the shelf.

Apart from the differences with Cognac on the method of distillation, the strength from the still and character, Armagnac differs in that the best (the Bas Armagnac) comes from a sandy area, as opposed to a distinctly chalky zone with Cognac, with different climates. The ageing of Armagnac is undertaken in the diminishing Armagnac wood. It is a spirit that is growing in popularity in Britain; it is often marketed by stressing the region's association with the Three Musketeers.

RUM

By definition, this is a spirit distilled direct from sugar-cane products in sugar-cane-growing countries. Rum was originally made in the West Indies to provide the natives with an alcoholic drink. In later years, it became a firm favourite with the Royal Navy.

Geographical Location

British imports tend to come from Guyana (about 43 per cent), Jamaica (about 29 per cent) and the balance from other states. Sugar-cane for rum production is grown in the U.S.A., Indonesia, Australia, Brazil and Mexico. Trinidad and Barbados are sources of increasing importance to the U.K. In style, the rums may be categorised as:

Jamaica:	Pungent, full-bodied.
Guyana:	Demerara rum (dark, relatively heavy) but less pungent than Jamaican.
Trinidad and Barbados:	Lighter, less flavoured.
Puerto Rico:	Light in style.

Production

An alcoholic mash is fermented from molasses, which is the residue after sugar-cane has been boiled. The stems contain the sweet, sugary sap. A centrifuge is used to extract as much sap as possible. The fermentation takes place under temperature control, usually with cultured yeasts.

If a lighter less pungent style is required, distillation is by the continuous still, but the pot still is used for the pungent rums, particularly in Guyana and Jamaica. When rum is first distilled, it is colourless. It derives its later colour from ageing in the cask and from the addition of caramel.

As with other distillates, demineralised water is added at the final prebottling stage to adjust the rum to its sale strength; this is often 70° proof. By law,* rum sold in the U.K. has to be a minimum 2 years old, but a longer maturation period is often given to the full-flavoured styles.

Service

Rum may be enjoyed in a variety of ways. The white styles are frequently

*Finance Act, 1974, Section 4.

served lightly chilled in long drinks with fresh fruit and fruit juices, such as the juice of fresh limes. The dark-coloured rums have a useful place in culinary work or mixed with coffee (see liqueur coffees, Chapter 8). They can also be mixed with soda water, with ice or ginger ale.

OTHER SPIRITS

Apart from those above and liqueurs (Chapter 8), there are some other spirits which should be considered:

Saké

Japanese fermented liquid using rice which is cleaned, steamed and fermented. It is subsequently filtered, matured in wood and has a tendency to be fairly sweet. It is served warm by the cup in Japan. It is usually 12 to 16 per cent alcohol by volume in strength.

Arak

A spirit from widely differing substances, sometimes spelt arrak, arrack, arack. It is made from grain in Greece; fermented palm sap and rice in the East Indies; and from dates in Egypt. Batavia in Java is known for an arak made on the lines of rum from molasses. An acquired taste!

Aquavit

A spirit made generally from a grain or potato base which is flavoured with caraway seed, although herb and citrus peel can additionally be used or alternatively. It is colloquially known as *schnapps* and is popular in Norway, Denmark, Sweden and Iceland.

8. Vermouths, Liqueurs and Cocktails

'I am willing to taste any drink once', James Branch Cabell.

Vermouth and Aromatised Wines

Vermouth and aromatised wines are wines flavoured with herbs and other substances. Spiced wines have a long history with preparations dating from the days of Cicero and Hippocrates. Aromatisation was originally undertaken to preserve wines and hide any off-flavours by adding sea water, tar and other substances. By the Middle Ages oriental spices, such as almonds, cloves, myrrh, myrtle, ginger, nutmeg and sandalwood, were used in aromatised wines which were made for medicinal purposes.

The term 'vermouth' is thought to originate from the German *wermut*, a shrub, *Artemisia absinthia*, whose flowers flavoured sixteenth-century Rhine wines. It had developed on a commercial scale in Italy by the late eighteenth century, using many of the flowers and herbs of the foothills of the Alps. Benedetto Carpano is credited with producing the first Turin vermouth in 1786. Today it is an important industry and comprises a sizeable section of the alcoholic drinks market. The producers keep their exact ingredients secret but the production sequence is generally as follows.

1. Production of the Base Wine:

Some 80 per cent of the final blend is wine and therefore care is taken with the selection of the base to be used. French vermouths tend to use southern French wines (the Hérault, Languedoc and Roussillon) from the Picpoul, Bourret and Clairette vines; while the Italian vermouths mainly use grapes from Piedmont, Emilia, Apulia and Sicily.

2. Infusion:
A proportion of the base wine is seeped for 14 days in a variety of spices, seeds, flowers, roots, bark, plants and leaves. Among the ingredients are balm-mint, germander and sage for their flowers and leaves, dittary for its bitter leaves, the rind of bitter orange, vanilla pods, lemon-peel, perfumed seeds of the coriander, flowers of the Roman camomile, flowering tops of some Artemisias, aromatic roots of the calamus, bitter roots of the gentian, tea, savory, origan, centaury, cinnamon, sandalwood, Cinchona bark, violets and roses. Infusion is usually undertaken in large steel cylinders which rotate to allow mixing. Contrary to popular belief, wormwood is not used today (see below – Other Aromatic Wines).

A still is used to refine certain aromas; it may be that the intensity of the infusion is such that several months elapse before the third stage.

3. Clarification:
Fining, often using bentonite rather than egg white, is applied and then filtration.

4. Blending:
The aromatising infusions are now added to the basic filtered wine in the ratio of 2 to 3 per cent infusion to 97 to 98 per cent wine. Alcohol is added which raises the drink to 16 to 18° G.L. At this strength, the vermouth producers have found that the flavours are extracted most economically. Sugar is added to the final blend, depending upon the style. An extra dry would have less than 4 per cent, but a sweet style would contain over 14 per cent sugar. Caramel is frequently added to the red styles.

5. Maturation and Refining:
It is usual to age the blend for 4 to 6 months and to then chill it to around 16°F (–9°C) for 9 to 10 days which causes many impurities to precipitate. The blend is subsequently pasteurised to soften the taste and to render the yeasts harmless. Often the final blend is given a final ageing in wood, or more probably today, in glass-lined concrete vats, before bottling.

The total production time is therefore about 4 years and the final aromatised wine will have an alcoholic strength about 50 per cent higher than the original wine. There are variations in the production sequence with smaller makers, who still practise the custom of weathering the original wine, before blending, by exposing it to the sun for up to 2 years.

Styles of Vermouth

There are four main styles: crisp dry white (usually French); a rosé, which is relatively new; sweet white (nearly always Italian origin); and a slightly less sweet red.

The finest quality is Chambéry which was accorded an Appellation d'Origine Contrôlée status for its vermouth in 1932. Apart from its delicate dry white, Chambéry, which lies at the foothills of the Alps in Savoie, France, is also known for a style which is flavoured with wild strawberries. In the U.K., it is known as Chambéryzette. Italian vermouths tend to be made from a fuller-bodied base than French and use a greater amount of *mistelle* (fortified grape juice). Although France and Italy are the best known sources for vermouth, it is also produced in Spain, West Germany, Netherlands and the U.S.A. While most Italian is made in north-western Italy (Piedmont), French vermouth is centred around Marseilles on the Mediterranean.

Other Aromatised Wines

While vermouth has traditionally been based upon the flowers of wormwood, there are other spiced wines which fall into the general aromatised wine category that have not been flavoured by this flower. Some have quinine added and spices. St Raphaël is an example of quinine flavouring, using the bitter-tasting Peru bark, which gives it a distinctive taste. It was taken in the French colonies to ward off malaria. Other drinks, like retsina, have different flavouring; these Greek wines have pine resin added and are unfortified.

Absinthe, is based on the root of the wormwood. It was invented in the late eighteenth century but today it is formulated under the name of Pernod since absinthe was made illegal in 1915 because of the drugs in the original recipe. Aniseed replaced the wormwood and the drink is also frequently called pastis. Ricard and Berger are other examples. Byrrh, another French apéritif invented in 1866 in Roussillon, is a bitter-sweet selection, reddish-brown in appearance. Gentian, rather than quinine as with Byrrh, is an ingredient of the Auvergne drink, Arvèze, and of the bright yellow Suze. Both are good digestives to help large meals.

Orange flavour is evident in Amer Picon, which originated with the French army in Algeria in 1835; it has a pinky-red hue by comparison with the darker red of Dubonnet, although there is additionally a pale gold Dubonnet Blonde. Slightly less sweet than Dubonnet is Cap Corse, which is made near Bastia in Corsica and has a vanilla taste but a dark reddish-brown appearance. Similarly dark in colour, but both lighter and drier, is Ambassadeur.

The French have a large number of such drinks, usually under brand names. Lillet, for instance, is a Bordeaux white wine flavoured with Armagnac. Two French exceptions which are given general names are Pineau des Charantes, where brandy is added to the fermenting juice of fresh grapes and is sweet because of the residual sugar left unconverted; and Ratafia de Champagne, a rich, peach-coloured apéritif which is spirit added to freshly pressed Champagne A.O.C. grape juice.

Serving Vermouths and Aromatised Wines

The better quality vermouths can be enjoyed straight with the drier styles lightly chilled. Frequently ice and lemon are added, or water or soda to the drier versions. Many are used as a base for a spirit, such as a neutral one like white rum, or with gin, vodka or tequila. Olives can appeal, mainly again with the drier styles.

COCKTAILS

It is not clear who invented the term 'cocktail' but it may have come from France where the *coquetel* was a mixed drink from the Bordeaux region. It was allegedly introduced into the U.S.A. by French officers serving with Washington's army. An alternative derivation is the 'cocktray' in which a New Orleans pharmacist used to serve heady drinks of brandy, bitters and sugar.

Cocktail Equipment

1. Mixing glass for stirring clear drinks (e.g. for Manhattan).
2. Bar spoons.
3. Cocktail shaker.
4. Fruit knife and board.
5. Ice pick or ice chopper, ice bowl, ice shaver.
6. Fruit squeezer, nutmeg and nutmeg grater.
7. Sticks (for cherries and olives), drinking straws.
8. Strainer, preferably in stainless steel.

Among food accessories, include olives, cherries, cocktail onions, oranges, lemons, crisps, mint, fresh eggs, milk and cream.

Cocktail Measures

Only when either the customer specifies a different quantity, or when 3 or more liquids are being used together, may you move from the measured size that is declared in your bar. By the Weights and Measures Act, 1963, Schedule 4 Part VI, rum, gin, vodka and whisky may only be sold in $\frac{1}{4}$, $\frac{1}{5}$ or $\frac{1}{6}$ gill measures (35, 28 or 24 millilitres).

Methods

When making cocktails, speed is important as the ice should not melt. Do not allow the cocktail ingredients to exceed half the shaker's volume in order to allow room for the shake. Do not shake when mixing is specified, as cloudyness will result.

Market your cocktails by making them look appealing. Consider using a frosted glass for the presentation by rubbing the rim against the side of a cut lemon and then dipping it in sugar.

Where possible, use fresh fruit juice for the flavour. When shaking cocktails, use the ice only once; it absorbs the flavour which is then passed to the next drink. It helps to keep glasses for cold drinks in the refrigerator.

SOME COCKTAIL RECIPES

Among the many and varied cocktails to try are:

White Lady: 1 dessertspoonful fresh lemon juice, $2\frac{1}{2}$ fluid ounces (70 ml) London gin, 1 fluid ounce (28 ml) Cointreau, ice. Shake vigorously and strain into 2 cocktail glasses.

Chocolate Flip: 1 egg, 1 teaspoon powdered chocolate; $\frac{3}{4}$ fluid ounce (20 ml) sloe gin, $\frac{3}{4}$ fluid ounce (20 ml) Armagnac, 2 teaspoons double cream.
Shake well with cracked ice; strain into a 5 ounce (140 ml) flip glass; add grated nutmeg.

Harvey Wallbanger: 4 measures orange juice, 1 measure vodka; add ice and stir; add in half measure Galliano.

Silver Fizz: 3 parts gin, 1 egg white, 1 part fresh lemon juice, $\frac{1}{2}$ teaspoon sugar or sugar syrup, soda water and ice cubes.
Place ice into shaker; pour the sugar, gin and lemon juice over the ice. Add the egg white to the mixture. Shake vigorously until a frost forms. Strain and pour. Top with soda water and serve.

Lombardo: Add ice, lemon, American dry to 1 measure St Raphaël Extra Dry.

Bianco Verde: Two measures bianco, add ice, $\frac{1}{2}$ measure crème de menthe and stir. Add dash of soda water.

Traditional Selections

Apart from the lesser-known cocktails given above, there is a good call for the following traditional selections:

Dry Martini:* One third French dry white vermouth, $\frac{2}{3}$ London gin, 2 dashes orange bitters. Add broken ice to a mixing glass and stir well; strain; serve with lemon peel squeezed on top.

*A Dry Martini is this cocktail and not the dry brand of this famous vermouth house.

Sweet Martini: Half sweet Italian vermouth, $\frac{1}{2}$ London gin. Stir and strain as for Dry Martini; add cherry to decorate.
Do not confuse either of these Martini cocktails with a straight vermouth and ice order.

Pink Lady: Half London gin; $\frac{1}{2}$ white of egg, dash of Grenadine. Shake well; strain into a frosted glass.

Pimms: There are now only two Pimms (gin and vodka based respectively). Use a tumbler, placing borage or cucumber peel at its base with ice, the Pimms required and top up with lemonade.

John Collins: One measure gin, juice of $\frac{1}{2}$ lemon, $\frac{1}{2}$ teaspoon sugar, ice cube. Stir in tall glass with long spoon, adding soda to taste. Serve with straw.

Manhattan: One-third sweet vermouth, $\frac{2}{3}$ rye whiskey and dash of Angostura bitters. Stir and strain, adding a cherry.

Bacardi: Half Bacardi white rum, $\frac{1}{2}$ fresh lime (or lemon) juice, dash of Grenadine. Shake well and strain.

Daiquiri: 3 fluid ounce (85 ml) white rum, 1 teaspoon Cointreau, $\frac{3}{4}$ fluid ounce (20 ml) lemon (or fresh lime) juice, 1 level teaspoon sugar, ice cubes, and (optional) one egg white. Mix lemon juice or lime with sugar to dissolve the sugar. Add rum, Cointreau and ice. Place shaker on top of mixing glass, shake and strain. Add dash of egg white before shaking if a foamier cocktail is required.

Bloody Mary 3 fluid ounce (85 ml) vodka, 4 fluid ounce (110 ml) tomato juice, 2 teaspoons fresh lemon juice, 2 drops Worcester sauce, 2 drops Tabasco, ice cubes, freshly ground black pepper. Fill a mixing glass with ice, add lemon juice, tomato juice, vodka, Worcester sauce and Tabasco. Season with black pepper. Place a shaker on top of the mixing glass, shake and strain. A **Danish Mary** uses aquavit in place of vodka.

Sidecar: Quarter Cointreau, $\frac{1}{2}$ Cognac, $\frac{1}{4}$ fresh lemon juice. Shake and strain.

LIQUEURS

Liqueurs are sweetened and flavoured spirits. They have a long tradition, dating back to 800 B.C. One can see stills in Egyptian bas-reliefs. Many liqueurs owe their origin to the Church: the monks acted as apothecaries and added sugar to make medicines taste less unpleasant. The flavouring agents used are the significant ingredients and the method of production employed will depend upon what these are.

Production of Liqueurs

1. Percolation:
This is the method of hot infusion. The hot spirit is cycled on a closed circuit to extract essential oils by passing the spirit through a filter of the pulverised flavouring agent.

2. Cold Maceration:
The flavouring materials are soaked for 24 hours to 1 year to extract the flavour, particularly where delicate colours or flavours are involved which would spoil with percolation.

3. Distillation:
Either the distillation of a mixture of alcohol and water with the flavourings, or the passing of alcohol vapour through a filter of pulverised flavouring materials. As the distillate is almost colourless, both colour and sweetener are added.

4. Mechanical Pressure:
Effective in such cases as citrus fruit peel.

Compounding plays an important part in liqueur production. Most liqueurs are a mixture of ingredients, obtained by several methods. It is the compounder's skill which achieves a consistent harmony of style; although the order of mixing is also a significant factor.

Subsequently most liqueurs need time for their constituent parts to 'marry' together in oak at an even temperature. This is followed by fining and filtration.

Liqueur Classification

1. Citrus Peel:

Originally these were liqueurs using fruit from the island of Curaçao in the Caribbean near the coast of Venezuela, but today are applied generically to those using bitter peel of citrus fruits from other countries. Well-known brands include Cointreau, Grand Marnier, Parfait Amour and Van der Hum.

2. Fruits:

This category covers the fruits themselves, rather than the peel and, should not be confused with fruit brandies (see below). Apples, pears and quinces are used as well as berries, stoned fruit like cherries, and tropical fruit such as pineapple and banana. Among the liqueurs in this category are Maraschino, using fermented maraschino cherries and their crushed kernels; Southern Comfort, using mainly peach and orange; Sabra, orange and chocolate and named for the desert cactus; and the Burgundian Crème de Cassis (using macerated destalked blackcurrants in a Marc).

3. Seeds and Herbs:

This covers either single or mixed categories, such as aniseed and caraway seed as well as mint-based liqueurs. Brands include Drambuie, Bénédictine, Glayva, green and yellow Chartreuse, Izarra, Strega, Kümmel, Anisette, Ouzo, Crème de Menthe, Galliano and Vieille Cure.

4. Egg:

Advocaat.

5. Beans and Kernels:

Coffee, cocoa and vanilla are among the ingredients used. Coffee brands include Tia Maria, Mokka and Kahlúa while Crème de Caçao is a chocolate one. Noyau is an example of an extract of peach and apricot kernels.

Fruit Brandies in Eaux-de-Vie

Fruit brandies or *eaux-de-vie* (meaning 'waters of life') are not fruit liqueurs. They are produced in a sequence where the sugar of the fruit is used initially for the fermentation; this yields a wash which is then distilled. Examples include Calvados (apple), Kirsch (cherry) and Slivovitz (plum).

Use of Liqueurs

Traditionally liqueurs are served at the end of meals as digestives, but enterprising marketing has developed liqueur-based cocktails and such iced drinks or *frappés* as Crème de Menthe, which is delicious on a warm day. Liqueur flavours are developed by serving on ice or chilled. Two summer drinks to serve are:

Blue Lagoon: Blue Curaçao, lemonade and topped with fresh cream.

Valencia: Apricot brandy, orange and ice.

As much pleasure is derived from the nose of a liqueur, serve in balloon-shaped glasses and not in thimbleful-sized ones. When pouring, turn the bottle so that the label is facing upwards to prevent drips from staining the labels.

Liqueurs make ideal flavourings in the kitchen. *Soufflé Grand Marnier* is a good example, while Cointreau and Southern Comfort are popular for flaming pancakes. Fruit salads are improved with anis-flavoured liqueurs and chocolate cakes by adding Crème de Caçao or Royal Mint Chocolate liqueurs.

LIQUEUR LIST

Liqueur	Strength	Source	Ingredients
Advocaat	Up to 30	Netherlands	Egg yolk, brandy and sugar
Anis	45	Spain	Aniseed
Anisette	45	France, Italy	Anise, coriander, fennel, etc.
Apricot Brandy	50	Various	Apricots and brandy
Bénédictine	73	France	Herbs, plants, peels and brandy
Calisay	56	Spain	Herbs
Chartreuse (Green)	96	France, Spain	Herbs
Chartreuse (Yellow)	75	France, Spain	Herbs
Cherry Brandy	42	Various	Cherries and brandy
Cointreau	70	France	Oranges
Crème de Caçao	47	France	Cocoa and vanilla beans
Crème de Cassis	28	France	Blackcurrants
Crème de Menthe	52	France	Mint
Curaçao	70	Various	Orange peel

Drambuie	70	Scotland	Herbs, honey and Scotch whisky
Grand Marnier	67	France	Oranges and mature brandy
Izarra (Green)	85		
(Yellow)	64	France	Herbs, flowers and Armagnac
Kahlúa	46	Mexico	Coffee beans
Kirsch	70	France	Cherries
Kümmel	68	West Germany, Austria	Caraway seeds
Maraschino	50	Various	Maraschino cherries
Mirabelle	70	France	Mirabelle plums
Tia Maria	55	Jamaica	Rum, coffee and Jamaican spices
Van der Hum	54	S. Africa	Tangerine, rum and Cape brandy
Vieille Cure	75	France	Roots and herbs

The strengths quoted above are the usual ones sold in the U.K., but they may vary. They are given in degrees British proof (for strength explanation, see Chapter 2).

Liqueur Coffees

A useful liqueur marketing exercise is to offer a range of attractive combinations with coffee. It is usual to pour black coffee on to the liqueur measure, stir in sugar to taste and top with cream.

Speciality	**Spirit**
Calypso	Tia Maria
Caribbean	Rum
Coffee of the Glens	Glen Mist
Dutch	Geneva
French	Cognac (or sometimes Armagnac)
Gaelic	Irish whiskey
German	Kirsch
Italian	Strega
Mexican	Kahlúa
Monks'	Bénédictine or Chartreuse
Normandy	Calvados
Prince Charles	Drambuie
Russian	Vodka
Scandinavian	Aquavit
Scotch	Scotch whisky

Flavoured Spirits

A number of spirits are appropriately flavoured, such as gin with the juniper berry, angelica, caraway, cardamom, coriander, aniseed and orris root and then steeped in a particular flavour or fruit; gins may be flavoured lemon, orange or blackcurrant.

Bitters are additives to mixed drinks and are particularly used with dry spirits like gin and aquavit. They are sometimes taken as apéritifs or digestives on their own. Brands include Underberg (West German), Angostura (Trinidad), Fernet-Branca (Italy), Campari (Italy) and Amer Picon (France) (see above). Peach and orange bitters are also popular.

9. Beers and Ciders

'Good ale, the true and proper drink of Englishmen,' George Borrow.

By definition beer is the alcoholic beverage obtained through converting malt sugars, flavoured with hops, by a fermentation using brewer's yeast.

Historical Background

In ancient times, a fermented drink was made from barley and wheat. By the seventh century A.D. in Britain, it had developed into three forms of clear, mild and Welsh ale. In the tenth century A.D., regulations were brought in to control both beer measure and the number of outlets, by declaring a maximum of one per parish. Two centuries were to elapse before taxation on beer was introduced. Most of it was alcoholically weak, referred to as 'small beer', which explains how 8 pints (4·5 litres) per day could be allocated to the nuns at Syon convent in 1371.

Greater control was attempted under Cromwell during the Commonwealth and again over a century later, in 1787 with a Royal proclamation to correct the proliferation of taverns. However this was more against cheap gin than beer. In 1830, the Beerhouse Act was passed which facilitated the sale of ale without the need for a justices' licence. It was normal for beer to be brewed in each public house. Breweries only developed when transport was sufficiently improved to allow the movement of beer in bulk. The pendulum swung several ways and, by 1869, social pressures restored the justices' control over all licensed premises under the Wine and Beerhouse Act. This was followed by a series of licensing acts which extended the controls on licensed premises including the Licensing Act, 1904, which established compensation funds under which redundant ale and beerhouses were weeded out. In World War I, the swing reversed and there was a gradual relaxation.

With modern transport, the number of small brewery points declined through amalgamation. It has been estimated that some 16,000 brewers existed around 1890, declining to about 75 today, of whom six are important because of their size in the mass-production field. There has been a trend in the 1970s towards exchanging public houses between brewers. This avoids any reference under monopolies legislation whereby one brewer could be said to have more controlled outlets than was reasonable for fair competition. A move by consumers has led to greater interest being taken by brewers in their traditional draught beers. Such bodies as The Society for the Preservation of Beers from the Wood and the Campaign for Real Ale have been influential.

Beer Production

The ingredients are yeast (*Saccharomyces cerevisiae*) for top fermentation – lager is bottom-fermented using *Saccharomyces uvarum* – malt, hops, and water which the brewers call the 'liquor'. Some brewers use substitutes for malt, which they term 'adjuncts', such as wheat flour, potato starch and rice. The Food Standards Committee Report on Beer, March 1977 recommended that the malt content of each brew should be declared.

1. Malting:

The first stage in the brewing process is the malt preparation. This is frequently carried out away from the brewery by specialists, known as maltsters, but some breweries own their own maltings. Barley is the main grain used, but small amounts of other unmalted cereals, such as maize and wheat, are often included. The grain is steeped in water and spread on a 'malting floor' where temperature and humidity are carefully controlled so that germination takes place. After about five days, rootlets will have appeared and the malt – as it has become – is 'kilned' (heated) to prevent further growth and to improve the flavour. Natural changes occur during germination within the grains including the formation of enzymes; this makes it possible for the starch they contain to be converted to sugar at the next stage.

2. Milling and Mashing:

In the brewery, the malt grains are lightly crushed by roller mills before being mixed with hot water in a vessel, known as the 'mash tun'. Brewers refer to the mixture at this stage as 'grist'. Great care is required with the mixing to ensure that there is a good balance between the grist and the water; this is known as 'mashing'. The malts for different beers may be mashed at slightly different temperatures but all are around 150°F (65°C).

Mashing converts the starch in the grist to a number of different sugars, which are dissolved in the water to form the 'wort', a sweet extract. After 1 to 3 hours, depending upon the grist, the wort is slowly drained from the mash tun and passed to the coppers. During the draining, more hot water is sprayed on to the mash to wash the last of the sugars out of the grain; this process is called 'sparging'. The spent grains are sold for cattle food.

3. Boiling:

The wort is boiled in the copper, together with the hops, for about 2 hours. The golden dust at the base of the hop cone petals contains insoluble resins which become both soluble and bitter during boiling. It is this which contributes to beer's traditionally bitter flavour. The hop cones are dried in oast houses before they are despatched to the brewery. Sugar may be added at the copper stage for either taste or strength purposes.

After boiling, the wort is drained through coolers to the fermenting vessel. The spent hops are removed in the process, sometimes by straining the hopped wort through a giant sieve (a hop back) or by centrifugal force; the spent hops are sold for fertiliser. After the hopped wort is cooled and aerated, it is measured in the fermenting vessel by H.M. Customs and Excise for the volume and specific gravity (or potential alcohol) in order to calculate the duty payable by the brewer.

4. Fermentation:

Fermentation commences with the introduction of yeast, a living organism that feeds upon the nutrients in the wort and uses sugars as it does so. If temperature is maintained correctly about 57–68°F (14–20°C), the yeast will multiply and, in the process, yield alcohol, carbon dioxide and flavour components. The yeast collects on the surface and is carefully skimmed off periodically, producing about five times as much as at first. The surplus yeast is sold for tonic and food preparations, no by-products being wasted. The fermenting process takes about 5 days, after which the wort has become beer. It is then run off into storage tanks or containers and matures to the right condition for taste.

5. Conditioning:
The final stage will depend upon the beer style to be produced. Some, which have been run directly into containers of up to 36 gallons (164 litres/ a barrel) may have a handful of dry hops added to give extra flavour to the aroma. They will continue to develop in the cask in the retail outlet right up to, and including, the time it is dispensed. Prior to leaving the brewery, finings are added to clarify the beer which sink to the bottom, precipitating any solids which have been left in suspension. As this is a 'living' beer, it should be dispensed in a short time to avoid deterioration.

An alternative end treatment is for fining to take place on a bulk scale, prior to the beer going into a container from which it is dispensed to the outlet. Some beers may be filtered (instead of being fined) and are termed 'keg'; they usually have a carbon dioxide injection to restore the sparkle that would otherwise be missing. Such keg or 'bright' beer keeps longer than the cask-conditioned beers, because there is no danger of refermentation. Most beer which is 'kegged' is also pasteurised. Much bottled and canned beer is given this latter 'bright' beer treatment, since it gives a longer shelf life. Bottled beer was introduced at the beginning of the twentieth century, but only started to take a significant place in the beer market after World War I. By 1939, bottled beer accounted for around one-third of beer sales and today bottled and canned together form over 25 per cent of the beer market (see page 20).

BEER STYLES

Bitter

This is usually a draught beer, yellow-golden in appearance, with a distinctive hop taste. If a bitter is made into a keg, it frequently tastes sweeter; although the true flavour can be obscured by the low temperature that it is sometimes served at.

Mild

Currently, this accounts for 13 per cent of the market and is a declining sector. It is brewed like bitter but using darker malts, fewer hops and more caramel or sugar. It is the weakest of draught beers, tends to be sweeter than bitter and is red-brown in appearance. There are some pale milds, alcoholically weaker but approaching bitter in taste. In the North-

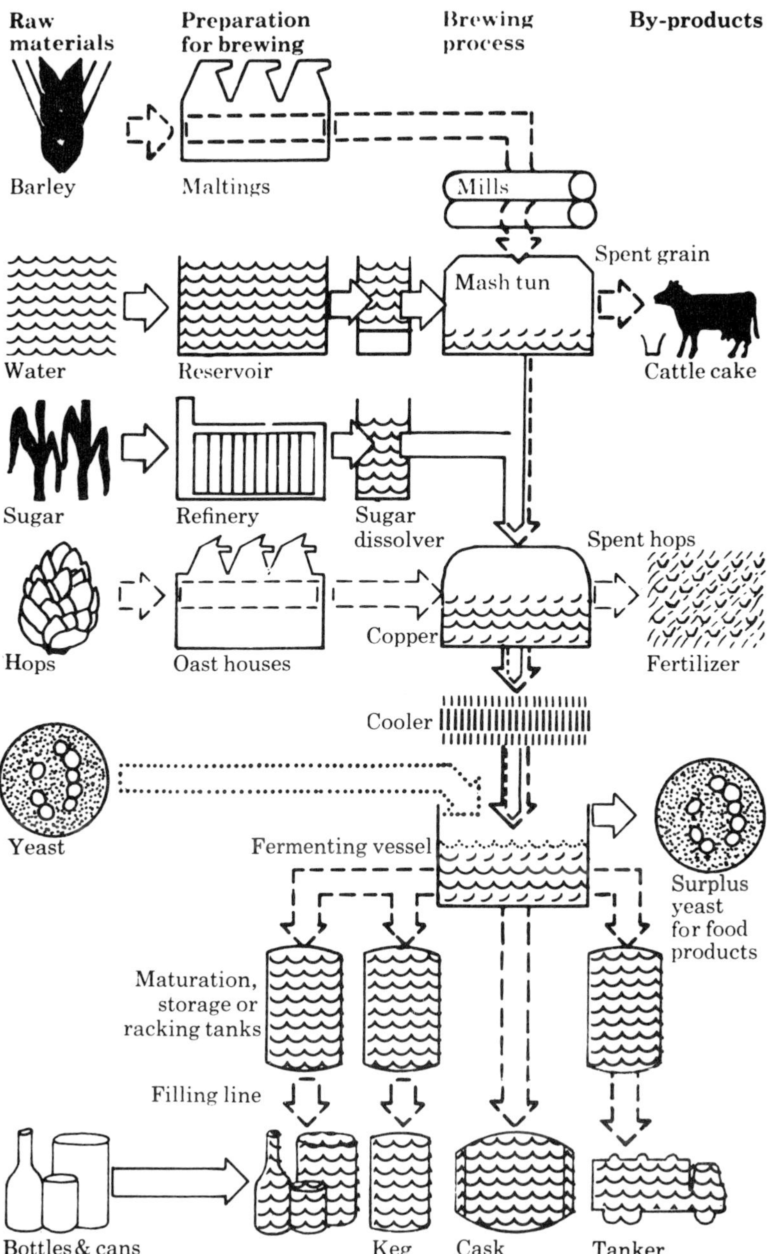

Different stages of the brewing process and resulting by-products.

West and Midlands, a fair catering demand exists for mild. Brown ale is the bottled version of mild.

Strong Ale

This is a beer where the fermentation has been allowed to continue for a longer period; it is sometimes known as Old Ale. It tends to be strong alcoholically and is frequently on the sweeter side in taste. It is brewed almost exclusively by independent brewers for the winter trade.

Stout

A well-hopped, dark-coloured beer that is often sweet in taste. Guinness is the only stout available both on draught and in bottle; it can also be obtained in cans.

Brewers apply several terms to the same style, often dependent upon the method of packaging. A Barley Wine, for instance, is usually a bottled version of a strong ale. Light Ale is the bottled equivalent of ordinary bitter; I.P.A. or Pale Ale are best bitters.

Lager

The name originates from the German term *lagerbier* or store beer. It is an entirely different type of beer, fermented with a yeast which works on the floor of the fermentation vessel (rather than on the top with other beers). The fermentation takes place at a low temperature for periods of between 8 and 24 weeks; this includes the conditioning and chill-proofing. Many are carbonated.

Lager brewing is recorded at Glasgow and Wrexham in the 1880s with lager brewing facilities developed in the early 1900s at Alloa, Burton on Trent, Edinburgh and London. Yet for decades lager's share of the beer market was less than half per cent and it remained virtually at that level until 1960. Lager is now a growth sector of the beer market, holding about 24·8 per cent in 1977 and likely to command nearer 30 per cent by 1980.

Some brewers, looking at the switch to lager in such countries as Australia and Belgium, consider a similar move will occur in Britain. The trend is not overall for some regions have taken to lager much more than others. In Scotland, for instance, lager has a 40 per cent share of the beer market, while it is around 45 per cent in Ulster.

Beer Strength

The alcoholic strength of beer is calculated by H.M. Customs and Excise on the specific gravity reading of the wort, prior to its fermentation into beer. It is therefore the potential that is being measured. However, this is accepted, apart from excise duty purposes, by brewers as an indication of the comparative strength of beers. Water is taken as having a specific gravity of 1000°. Any measure of the sugars and malt present in the wort will show by a reading above 1000°. The specific gravity drops once fermentation commences, because the yeast converts the sugars into alcohol and carbon dioxide. The brewer will stop fermentation when the specific gravity reaches between one-fifth to one-quarter of the original gravity.

British beer has been gradually declining in original gravity as shown by these average readings:

1900	1055
1928	1043·17
1938	1041·02
1948	1032·66
1958	1037·48
1968	1037·36
1973	1036·99

Since it is currently voluntary for brewers to publish figures for each style they produce, the Beer Report from the Food Standards Committee recommended, in March 1977, that the original gravity should be designated by bands:

Suggested Classification	Description	Original Gravity Band
X	Light	Up to 1035
XX	Special, Heavy	1035–1040
XXX	Export, India Pale Ale (I.P.A.)	1041–1046
XXXX	Strong	1047–1061
XXXXX	Extra Strong, Barley Wine	1062 and above

This is the Committee's recommendation and does not have Government support to date. Caterers are unlikely to find the further information of much help, as some 80 per cent of all beers brewed in Britain fall into the first two bands.

Beer Dispensing

The many different methods of dispensing draught beer reflect the separate styles. Beer conditioned in cask is generally dispensed by:

1. Gravity.
2. Hand pump.
3. Compressed air beer engine.
4. Electrical pump.
5. Carbon dioxide pressure (occasionally).

As the level of the beer in the barrel falls, air enters and causes the beer flavour to deteriorate and it to go flat. If the beer is not used within a few days, spoilage micro-organisms (like acetic acid bacteria) multiply, causing a sour quality in the remaining beer. Gravity simply means that two holes are made in the barrel – one for dispensing and the other for oxygen – and the beer is served through a simple tap. The beer engine can take the form of a suction pump on a bar counter or as a metered electric pump, which removes the harder work involved with hand pumps.

An alternative is for a cylinder of carbon dioxide, which may be mixed with nitrogen, to be applied to the head space of the barrel, keg or tank. Where beer is drawn using this method in place of oxygen, it is termed 'top pressure'. Caterers should be careful, when using the top pressure method, not to increase the gas level beyond the generally acceptable 4–5 lb per square inch pressure. Above that, carbon dioxide gas alters the true flavour of the beer. Some cellar tanks are fitted with a flexible liner in order that the gas pressure can be applied to the outside of the liner and so does not come into direct contact with the beer.

If you are using a system which involves carbon dioxide pressure, ensure the gas supply is turned off between serving times, so that excess gas is not released into the beer. The measuring dispenser, used with keg and certain other styles, gauges the correct quantity into each glass. Such dispensers are available with cooling and temperature devices which allow beer to be served at its correct temperature and remove the necessity to have a specially constructed cellar. For a traditional beer cellar, which can be either below or above ground, 7 foot (2·1 metres) is a good height.

The 'thrawls' on which the casks stand, should be 3 feet (90 centimetres) wide and about 15 inches (38 centimetres) thick. An overlapping brick will protect the pipe for it has a $1\frac{1}{2}$ inches (4 centimetres) projection. Most caterers operate portable 'stillages' (metal cradles with a tilting device), rather than fixed position thrawls, as this means your bar staff can change casks at a peak time without upsetting the beer quality by a rapid change of position of the cask. When constructing a beer cellar, allow channels for drainage.

The enterprising will want to show a helpful consumer trend, ahead of legislation, by indicating at the dispensing point the method of conditioning of each beer (cask conditioned or bulk conditioned), method of dispensing (drawn or pressure dispensed for draught), and a note of those beers, if any, where the carbon dioxide content exceeds 1·5 volumes. The original gravity bands suggested by the Food Standards Committee could be displayed on a notice near the bar.

Top fermented beer should be served around 55°F (13°C), while poor quality and many keg beers are served at lower temperatures, partly to mask the full flavour. Lager is traditionally served around 46 to 50°F (8 to 10°C). During the winter, enterprising caterers offer warmer beer in punches, mulled ale and 'wassail', such as below.

Lamb's Wool: Heat 1pt (570 millilitres) brown ale to 8 fluid ounces (225 millilitres) apple sauce; add ginger and sugar to taste.

One can add honey and lemon as well as a variety of spices to warm beer punch, but ensure it is heated and not boiled as this impairs the flavour. There is a glossary of beer terms at the back of this book.

CIDER

By definition cider is the alcoholic beverage derived from the fermentation of apple juice and sugar.

Historical Background

In Celtic mythology, the apple was sacred and an Apple God was worshipped. Early cider was made from bitter apples that grew wild in the forests. Cider was introduced to England from Normandy in the mid-twelfth century and at that time the apples were beaten in wooden troughs using pestles. Monastic writings in the Middle Ages made many allusions to the drink. William of Shoreham, in the fourteenth century, reflected on the Church's concern for the niceties of sacramental rites by saying that young children were not to be baptised with cider! Cider became a substitute for French wine when supplies were stopped during the Hundred Years War (1337–1453). William Langdon referred to cider in *Piers Plowman* and so did Shakespeare in *A Midsummer Night's Dream.*

Large amounts of apples were crushed in horse mills. The first specially-constructed cider mill appeared in the seveteenth century, using a wooden cylinder and rotated by hand. Royal Cider was distilled, and frequently fortified with other spirits and sugar. Further home production of cider received a boost by an Act of 1703 which sought to curb smuggling and the importing of French brandy. Cider production was essentially a craft of the cottage and farmhouse with apple orchards planted to provide fruit for culinary, dessert and cider uses as well as sheltered grazing for the livestock. Between the seventeenth and nineteenth centuries, this was a significant item in the mixed self-sufficient farming system.

Home cider brewing dropped, owing to the cheapness of beer and the unpredictable fermentation that resulted from wild yeasts; and the farmers began to sell their fruit to the cider mills. However this practice was uneconomical owing to the conflicting interests of the farmer, the type of apples produced and the overall economics of the exercise. To keep pace with the expanding market, large quantities of apples – chiefly from Normandy and Brittany owing to their proximity and the similarity of their apples to those of the West Country – were imported. This practice continues today. Large-scale production became viable in the late nineteenth century with the isolation of a yeast that dominated the fermentation process. Since World War II, there has been concern over the scarcity of apples. This is because there have been no appreciable plantings of cider apple trees in France; this is against a world rise in demand for apple juice. The full fruiting time of 15 years required for cider apple trees is therefore being augmented by intensive bush style orchards. Cider demand in the U.K. is markedly on the increase, it rose between 1963 and 1970 from 29,400,000 gallons to 41,200,000 gallons (133,655,300 litres to 187,299,300 litres).

Cider Production

The major English counties for cider apples are Kent, Somerset, Herefordshire, Norfolk and Gloucester. The apples are tipped into concrete silos, washed, milled to a pulp and the juice extracted usually by hydraulic presses. The juice is moved to settling vats and subsequently pumped into a vat for the 3 to 4 weeks of fermentation. The residue apple 'pomace' is further processed to yield pectin for sale to confectioners and jam-makers. The very final residue is sold as cattle food. Since apple pressing is undertaken only once annually, storage is necessary on a substantial scale.

Special yeast cultures are introduced to the fermentation vats with blending usually following the full fermentation, depending upon the cider varieties to be produced. The cider is usually chilled to about 35°F (1·6°C), before being passed through a sterilising filter or flash pasteuriser to the bottling.

Marketing

Most production in Britain is concentrated between three firms who have started to promote draught cider dispensation in catering and other outlets in the last few years. Drier styles are being promoted, moving away from the sweeter brands. Some firms age their cider for up to a year in oak vats; this gives a more mellow texture. Some semi-sparkling styles have been created which are twice fermented.

Cider is greatly underestimated in cooking and many recipes using cider are available today. They range from pâté to Cider Syllabub and stews, like Hereford Tomato Hotpot, which allow the enterprising caterer to promote the drink in both the food and in accompanying the dish.

Several Normandy ciders are imported in both dry (*cidre brut*) and sweeter (*cidre doux*) styles. A semi-sparkling, twice-fermented competitor from the same region (*cidre bouché*) is also available. A popular cider-based spirit is Calvados (see Chapter 8, Fruit Brandies).

Glossary of Wine Terms

Acetic Sour smell of vinegar with rasping taste resulting from the action of acetobacter; the wine has been soured.

Acidity Present in all wines as a natural component helping to develop the **aroma,** sharpen the final taste and act as a preservative. Most usually seen in immature whites and reds, particularly in poor vintages where there has been a lack of sun. Absence of acidity leads to a **flabby** wine that lacks **distinction**.

After-taste A semblance of the **nose** and taste that returns to the mouth after the wine has been tasted. Lovely on a well-aged wine; not to be confused with **finish.**

Agreeable A fairly balanced wine that is currently pleasant to drink.

Amontillado Medium-dry style of Sherry of the **fino** class (in that they have experienced a light **flor** growth) and acquired an amber appearance with age and a **nutty** taste.

Anada Young Sherry of a single year, aged from 9 to 36 months, prior to its entry to the **criadera.**

Appley High malic acid evident by a wine's **fresh,** almost rasping **aroma**. Frequently the sign of a youthful wine.

Aristocratic An individual wine that has the **balance** of all of the qualities expected by the sensitive taster.

Aroma The **nose** of a wine that originates from the grape in contrast to the development in the bottle (**bouquet**); marked on a Sauvignon from the upper Loire with its

flintyness, or the **earthyness** of a Syrah Rhône red.

Aromatic A herbal or slightly **spicy** nose.

Assertive Firmness of character on **nose** and taste. A youthful single village Beaujolais shows this with its marked **fruity** nose of the Gamay vine.

Astringent Effect of excess **tannin** which gives a dry, mouth-puckering taste.

Austere A **severe,** usually undeveloped wine, but that is not necessarily a criticism. Dry white upper Loire wines, for instance – like Sancerre – have a rasping mouth-watering quality in the final taste. The term can also be used for the **aroma** of very youthful wines that give future promise. Manzanilla sherry, with its rasping **finish,** and red vinho verde from northern Portugal are other examples.

Bad Eggs The harmless but not pleasant **nose** of hydrogen sulphide, usually resulting from poor cellar treatment. The pungency is removed by decanting vigorously prior to serving.

Baked An **earthy** or hot nose derived from a wine that has originated in a markedly warm region, such as North Africa or the southern Rhône Valley.

Balance A blend of physical factors that ensures an overall satisfactory wine. To achieve good balance, the wine should show correct development in its appearance, on the **nose** and on the taste. Therefore a youthful white Burgundy should display a pale straw appearance and not have a dark golden hue, which would imply that it was possibly **maderised** and not have a good balance. In a similar way, a youthful Beaujolais should show a bright cherry/pale ruby colour, characteristic of its vintage. In addition to appearance, the fruit of the predominant vine variety should be in harmony and the characteristics of **acidity,** alcohol, **tannin** and other factors be in correct alignment. If a wine is **oxidised** by premature decanting, and therefore loses most of its **aroma** but still retains the correct colour, it can be said to have bad balance at the time of serving.

Bead The effervescent bubble lines that rise in a **sparkling** wine. A good one will continue for hours after a quality sparkler has been opened. Look for regular small bead size.

Bereich Vineyard district in West Germany which covers several villages; each **bereich** may be thought of as a subdivision of the large regions (e.g. there are three **bereichs** in the Franconia region).

Big A wine full of taste and **rich** in **acidity,** alcohol, **tannin** and extracts.

Bitter A generally disagreeable taste which may become less evident with age. Improperly cleaned wood casks as well as colour derived from the grape skins can leave this flavour, which can be attractive in vermouths.

Blackcurrant **Aroma** associated with the main Bordeaux red grape, the Cabernet Sauvignon. It has a **rich,** inviting **fruityness.** See it markedly on wines from the Pauillac village of the Médoc.

Blue Fined The smell of bitter almonds which indicates excessive use of potassium ferrocyanide. Shippers use it to react with heavy metals like iron, copper, zinc, etc., to form an insoluble prussian blue compound. This should settle out to result in a clear wine after subsequent filtration.

Body The extract or weight which is the result of a wine's alcoholic content and other properties. If well constituted it will normally appear to fill the mouth. Full flavoured Italian wines, like Barolo, will have more body than a slight Swiss or English vineyard wine.

Boiled Beetroot The **aroma** associated with the Pinot Noir vine. The classic region is Burgundy, but the Pinot is successfully cultivated in other regions, like Champagne and Australia.

Bone Dry A wine with no residual sugar on the taste and therefore frequently almost an **austere** dryness. Often applied to *flor* fino sherry and to **crisp**, youthful Chablis.

Bottle Age Evidence on the **nose** of wine's development in bottle, signified by a **mellow** quality on reds and a soft, honeyed style on whites.

Bottle Sickness Temporary **oxidation** seen sometimes in wines recently bottled. This is a condition that results from the change in the wine's environment from a large vat to a bottle.

Bouquet The smell of a wine derived from its development, largely in bottle. Seen best in wines of some maturity. Not to be confused with **aroma** (the smell of the grape).

Breathing Development of the **nose** and flavour of a wine after its closure has been removed. It is aided by decanting.

Breed A wine of character that shows the hallmarks of quality. Opposite of a **coarse, rough** style that only should be purchased for cooking with or turning into Sangria for a summer punch. Regional characteristics should be evident.

Bright A wine that is perfectly clear and has no floaters, **haze** or other visual faults. Excessive filtering and fining, often undertaken on the branded *vin de table* lines, should result in a 'star bright' clarity, but slight particles are not a fault in a quality wine.

Broad A wine of an open style in **nose,** taste and **after-taste;** not clear cut.

Caramel A taste like burnt toffee, often found on Madeira and Marsala. It is used in spirits, particularly Scotch whisky, to ensure colour consistency.

Casse A haze or cloudiness in wine, often in addition to precipitation, created by the presence of excess oxidation, protein, copper or iron.

Cedarwood A lovely light **fruityness** detected on the **nose** of quality clarets.

Chewy A wine that is sufficiently substantial as to give the appearance (largely **tannin**) that one could chew on it.

Clean Absence of unnatural esters on the nose.

Cloudy Antonym of star-**bright**. All wines should be clear. Do not confuse cloudiness with either a bottle recently drawn from the cellar, or where the decanting has not been done properly. Sherry and other wines can throw a protein or other **haze;** such stock should be returned.

Cloying **Rich** and **heavy** characteristic, lacking **acidity,** that is unbalanced. Unctious.

Coarse Lacking both quality and elegance; not to be confused with the immaturity of a young wine.

Common An undistinguished, sound, but ordinary wine.

Complete A unified wine that has correct **balance** and has matured according to expectation.

Cooked A **heavy,** almost **rich nose** which implies the wine may have been over-chaptalised (where sucrose or unfermented must is added disproportionately during fermentation). Many tasters do not find this condition unpleasant.

Corked Unhealthy, often **musty** smell given to a wine from a diseased cork; the flavour may also be tainted. Noticeable when the cork is drawn, usually caused by the cork weevil or by wine seeping through the cork if it has not been properly applied or stored horizontally.

Creaming A light sparkle, beyond **pétillant** stage, but not a full **mousse.** Its **lightness** and lower atmospheric pressure make it an attractive style of wine to accompany poultry and fish courses.

Criadera Spanish term for nursery, used in connection with Sherry (and Montilla) which is a group of butts of wine of the same age drawn from the **anadas** before the **solera** stage.

Crisp Definite taste, the antonym of **flabby**. Created by balanced **acidity;** evident particularly on good Alsatian wines.

Delicate Showing more than usual qualities of charm and **balance** on **nose** and taste, such as the wines from the middle Loire like Savennières.

Demi-Sec Medium-sweet to sweet on labels for the U.K. trade, although it literally means 'half-dry'.

Depth Many layers of flavour; a subtle wine worthy of study. Applicable to most good vintage claret.

Distinguished A wine evidently displaying exceptional character.

Dry Not sweet, but less **austere** than **bone dry.**

Dumb Immature wine but with the promise of development. Sometimes seen immediately after filtering or transporting a wine. Some lesser regions yield wines with very few positive **nose** and taste qualities and these would therefore also be described as dumb.

Earthy Special taste ascribed to the soil on which certain vines are cultivated.

Fat Wine of **full body,** high in extracts like glycerine, which is often seen by the lines which are set up around a glass when the wine is moved. More often seen on a young wine, but may have additionally a **cloying** edge if it is a dessert wine.

Fine Wine showing **breed** and character; an overworked term but evident in most great wines by their nature.

Finish The final taste impression which depends upon the correct **balance** of **acidity.** An important factor in overall appraisal. A poor or short finish will be watery with the flavour inconclusive; a good or long finish will have a **crisp,** distinctive edge.

Fino The lightest, most delicate style of Sherry. A dry wine which has acquired its character largely through **flor** growth. Pale colour and refreshing.

Flabby Lacks distinction on taste.

Flat A **sparkling** wine that has lost its **bead** or a lifeless still table wine.

Fleshy A lively wine with good **acidity, chewy** and usually **full-bodied.**

Flintiness Aromatic nose like gooseberries that is associated with upper Loire wines like Pouilly Blanc Fumé. There is an associated taste.

Flor A film-forming yeast, *Saccharomyces Ellipsoideus,* which develops naturally after the first fermentation in the Sherry region. It forms a yellow-white film on top of the wine. It imparts a delicate **nutty** quality which creates the subsequent division between **fino** and **oloroso.** It has been developed in other countries and is said to grow naturally in some casks of Château Chalon, the unusual Jura wine of eastern France.

Flowery Flower-like fragrance on the **nose;** part of the **aroma** as it is a constituent of the grape's character. Distinctive in an Alsatian Gewürztraminer.

Forthcoming An appealing wine that evidently shows its character, often through the first impression of **nosing** or tasting.

Foxy A curious **earthy** quality on the taste which is normally derived from a hybrid vine variety, rather than from the classic *vitis vinifera.* Most well-known wine regions do not grow hybrid American vines directly, but it can be found on several English vineyard wines and on many American wines, particularly from the New York Finger Lakes area. The description does not indicate an animal smell, but relates to the wild or 'fox' grapes; this peculiar flavour cannot be removed, even by the use of charcoal in the cellars. Not to be confused with the spicy style seen in Alsace and sometimes Austria.

Fresh A wine that exhibits natural youthful vitality and charm, often associated with fair **acidity.** Wines are kept fresh by the addition of sulphur dioxide.

Fruity Attractive quality of a **fleshy,** generally youthful wine. Some, like the Muscat vine, smell **grapey**, but the term may be applied to other fruit esters and flavours.

Full-bodied A wine rich in alcohol and flavour. Its extract fills the mouth. Used about fortified wines, like Madeira and port, or heavy reds, like those from the northern Rhône.

Geranium Comparison with the unpleasant smell of this flower, largely indicating 'off' esters formed during fermentation.

Goaty A ripe smell, like the animal of the same name, that can often be a characteristic of **fatty** wines. Seen often in such instances as the southern German Palatinates, often from the Traminer vine, and the Moscatel de Setúbal, made near Lisbon.

Grapey An **aroma** that clearly shows its grape origin; noticeable on good Rieslings, for instance.

Green Immaturity which is frequently associated with **austerity** on taste. Caused by unsettled or excess **acidity,** particularly if unripe grapes have been picked or the result of a poor vintage.

Grip An **assertive** depth of flavour; the antonym of **flabby.** A good characteristic in port.

Hard A **severe** flavour of excess **tannin,** leaving a film across one's teeth. Additionally there may be excess **acidity** with insufficient weight of alcohol. This is the effect of fermenting the wine for too long in contact with the skins; or the addition of excess **tannin**; or simply too hot a harvest.

Harsh An uninviting combination of **hardness, austerity** and **bitter** flavours on the palate. Not a well-made wine.

Hazy **Cloudyness** owing to poor bottling, poor service or poor re-bottling quality control.

Heavy More than **full-bodied:** excess of extract, alcohol and other qualities. It is a term that can be used out of context, dependent upon the season and type of food. A North African wine of heavy **body** will appear quite unsuitable on a light summer luncheon menu and be accordingly described as heavy, but will appear quite in order to accompany game or steak in winter.

Legs Lines that fall down a glass after it has been swirled, indicating a **rich** combination of glycerine, alcohol and other esters. Their presence signifies a quality wine. Not to be confused with **bead.**

Length The time taken for the total impression of taste to remain in one's memory after spitting. Usually applies to taste but can occasionally refer to **nose.** Long length signifies a quality wine.

Light A low degree of alcohol, probably in practice under 11 per cent v/v. A light-bodied wine may be characteristic of a region, like most of the Loire, or a country, like England.

Little A minor wine that is produced for entirely local consumption and where few – if any – of the classic viticultural and vinification aspects have been adhered to.

Luscious A **rich,** soft **mellow** wine that shows these characteristics in **balance,** such as Sauternes or a fine Quarts de Chaume from the Loire.

Maderised The dull, **flat nose** of an **oxidised** wine which has usually also acquired a darker, tawny-tinged hue and taste reminiscent of Madeira. It is a condition that can occur when bottles are stored vertically and the corks dry out.

Malic Acid A **nose** like a raw cooking apple with a rasping taste. Originates from the use of unripe grapes and can lead to a secondary fermentation, which is attractive in the northern Portuguese vinho verde.

Meaty Full-flavoured wines of character; usually also **full-bodied.**

Medium-Dry/ Medium-Sweet A wine with some residual sugar, used about many 'house' carafe wines. Shippers apply the terms in differing ways.

Mellow A wine that has softened so that all its **harsh** character has gone and the **tannin** and other ingredient parts have broken down chemically. It usually comes with **bottle age** and shows itself generally on a long **finish.** A soft harmonious quality is also evident on the **nose** of such a wine.

Metallic Unpleasant tinny taste, probably owing to contamination during bulk storage or transportation prior to bottling.

Mousse The effervescence to be seen on a sparkling wine when it is first poured; distinguished from **bead.**

Musty A mouldy, unpleasant smell, usually from a cask with a rotten stave.

Noble A wine of **breed** and quality and therefore by implication one of stature. Certain legislation speaks specifically of 'noble' vines, as in Alsace, for the noble varieties yield the best quality style in terms of their fruit, **balanced acidity,** alcohol and overall qualities of development.

Nose The combined **aroma** and **bouquet.**

Nutty A crisp, **balanced** taste, evident of a well-aged wine with good **length,** frequently found on good medium-dry Madeiras or **full-bodied** classic white Burgundies.

Off-taste Unclean flavour, although the wine may still be drinkable.

Oloroso Soft, mellow Sherry, usually amber or dark gold in appearance, where **flor** has not grown. The wine is usually medium-sweet to sweet, but occasionally is found on the dry side.

Over the top A wine that is past its best; it has developed all its quality characteristics and will now start declining, although still remaining of interest.

Overchilled Self-evident but a cause for concern. Ensure that your refrigerator for wines is set at a modest number and try more often to use ice and a bucket, which reduces the temperature more evenly. Wines exposed to overchilling for too long may become unsaleable as the colour may alter and tartrates may form as crystals at the bottom of the bottle. An overchilled wine makes the **nose** and taste virtually **dumb.**

Overheated Wines can be ruined either by being left on display for a time in the sun or by being deliberately overwarmed. Do not store near strong sunlight. It is better to decant a red wine, even if it is too cold, thereby allowing it to **breathe**. Warm by hand to bring the wine towards the approximate 55°F (12·5°C) level.

Oxidised A wine that has been exposed to excess oxidation which has generally soured the wine. Often the result of storing the bottles vertically, thereby allowing the corks to dry out.

Peach The balance of **fruit** and **acidity** found on the palate, such as on certain Loire wines.

Peppery Immature **nose** where component parts have not yet blended satisfactorily together, often on **full-bodied** wines, such as young vintage ports and youthful red Rhônes.

Pétillant A very slight sparkle, evident as only a **bead** or two of bubbles and a slight rasping **acidity** (owing largely to **malic acid** presence). Often seen in Beaujolais Nouveau and vinho verde – the 'green' wine of northern Portugal.

Pinched Limited, almost mean, qualities and, accordingly, disappointing. Often the sign of a poor vintage.

Piquant **Crisp,** almost rasping **acidity**, which is attractive in Mosels or upper Loires like Quincy, but unpleasant in other youthful wines that have excess acidity.

Pricked Unattractive **sharp** taste owing to excess volatile **acidity**; one stage from vinegar.

Pungent **Assertive**, powerful **nose,** usually high in esters and alcohol.

Rancid **Oxidised nose** of a fortified wine; seen particularly in eastern Spain and south-western France.

Reserved Slow to reveal its qualities; a wine that will both develop further upon opening and in the bottle.

Resinous The flavour of resin, which is actually added to certain wines; an old tradition seen today on Greek table wines. An acquired taste.

Rich A combined **fruit,** extract, alcohol and flavour taste which implies sweetness. Applied to dessert fortified wines or, in the case of Champagne, to mean it will be very sweet.

Robust A weighty wine of full flavour, but **balanced.**

Rough A **harsh,** disagreeable, even rasping taste; often found with high **tannin** content and below average quality.

Round Correct total **balance** on **nose** and palate; this will vary with the quality of the wine.

Salty Self-evident term applied to fresh Manzanilla sherry.

Severe **Austere hardness** caused probably by the insufficient development of the **acid** and **tannin** properties.

Shadowy An aged wine which is only a light replica of its former self at its peak; beyond the stage of **mellow.**

Sharp **Acidic** character between **piquant** and **pricked.**

Sick Out of condition; often referred to in the temporary condition of **bottle-sickness.**

Silky A **rich,** almost **mellow,** but still distinctive taste; quality dessert wines, like old Sauternes, show this characteristic.

Smoky A delicate **aroma** that is seen in several whites and on the nose of Madeira as a result of the latter's special *estufado* heat treatment. Not to be confused with the clove-like aroma of certain vine varieties.

Smooth A **mellow** wine with no **harsh** edges.

Solera Method of ageing particularly in Sherry and Madeira, based upon the principle that old wine can be refreshed by the addition of a younger wine, which itself will acquire the characteristics of the older wine. It consists of a range of butts of the same basic type of wine, divided into a number of **criaderas.**

Sour Taste of excess **acidity;** one stage removed from **pricked.**

Sparkling A wine containing an induced degree of effervescence amounting to approximately 5 atmospheres pressure behind the cork; see **bead.**

Spicy Herbal **aroma** and flavour characteristic of certain vines; can be inviting, as on the Alsatian Traminer (which is the vine for Gewürztraminer).

Stalky Usually an unripe characteristic, caused by excess **tannin** in relation to the wine's **balance,** probably originating from the fermenting juice staying in contact with the stalks too long.

Straightforward Clean, distinctive wines where the various elements blend satisfactorily and give an immediate impression.

Sulphury The effect on **nose** and taste of sulphur dioxide to excess, masking other flavours and giving the wine a dull edge. If decanted, the wine may be restored to its more normal character.

Sweet Contains a high residual sugar, which has not been transferred into alcohol.

Tannin An essential element, derived from the skins, stalks and pips that gives longevity to a wine. It forms a film across one's teeth and gives a drying effect in the mouth on tasting youthful reds.

Tart **Astringent** excess **acidity**, sometimes accompanied by excess **tannin**. Sign of a poor vintage or bad production.

Thin A **light**-bodied watery wine; the antonym of **round.**

Tired Past its best for wines do not keep for ever. Check stock regularly by sampling to avoid listing such lines.

Tough Youthful wine with excess **tannin** and **body**. Not unattractive in cheaper wines that will be consumed with strongly-flavoured food.

Vanilla **Nose** obtained from **tannin** which has come from ageing the wine in oak.

Velvety	An extremely **smooth,** almost lusciously **silky** wine of **length.**
Vigorous	Youthful, lively wine of promise.
Vinegar	The **nose** of ethylacetate, an ester that suggests bacteriological infection.
Vinosity	**Assertive, balanced.**
Violets	Self-descriptive term applied to **nose.**
Well-balanced	A combination of qualities which are perfectly harmonious; this includes **acidity, body, fruitiness** and **tannin.**
Woody	The smell from keeping a wine too long in cask or in a cask made of defective wood. Not unpleasant on an immature wine, but a fault on a mature one.
Yeasty	The **nose** of ferments; a **flat** smell may come from dead yeast cells or from asbestos filtration, while an active yeastyness indicates refermentation in the bottle.

Glossary of Beer Terms

The production of beer will be better understood, and an appreciation of the terms involved in discussions with both brewers and customers better conducted, by an awareness of this glossary.

Adjunct A carbohydrate source, other than malted barley, which yields sugars to the **wort.** They are largely cereal based (such as barley, wheat and rice) and are then converted to sugars during **mashing;** if they are sugar based, they will dissolve in the **wort** in the copper.

Bottom fermentation A fermentation where the yeast cells (normally *Saccharomyces uvarum*, formerly called *Saccharomyces carlsbergensis*) settle to the floor of the vat. The actual fermentation – as in top fermentation – is accomplished by the cells circulating through the **wort.**

Cask Barrel-shaped container. Brewers traditionally refer to the 36 gallon (164 litres) cask for statistical purposes. A 'hogshead', is 54 gallons (245·5 litres) while the smallest is a 'pin' of 4·5 gallons (20·5 litres).

Dry hopping The addition of hops to beer (either in the barrel or conditioning tank). Over several days the beer will extract the **hop oil,** imparting a hoppy aroma to the beer. Hop oil is sometimes used in place of dry hops.

Extract The material dissolved in the **wort** during **mashing.**

Finings Agents used to clarify beer by causing the yeasts and other suspended solids to settle. Brewers use such fining agents as fish collagen, which has been soaked and dissolved in dilute acid.

Fobbing The practice of inducing bottled beer to foam, so that air in the headspace is displaced by carbon dioxide immediately before sealing.

Grist The mixture of flour, coarsely milled cereals, sugars and malted barley used to make a **wort** ready for fermentation.

Haze Lack of clarity. This may be because there are suspended yeast cells or for other reasons.

Hop back Vessel with a perforated bottom plate in which the hopped **wort** from the copper is collected. The spent hops act as a filter for the **wort**.

Hop extract Alpha-acids in concentrated preparation from which bitter compounds are obtained during the boiling of the **wort.**

Hop oil The essential oil in hops which gives their aroma; it is a mixture of volatile compounds.

Hop powder Ground hops in powdered form for easier handling and storage.

Keg Bulk metal container for beer dispensing under gas (usually carbon dioxide) pressure; normally under 22 gallons (100 litres).

Keg beer Bulk-conditioned beer that is highly carbonated and distributed in kegs.

Kilning Drying of **malt** by a regulated draught of heated air.

Liquor Water used during beer production; it may be chemically treated to ensure a specified salt concentration.

Malt extract Malt **wort** concentrated to a syrup by evaporation. Some brewers call this malt syrup.

Malted barley Barley which has germinated to yield enough enzymes so that, by subsequent **mashing,** a **wort** suitable for fermentation is made. Growth may be stopped in the malted barley by **kilning,** which also has the effect of providing flavour and colour.

Mashing The process whereby crushed **kilned malt** is mixed with water in a vessel (mash tun) about 150°F (65°C) in order that enzymic reactions in the **grist** and water can convert starch to sugars and reduce the proteins.

Original gravity The specific gravity of the **wort** from which beer is made. It is usually expressed at 60°F (15·6°C), multiplied by 1,000; e.g. a **wort** specific gravity of 1·055 becomes O.G. 1055°.

Primings The **wort** added to beer, which has finished its primary fermentation; to add sugars mainly for the secondary fermentation, but also to give a sweetness to the final beer.

Proof spirit A spirit which, at 51°F (10·5°C), weighs $\frac{12}{13}$ of the weight of an equal volume of distilled water; proof spirit contains 49·28 per cent by weight of alcohol or 57·06 per cent by volume.

Racking back The vessel in which beer is stored before being transferred to barrel or container.

Sparging The addition of hot water on to the grains remaining in the mash tun before the last transfer of the **wort** to the coppers. This spraying of hot water should wash out the last of the sugars remaining in the grains.

Specific gravity The weight of a given volume of a liquid, divided by the weight of the same volume of water at the same temperature.

Top fermentation A fermentation where the yeast cells (normally *Saccharomyces cerevisiae*) cling to the foam formed during fermentation at the top of the vessel.

Wort A mixture of **grist** and water after the processes of **mashing,** filtering and **sparging.** 'Sweet' **wort** is the term before boiling with hops; 'hopped' **wort** is the term after boiling.

Wort syrup Liquid which is nearly saturated with sugar. It has a carbohydrate composition similar to **wort** and is made from cereals or cereal starches.

Bibliography

General

Amerine, M. A. & Singleton, V. L. – *Wine, an Introduction* (2nd Ed., 1977)

Berry, C. W. – *In Search of Wine* (1935)

Born, W. – *The Concise Atlas of Wine* (1974)

Carling, J. E. – *The Complete Book of Drink* (1951)

Don, R. S. – *Wine* (2nd Ed., 1977)

Dumay, R. – *Guide du Vin* (1967)

Grossman, H. J. – *Grossman's Guide to Wines, Spirits and Beers* (6th Ed., 1977)

Hyams, E. – *Vin* (1959)

Jeffs, J. – *The Wines of Europe* (1971)

Johnson, H. – *Wine* (2nd Ed., 1974)

Johnson, H. – *The World Atlas of Wine* (Revised Ed., 1977)

Lausanne, E. (Ed.) – *The Great Book of Wine* (1970)

Lichine, A. – *Encyclopedia of Wines and Spirits* (2nd Ed., 1974)

Morrell, J. – *An International Guide to Wines of the World* (1974)

Penzer, N. M. – *The Book of the Wine-Label* (1947)

Price, P. V. – *A Directory of Wines and Spirits* (1974)

Price, P. V. – *Entertaining with Wine* (1976)

Saintsbury, G. – *Notes on a Cellar Book* (1920)

Schoonmaker, F. – *Encyclopedia of Wine* (2nd Ed., 1977)

Simon, A. L. – *Gazeteer of Wines* (1972)

Winkler, A. J. & others – *General Viticulture* (Revised Ed., 1974)

Tasting

Amerine, M. A. & Roessler, E. B. – *Wines, their Sensory Evaluation* (1976)

Brillat-Savarin, J.-A. – *The Physiology of Taste* (1926)

Broadbent, J. M. – *Wine Tasting: enjoying understanding* (5th Ed., 1977)

Durac, J. – *A Matter of Taste: Wine and Wine-Tasting* (1975)

Lake, M. – *The Flavour of Wine* (1969)

Price, P. V. – *The Taste of Wine* (1975)

Vedel, A. & others – *Essai sur la Dégustation des Vins* (1972)

Technical

Amerine, M. A. & Joslyn, M. A. – *Table Wine: The Technology of Their Production* (2nd Ed., 1972)

Austin, C. – *The Science of Wine* (1968)

Frumkin, L. – *The Science and Technique of Wine* (1965)

Massel, A. – *Applied Wine Chemistry and Technology* (1969)

Matthews, C. G. – *Manual of Alcoholic Fermentation* (1901)

Ordish, G. – *The Great Wine Blight* (1972)

Rozier, J. – *Code du Vin* (1957)

Schanderl, H. – *Mikrobiologie des Mostes und Weines* (1950)

Troost, G. – *Technologie des Weines* (1961)

Vogt, E. – *Weinchemie und Weinanalyse* (1953)

Historical

Crozet, R. – *Histoire de Champagne* (1933)

Davis, S. F. – *History of the Wine Trade* (1969)

Delamain, R. – *Histoire du Cognac* (1935)

Dion, R. – *Histoire de la Vigne et du Vin en France* (1959)

Dreyer, J. – *Vines and Wines of Alsace throughout the Centuries* (1966)

Hyams, E. – *Dionysus: A Social History of the Wine Vine* (1965)

Kerdeland, J. de – *Histoire des Vins de France* (1964)

Redding, C. – *A History and Description of Modern Wines* (1860)

Seltman, C. – *Wine in the Ancient World* (1957)

Simon, A. L. – *The History of the Wine Trade in England* (3 vols, 1905–06; re-issued 1965)

Warner-Allen, H. – *A History of Wine* (1961)

Legal

The Institute of Masters of Wine Ltd. – *The Protection of Names of Origin* (1971)

Martin, N. J. (Ed.) – *Paterson's Licensing Acts* (87th Ed., 1978)

Solicitor to the National Union of Licensed Victuallers – *An A.B.C. of the Licensing Laws* (59th Edition, 1977)

Underhill, M. – *New Licensing Guide* (7th Ed., 1979)

France: General

Baynes, J. M. – *The Vineyards of France* (1950)

Berget, A. – *Les Vins de France* (1900)

Jacquelin, L. & Poulain, R. – *The Wines and Vineyards of France* (1962)

Lichine, A. – *Wines of France* (7th Ed., 1969)

Morris, D. – *The French Vineyards* (1958)

Morton Shand, P. – *A Book of French Wines* (Revised Ed., 1964)

Price, P. V. – *Eating and Drinking in France Today* (1972)

Scott, J. M. – *The Vineyards of France* (1951)

Simon, A. L. – *The Noble Grapes and the Great Wines of France* (1957)

Vizetelly, E. & Ar. – *The Wines of France* (1908)

Warner Allen, H. – *Wines of France* (1924)

Wildman, F. S. (Jr.) – *A Wine Tour of France* (1976)

France: Alsace

Hallgarten, S. F. – *Alsace and Its Wine Gardens* (Revised Ed., 1978)

Wolff, C. – *Riquewihr, son Vignoble et ses Vins à Travers les Ages* (1967)

France: Bordeaux

Beatty-Kingston, W. – *Claret* (1895)

Cocks, C. & Feret, E. – *Bordeaux et ses Vins* (Revised Ed., 1969)

Duijker, H. – *The Great Châteaux of Bordeaux* (1975)

Dupont & Nemours – *Cultivation of Vineyards of South Western France* (1920)

Farnoux-Reynaud, L. – *Vins de Bordeaux, Vins de Châteaux* (1950)

Healey, M. – *Claret and the White Wines of Bordeaux* (1934)

Lamb, D. – *Guide to Bordeaux Wines* (1948)

Penning-Rowsell, E. – *The Wines of Bordeaux* (3rd Ed., 1973)

Price, P. V. – *Guide to the Wines of Bordeaux* (1977)

Roger, J. R. – *The Wines of Bordeaux* (1960)

France: Burgundy

Arlott, J. & Fielden, C. – *Burgundy: Vines and Wines* (1976)
Chidgey, G. – *Guide to the Wines of Bordeaux* (1977)
Guillaume, A. – *La Côte d'Or* (2nd Ed., 1963)
Gunn, P. – *Burgundy, Landscape with Figures* (1976)
Gwynn, S. – *Burgundy* (1934)
Hatch, E. M. – *Burgundy Past and Present* (1927)
Moissy, R. – *Beaujolais* (1956)
Moucheron, E. de – *Grands Crus de Bourgogne* (1955)
Poupon, P. & Forgeot, P. – *The Wines of Burgundy* (New Ed., 1974)
Rodier, C. – *Le Vin de Bourgogne* (1920)
Yoxall, H. W. – *The Wines of Burgundy* (1968)

France: Champagne

Arlott, J. – *Krug: House of Champagne* (1976)
Catel, M. – *Visages de la Champagne* (1945)
Forbes, P. – *Champagne: The Wine, The Land and The People* (1967)
Gandon, Y. – *Champagne* (1958)
Hollande, M. – *Connaissance du Champagne* (1952)
Kaufman, W. I. – *Champagne* (1973)
Pacottet, P. – *Wines of Champagne and Sparkling Wines* (1930)
Ray, C. – *Bollinger* (1971)
Simon, A. L. – *Champagne* (1934)
Simon, A. L. – *A History of Champagne* (1962)

France: Loire & Rhône

Hallgarten, P. A. – *Côtes du Rhône* (3rd Ed., 1976)
Layton, T. A. – *Wines and Châteaux of the Loire* (1967)
Livingstone-Learmonth, J. & Master, M. C. H. – *The Wines of the Rhône* (1978)

West Germany

Baumann, C. M. & Michel, F. W. – *German Wine Atlas and Vineyard Register* (1977)
Hallgarten, S. F. – *German Wines* (1976)
Hallgarten, S. F. – *Rhineland Wineland* (4th Ed., 1965)
Huggett, H. E. – *Rheinish* (1929)
Langenbach, A. – *German Wines and Vines* (1962)

Langenbach, A. – *The Wines of Germany* (1951)
Loeb, O. W. & Prittie, T. – *Moselle* (1972)
Meinhard, H. – *The Wines of Germany* (1976)
Rouel – *La Vigne et les Vins Allemands* (1950)
Rudd, H. R. – *Hocks and Moselles* (1935)
Schoonmaker, F. – *The Wines of Germany* (1956)
Simon, A. L. & Hallgarten, S. F. – *The Great Wines of Germany* (1953)

Italy

Bode, C. – *Wines of Italy* (1956)
Dallas, P. – *Italian Wines* (1974)
Deltori, R. – *Italian Wines and Liqueurs* (1953)
Flower, R. – *Chianti: The Land, the People and the Wine* (1978)
Layton, T. A. – *Wines of Italy* (1961)
Paronetto, L. – *Chianti* (1st English Ed., 1970)
Ray, C. – *The Wines of Italy* (1966)
Roncarati, B. – *Viva Vino – D.O.C. Wines of Italy* (1976)
Veronelli, L. – *The Wines of Italy* (1960)

Iberian Table Wines

Belda, J. – *Vinos de España* (1929)
Castillo, J. del – *Los Vinos de España* (1971)
Postgate, R. – *Portuguese Wine* (1969)
Rainbird, G. – *Sherry and the Wines of Spain* (1966)
Read, J. – *Guide to the Wines of Spain and Portugal* (1977)
Read, J. – *The Wines of Spain and Portugal* (1973)

Australia

Cox, H. – *The Wines of Australia* (1967)
Despeisses, A. – *Handbook of Horticulture and Viticulture in Australia* (1921)
Evans, L. – *Australian and New Zealand Complete Book of Wines* (1976)
Evans, L. – *Guide to Australian Wines* (1966)
Fallon, J. T. – *Australian Vines and Wines* (1874)
James, W. – *Wine in Australia; a Handbook* (Revised Ed., 1955)
Laffer, H. E. – *The Wine Industry of Australia* (1949)
Lake, M. – *The Classic Wines of Australia* (1966)
Mills, S. L. – *The Wine Story of Australia* (1908)

Simon, A. L. – *The Wines, Vineyards and Vignerons of Australia* (1966)
Slessor, K. – *The Grapes are Growing: A Story of Australian Wine*
Whitington, E. S. – *Australian Vintage* (1903)

South Africa
Dicey, P. – *Wine of South Africa* (1951)
Klerk, W. A. de – *White Wines of South Africa* (1967)
Maxwell, K. – *Fairest Vineyards* (1966)
Opperman, D. J. (Ed.) – *Spirit of the Vine* (1968)

Sherry
Croft-Cooke, R. – *Sherry* (1955)
González Gordon, M. M. – *Sherry – The Noble Wine* (Revised Ed., 1972)
Jeffs, J. – *Sherry* (1971)
Wyndham, R. – *Sherry, from the Grape to the Glass*

Port and Madeira
Biddle, A. J. D. – *Land of Madeiras* (1900)
Bolitho, H. – *The Wine of the Douro* (1956)
Bradford, S. – *The Story of Port: The Englishman's Wine* (Revised Ed., 1978)
Brazao, E. – *The Anglo-Portuguese Alliance* (1957)
Brown, A. S. – *Madeira, Canary Isles and Azores* (1922)
Croft-Cooke, R. – *Madeira* (1961)
Croft-Cooke, R. – *Port* (1957)
Fisher, H. E. – *The Portugal Trade* (1969)
Fletcher, W. – *Port: an Introduction to its History and Delights* (1978)
Lewis, R. A. – *Maderia* (1968)
Robertson, G. – *Port* (1978)
Sanceau, E. – *The British Factory – Oporto* (1970)
Sandeman, P. W. – *Port and Sherry* (1955)
Simon, A. L. & Craig, E. – *Madeira* (1933)
Simon, A. L. – *Port* (1934)
Symington, J. D. – *Portugal, The Ancient Alliance* (1960)
Tait, G. M. – *Port from the Vine to the Glass* (1936)
Todd, W. J. – *Port* (1926)
Valente-Perfeito, J. C. – *Let's Talk about Port* (1948)
Wyndham, R. – *Port, from Grape to Glass* (1940)

Other Wines

Barty-King, H. – *A Tradition of English Wine* (1977)
Gunyon, R. E. H. – *The Wines of Central and South Eastern Europe* (1971)
Hogg, A. – *A Guide to Visiting Vineyards* (1976)
Ordish, G. – *Vineyards in England and Wales* (1977)
Schoonmaker, F. & Marvel, T. – *American Wines* (1941)

Scotch Whisky

Brander, M. – *A Guide to Scotch Whisky* (1975)
Daiches, D. – *Scotch Whisky: Its Past and Present* (1969)
Lockhart, R. B. – *Scotch* (1967)
McDowall, R. J. S. – *The Whiskies of Scotland* (2nd Ed., 1971)
Ross, J. – *Whisky* (1970)
Wilson, R. – *Scotch: Its History and Romance* (1973)
Wilson, R. – *Scotch Made Easy* (1959)

Cognac

Lafon, R. & others – *Le Cognac, sa Distillation* (5th Ed., 1973)
Layton, T. A. – *Cognac and other Brandies* (1968)
Ray, C. – *Cognac* (1973)

Other Alcoholic Beverages

Brevans, J. de – *La Fabrication des Liqueurs* (1948)
Charley, V. L. S. – *Principles and Practices of Cider Making* (1949)
Dejey, M. – *Victorian Cups and Punches and other Concoctions* (1974)
Doxat, J. – *Booth's Handbook of Cocktails and Mixed Drinks* (1966)
Embury, D. E. – *The Fine Art of Mixing Drinks* (1953)
Fisher, M. I. – *Liqueurs* (1951)
Hallgarten, P. A. – *Liqueurs* (1967)
Hallgarten, P. A. – *Spirits and Liqueurs* (1979)
Kinross, Lord – *The Kindred Spirit (Gin)* (1959)
McGuire, E. B. – *Irish Whiskey* (1973)
Pesquidoux, J. de and others – *L'Armagnac* (1937)

Beer

Findlay, W. P. K. (Ed.) – *Modern Brewing Technology* (1971)
Hough, J. S., Briggs, E. E. and Stevens, R. – *Malting and Brewing Science* (1975)

Index